THÉRÈSE
OF LISIEUX

Also by Monica Furlong:

Merton: A Biography
Zen Effects: The Life of Alan Watts

Also in the Virago/Pantheon Pioneers Series:

George Eliot by Jennifer Uglow
Emily Dickinson by Helen McNeil
Simone de Beauvoir by Judith Okely

THÉRÈSE
OF LISIEUX

MONICA FURLONG

· VIRAGO ·
PANTHEON
PIONEERS

All rights reserved under International and
Pan-American Copyright
Conventions. Published in the United States by
Pantheon Books,
a division of Random House, Inc., New York.
Published in Great Britain
by Virago Press, Limited, London.

Library of Congress Cataloging-in-Publication Data

Furlong, Monica.
Thérèse of Lisieux.

(Virago/Pantheon pioneers series)
Bibliography: p.
Includes index.
1. Thérèse, de Lisieux—Biography. 3. Lisieux (France)
—Biography. I. Title. II. Series: Virago/Pantheon
pioneers.
BX4700.T5F87   1987   282′.092′4 [B]   87-43048
ISBN 0-394-53706-8
ISBN 0-394-75360-7 (pbk.)

Manufactured in the United States of America

Virago/Pantheon Pioneers

CONTENTS

Chronology vi

Introduction 1

Chapter 1
For Ever and Ever 11

Chapter 2
The Little Queen 24

Chapter 3
Born for Greatness 38

Chapter 4
A Drop Lost in the Ocean 51

Chapter 5
A Toy of No Value 64

Chapter 6
The Little Bride 74

Chapter 7
The Little Way 92

Chapter 8
A Very Little Saint 106

Chapter 9
The Shower of Roses 121

Conclusion 129

Bibliography 136

Notes 138

Index 141

CHRONOLOGY

1873	*2 January:* birth of Marie-Françoise-Thérèse Martin, the ninth and last child of Louis and Zélie Martin, at 36 rue Saint-Blaise, Alençon, Normandy. *4 January:* baptised, with her sister Marie as godmother. *March:* goes to live with a 'wet nurse' – Rose Taillé, at Semallé.
1874	*April:* returns to live with her family.
1875	Thinks that she will be a nun when she grows up.
1877	*28 August:* death of Thérèse's mother, Zélie. Thérèse's choice of Pauline as her substitute-mother, 'ma petite mère'. *November:* the Martin family go to live at Lisieux.
1879	First confession.
1881	Begins going to school at the Benedictine Abbey.
1882	Pauline enters the Lisieux Carmel.
1882–1883	*December–May:* Thérèse suffers from acute nervous illness.
1883	*13 May:* Thérèse's illness is cured by a vision of the Virgin.
1884	*8 May:* First Communion. *14 June:* Confirmation.
1886	Thérèse leaves school, studies privately with Mme Papinau. *25 December:* has the religious experience she described as 'conversion'.
1887	*March:* Louis Martin suffers his first stroke. *May:* Louis gives Thérèse permission to enter Carmel. *July:* Thérèse prays for the murderer Pranzini. *October:* Thérèse and Louis visit the Bishop of

	Bayeux in an attempt to win his approval for her entering Carmel at fifteen. *November:* Thérèse, Céline and Louis take a European tour. *20 November:* an audience with the Pope in which Thérèse begs him to let her enter Carmel.
1888	*9 April:* Thérèse enters Carmel as a postulant.
1889	*10 January:* Thérèse takes the habit at Carmel, and becomes a novice.
1890	*8 September:* Thérèse is 'professed' – takes her life vows. *24 September:* Thérèse 'takes the veil' – starts wearing the black veil of the professed nun instead of the white one of the novice, and is henceforth known as 'Soeur Thérèse de l'Enfant Jésus et de la Sainte Face'.
1891	*December:* influenza epidemic.
1893	Thérèse becomes assistant novice mistress.
1894	Thérèse writes the play *Jeanne d' Arc* and acts the title role. Has her throat cauterised for soreness and hoarseness. Death of Louis Martin. Ordered by Pauline – Mother Agnes – to write memories of her childhood.
1895	Becomes the 'spiritual sister' of a missionary and starts praying for him and corresponding with him.
1896	*January:* Thérèse gives the finished manuscript to Pauline. *April:* Thérèse suffers the first haemorrhage from her lungs. Finishes second part of her autobiography.
1897	*April:* becomes very ill. Is permitted a regime of rest, treatment and a slightly improved diet. *June:* Thérèse writes the third part of her autobiography. *30 July:* Extreme Unction given. *19 August:* Last Communion. *30 September:* death of Thérèse.
1898	*September:* 2000 copies of *Histoire d'une Ame* (The Story of a Soul) published.
1899	*October:* a second edition – 4000 copies – of

Thérèse's autobiography published.

1906–1923   Formal proceedings towards Thérèse's canonisation take place.

1923   *April:* beatification of Thérèse.

1925   *May:*canonisation of St Thérèse at St Peter's, Rome.

INTRODUCTION

Thérèse of Lisieux, sweet, childlike, obedient, tragic, has been until recent times a cherished icon of Catholic womanhood. Although close in time to our own period – she died shortly before the turn of the century and her sister Céline survived until 1959 – she has been cast in one of the favourite moulds of traditional female sanctity, the mould of virginity, of suffering, of drastic self-abnegation. Vita Sackville-West, even in the first flush of Catholic conversion, had another complaint about Thérèse. She accused her of what the French call *niaiserie*, sugariness.

It is a little embarrassing, therefore, to admit that I have been fascinated by Thérèse of Lisieux for years, ever since reading Ronald Knox's translation of her autobiography *Autobiography of a Saint* more than twenty years ago. Partly this was because her vivacious account of life in the Martin family touched upon something in my own experience – like her I was the youngest member of the family, was close to my father and had a fractured experience of my mother. More even than this, I was captivated by her account of her adolescent passion for God. Like many girls, I was haunted by God in my teens, but I sensed that this was an embarrassing, even slightly improper, state of feeling in twentieth-century England. Thérèse not only demonstrates the passion for God with great thoroughness, she also shows the devastating effect that it had on her life, cutting her off from ordinary human contact at the age of fifteen, to die at twenty-four. What health or pathology we are bound to ask, or what mixture of the two, pushed her into this obsession with ultimate relationship?

As we begin to ask these questions we find ourselves also asking hard questions of the Christian religion, of its interpretations of its basic doctrines, of its attitudes to women and the way these shaped European culture and affected women like Thérèse. One of the most interesting things about Thérèse's story is seeing the way Christian attitudes, Jansenist Catholic attitudes in her case, impinged upon a very intelligent, passionate and sensual little girl.

Christianity had inherited many of its attitudes to women from Judaism, a religion in which women exercised little or no power outside the family, and were explicitly regarded as inferior to men. Although Jesus clearly treated women with respect, even partiality, Christian attitudes, like those of Judaism, were shaped by the myth of Adam and Eve, in which woman was seen as the dangerous temptress who, unless firmly controlled, would drag man with her into destruction. Although it seems as if women played some part in the leadership of the early Church, teaching, caring for the poor, offering hospitality in their homes so that Christian rites could be enacted there, within a generation or two of Jesus' death they had been relegated to the silent role advocated by St Paul.

Other forces affected the role of women. The Middle East in the first century abounded in fertility cults in which women, as priestesses, enjoyed privileged status. In its need to find a separate identity, to be seen as distinct from a paganism which may have given a central importance to sexuality and sensuality, the young Church followed a different pattern and rejected women as potential leaders. Although many women died as martyrs, their voice, and therefore much of their formative influence on Christianity, was lost.

Greek thought also profoundly influenced the young Church. Mind or spirit were seen as distinctly separate from body, a dualistic concept very different from Judaistic ideas.

In the third century Manes developed the ideas which became known as Manicheism, a way of seeing the world as a total conflict between good and evil – another form of dualism. The religious believer, by practising all kinds of austerities, in particular by rejecting sexuality, sided with the forces of good. The Christian church rejected the ideas of Manes as heretical, but it never lost the idea of a dramatic split at the heart of experience, one which would resurface in Christian thought again and again. The split, and the agony it produced, seemed to appeal more to the Christian imagination than a sense of the unity of the world, of God and all the creatures within the world, of spirit and matter. Fantasies of conflict and punishment seemed to recur more often than fantasies of unity and bliss, although, as in all religions, mystics did speak of transcending the dualisms and achieving ecstasy.

On the whole, though, dualism remained dominant, despite a belief in a God who became human, of spirit becoming incarnated in flesh, and of the consequent sacramental understanding of a world in which matter showed forth the divine. In spite of the central Christian rite in which the body of God was eaten (literally or symbolically according to different schools of thought) Christianity retained an obstinately 'spiritual' or 'disembodied' attitude, preferring saints who had not been 'tainted' by sexual experience, priests (within Catholicism) who eschewed marriage, and followers who, often enough, showed a harsh and rigorous attitude to the body.

Sexuality, the outcome of attraction to creatures (matter), somehow turned into the enemy of the God who had invented it. Woman, the most attractive of the creatures, aroused the strongest sexual feelings and was therefore, if not the enemy herself, at least implicated on the wrong side of the struggle between good and evil. The writings of the Fathers saw woman as dangerous, a source of temptation. Saint Augustine did not believe that she was made in the image of God, a personal disaster she could only redeem by subordinating herself to a husband who *was* made in the image of God. (Later St Thomas Aquinas was to suggest that woman was a sort of botched male.) She must be dominated, supervised, by men so that her mischief could not wreak havoc.

By the Middle Ages celibacy had become the noblest option for men who loved God, an option that allowed, positively encouraged, them to avoid women as much as possible. Even the saintly Francis, who loved birds and animals and embraced lepers, advised his disciples, according to his biographer Bonaventure, never to so much as look a woman in the face if they could help it. Woman, in person, had somehow become 'the body', the contaminated matter against which the would-be spiritual person had to strive.

Quite why women should be drawn to a religion that treated them so woundingly is an interesting question. Perhaps on the deepest level they understood Christianity better than it officially understood itself, and were nourished and comforted by it as the black slaves of America would come to be comforted by it in a society that had no human place for them at all. Forbidden all leadership, not permitted to raise their voices in public, to perform rites, to preach or teach, women still clung to the religion which spoke of love, sharing and compassion, faithful in prayer, religious devotions, and acts of charity.

One of the ambiguities of their situation was the passionate devotion accorded to the Virgin Mary. Men who had separated themselves from any contact with flesh and blood women, or who at least thought it desirable to do so, nevertheless gave tremendous honour to the Mother of Christ. Undoubtedly some sense of self-worth and esteem, deriving from Mary, was felt by Christian women, though as an ideal for women she was seriously wanting. As celibate as the priests who were devoted to her, able, as no other woman was able, to conceive without the 'contamination' of sexuality, she offered a kind of model that could only very approximately be copied. Her self-abnegation, in accepting the will of God, and her suffering, in seeing her son die, were enjoined upon women as their religious role.

One way for women to follow her example was to embark upon motherhood with as little sexuality as was practically possible. Another way, though it involved sacrificing both sexuality and the opportunity to bear children, was by becoming a celibate in a religious community – a nun. Religious communities for women were ultimately governed by men – their abbesses controlled by monks, priests and bishops. The life, in theory, and very often in fact, was a penitential one, intended to redeem both the sin of Eve and the sinfulness of the world.

Despite considerable restrictions, however, convents often offered women opportunities that were not otherwise available to them – education, freedom not to marry, or not to be controlled by the family, freedom from uncontrolled child-bearing, freedom from the dangers of licentious societies with an exploitative attitude to women, the chance of exercising limited leadership (some of the medieval abbesses were very powerful, usually because of aristocratic connections), the pleasure of living with congenial women and leading a life of order, prayer, and maybe intellectual and aesthetic satisfaction.

Alongside the positive aspects of the life, however, and along-side the sacrifice of sexuality and motherhood, there was, in many convents, physical discomfort and hunger, brief periods of sleep, humiliations of various kinds and flagellation. The body was punished to exalt the spirit, and in the effort to achieve 'detachment from creatures' the simplest appetites and pleasures were denied. Inevitably, it seems to us now, many women who lived such lives succumbed to illness and early death.

It is this history that we need to have in mind when we consider Thérèse. Brought up in a household run rather like a convent, she inherited a religion that had shown an attitude of little more than toleration towards women for hundreds of years. (During the periods of the persecution of witches even toleration had broken down.) A secret ambition of Thérèse's, secret because it was forbidden to women, was to be a priest. Of course, she knew that there was no question of it, since there was no such thing as a woman priest in Catholicism, but the longing lodged in her mind, and as she lay dying she confided to her sister that she was glad she would be dead before the age at which young men were admitted to the priesthood, that she felt this was a great kindness on God's part to save her from dis-appointment.

Priesthood apart, for her, as for most young women of the middle class in nineteenth-century France, the choice was between marriage and the convent, that is to say between uncontrolled childbearing within a relationship which might, or might not, be of the girl's own choosing, or a life without sexual expression. Independence was scarcely a possible choice.

Thérèse had had the chance to observe the first of these alternatives. Her mother, Zélie Martin, had borne nine children within thirteen years, nearly all of them suffering a very sickly infancy. Four of them died within the first few years of life. In the later years of her childbearing Mme Martin was afflicted with breast cancer, and in addition to the exhaustion of her illness, and her grief at the loss of her children, she had the added stress of running her lace-making business.

Thérèse's early childhood was spent in a small Norman town, Alençon, whose claim to fame was its lace-making industry. After Zélie died the Martin family exchanged Alençon for another small town, Lisieux. The Martins lived the life of provincial bourgeois Catholicism.

It was a Catholicism still in reaction to the Age of Enlightenment and to Voltaire's attacks upon the Church. Normandy, and more particularly Lisieux, was the scene of an enormous struggle between Catholics, usually royalist and anti-Semitic (like Thérèse's uncle Isidore), and republicans, usually agnostic or atheistic and profoundly anticlerical. Two weekly newspapers, on different sides of the conflict, *Le Normand* and *Le Lexovièn*, continually exacerbated it. This bitter fight was the background to Thérèse's religious upbringing.

To their clericalism and sense of belonging to a religion under siege the Martins brought a peculiar rigour of their own, a Jansenist note that was by no means common to all Catholics. Jansenism, deriving from the seventeenth-century theologian Cornelius Jansen, propagated by his friend and disciple Saint-Cyran, and the convent of Port-Royal, offered an extraordinarily pessimistic interpretation of the Christian religion. Like Calvinism, with which it had many parallels, it believed grace to be irresistible, with the deterministic consequence that, as in the doctrines of predestination, one was set for salvation or damnation in spite of oneself. The longing to find oneself in the camp of the saved led to a moral rigorism, a tendency to despise the folly and vanity of this world, and to long for death and the joys of the hereafter. There was a profound suspicion of the life of the senses, and a method of continual self-examination which was meant to root out faults and cultivate virtues. What it cultivated less intentionally were morbid scruples, depression and a fear of damnation.

The world into which Thérèse emerged, therefore, was defensively Catholic, morbidly concerned with virtue, and fascinated by death. The life of her family was concentrated upon the Church, with a limited interest in matters outside religion, such as art or letters. There was warmth and love both within the immediate family circle and within the extended family of aunts and cousins, and there was, presumably, a sense of intimacy in the small town atmosphere of Lisieux, though this does not especially feature either in family letters or in Thérèse's writing. In practice this life may have been claustrophobic, but no one who grew up within it could believe themselves a matter of indifference to others – on the contrary every detail of life and of relationship was a matter of the utmost interest and the continual subject of reflection and speculation in family letters. Despite all her responsibilities Zélie Martin wrote letters almost daily to her brother and sister-in-law discussing her children, her business, and her health.

It is partly because there is such an immensity of detail known about the life of Thérèse and the life of her family that she is so interesting. Both she and her mother are natural writers and have a gift for fixing upon small, compelling details that bring an alien world vividly alive for us. Both of them have a taste for trivia (it is no accident that Thérèse's understanding of spirituality – the Little Way, as she called it – is a form of spirituality concerned with apparently trivial events and details) and we learn to understand Thérèse through minutiae. I have used many of these details to try to show the reader the saint and her life. They are not unlike a photographic record which can take us in an instant into a world very different from our own.

As it happens the life of Thérèse was contemporaneous with the growing popularity of photography, and Thérèse's sister

Céline loved to use a camera. So that alongside the descriptive gifts of the Martin family we have photographs of the saint as a tiny girl, as an eager seven-year-old wearing earrings, as a fifteen-year-old who had put her hair up in an attempt to look grown-up to impress the bishop, and throughout her brief years in the convent.

I think that it is rare to know as much about any dead person as we know about Thérèse; of some periods of her life we know not only what happened but exactly what she was feeling. It is an intimate knowledge that, usually, we have only of characters in a novel, and at times I find myself thinking of Thérèse as a character in a novel, as someone with whom I have enjoyed a literary intimacy. At one point in the book, the part where she enters Carmel, so confident was I of her thoughts and emotions that I have described the event with the innerness of a novelist, a slightly dangerous habit in a biographer but one which felt appropriate here since the innerness was so well documented.

Quite apart from the intrinsic interest of Thérèse's life – the life of a nineteenth-century French girl, the life of an enclosed nun in the Carmelite order – there is the fact that she is known as a saint. St Paul, and the earliest Christian writers, spoke of 'saints' rather than 'a saint' meaning the community of the faithful, God's holy people, a usage which appeared again among the Calvinist communities of the seventeenth century, who thought of the saints as, collectively, 'the elect'.

The lives of the martyrs from the first century onward were of a quality of such extraordinary heroism that a special term seemed to be needed and gradually the word 'saint' began to be applied to such individuals. Their bodily remains, together with their belongings, began to be collected and preserved as items containing some special spiritual quality, and their names became favourite names to give to Christian children in baptism. Already by AD 220 Tertullian, the Church Father, was protesting against the superstition and excess which surrounded the cult of saints.

The first saints were simply recognised and admired by local churches or by local bishops. Sometimes their fame would spread outside their own neighbourhood or country and they would come to be revered in places far away. Such saints were created as a result of popular enthusiasm and taste, a taste which the bishops then endorsed.

During the tenth century in the western church this informal method began to change and henceforward the Pope reserved the right to make saints. From 1634 a very formal method was established, what was and is called canonisation, one that involved a number of elaborate processes – the subject's writings and life had to be meticulously examined, and evidence was taken from relatives, friends and others. It was by this method that Thérèse of Lisieux was made a saint in 1925.

Saints were not, so far as the Church was concerned (the popular belief was different), people who led perfect lives, or who were without faults and failings. 'The saint', says the *Oxford Dictionary of Saints*, 'is the man or woman who gives himself, herself, to God heroically.' By this standard Thérèse, as we shall see, richly deserved her title.

What is sometimes difficult for a twentieth-century reader is a sense that motives which once seemed above suspicion – self-denial, bodily mortification, a life lived 'for others' – may contain hidden gratifications, covert claims for glory and power, masochistic solutions to intolerable situations, which for us destroy the sense of wonder. Whether we like it or not – and there is, in most of us, a tendency to enjoy making heroic projections – we find ourselves becoming critical about sanctity, spoiling the idealised picture with psychological questions which detract from the sense of perfection and awestruck admiration once accorded to saints. We note their childhood difficulties, their neurosis, their inability to adapt to normal adult life, their illusions and defences. It is a kind of reductionism which, at first sight, seems to leave us poorer, bereft of the example of those who once seemed to show us how life should be lived.

At first sight, but not at second perhaps. In many ways the women and men who have been called saints become more, not less, remarkable and lovable, when we see their frailty more clearly. We begin to see that their courage and heroism lay in their exploration of the human condition, that their originality resided in knowing the extremes of mind and spirit, as Columbus's lay in exploring the world geographically. Like artists they were able to do this not in spite of the wounding of their psyche but because of it, as neurosis opened them to realms that 'the normal' would never dream of entering. To yearn to know, or love God, as the saint yearned for it, was to want to know the geography of the spirit, to understand what it was to be a human being, but also to know more beside, to set humanity within a larger landscape of meaning.

It was such a landscape that Thérèse, despite hysteria and depression, or because of it, was prepared to explore, despite the low esteem in which she, as a woman, was held in the Church, or because of it. It was a desperate voyage, one so severe that, possibly, she died of its effects. Personally I love her in her pain and conflict in a way that I could never have loved the sugary little saint that so many biographies have depicted. I do not believe that it is true, as so many of her male biographers have suggested, that she was particularly gentle or obedient. Rather she was one who, whatever the obstructions, struggled from her earliest days to make sense of life, and who was prepared to pay any price in order to do so. This is an account of the struggle and the price.

Chapter One

FOR EVER AND EVER

On Monday 9 April 1888, Thérèse set off with her sisters Léonie and Céline and her father to walk to Carmel, the convent she was about to enter. The walk, first downhill from the steep little hill where they lived in a house called Les Buissonets, then uphill, took about twenty minutes. She took Papa's arm – he had tired easily since the stroke a year ago. Once when he saw tears in her eyes he said, 'Steady, my little queen', but he was much more tearful than she was.

It was a relief that she had actually set off at last, and the big adventure for which she had planned for so long had begun to happen. She had been so scared that something would prevent it. The last few days had been very difficult. She had to say goodbye to Les Buissonets, which she would never see again. She had visited all her favourite spots, the shrubbery in which she and Céline had played hide and seek, the tower where Papa liked to think his thoughts, the places in the garden where she had built little altars, the room where Pauline had taught her, the alley outside the garden where she had bowled her hoop, the bedroom where once, in delirium, she had seen a vision of the Blessed Virgin, the place where she had told her distraught Papa that she wished to enter Carmel like her two older sisters.

'Never again' – the words had a romantic appeal for her, as she played for the last time with her dog Tom (she felt guilty that she could not explain the situation to him), wandered in and out of the kitchen where she and various maids had played and chatted, chose the few simple possessions she was going to take with her into the convent, objects which the novice mistress might well take away from her.

The last days had been a torment of excitement, with Thérèse longing to start her new life, and then catching Papa's tearful glance resting upon her. Always given to easy tears, as well as to irritable tempers, lately he had got much worse.

On her last day at Les Buissonets the Martins had gone as usual to Sunday Mass at the cathedral of St Pierre and she had made her goodbyes to the chapel where she had prayed so often. That evening her uncle Isidore Guérin and Aunt Céline had come for a farewell meal with her cousins Jeanne and Marie. Victoire had cooked a special dinner, though she knew better than anybody that Thérèse was never very interested in eating. Thérèse looked pretty and Uncle Isidore was unusually complimentary. He proposed a toast to her, though he had strongly disapproved of her entering the convent at fifteen and it had taken all her determination to get her own way. Papa scarcely spoke a word.

When she and her cousin Marie were alone together for a few moments Marie begged her pardon for all the unkind things she had ever done to her. Thérèse could not remember any unkind things Marie had ever done to her, but something in her questions made her think that, unlike Jeanne who was engaged to be married, Marie had secret dreams about the convent herself.

Poor Léonie, despite her own failure to become a nun, was very loving and thoughtful towards Thérèse as always, but her suggestions and little gifts were never quite right, somehow. She always wanted to talk just when Thérèse was getting into something really interesting with Céline, and she never understood the jokes they had together.

Thérèse and Céline had one last night of sharing a room. Thérèse had shared all her dreams of the convent with Céline, as well as her plots to get herself accepted under age. Now that they had achieved what they had worked for, both were so excited it was hard to sleep. The thought of separation was only bearable as a temporary measure.

'Remember,' she had said to Céline, 'one day you must belong to the Carmel too.'

'What about Papa?' Céline had asked.

'Léonie could look after him. She doesn't seem to have a vocation like the rest of us.'

Léonie was the middle one of the five sisters. The two oldest were Marie and Pauline and they were already in Carmel. Léonie had tried her vocation with the Poor Clares and then with the Visitation nuns and had been sent home ignominiously from both convents. She had always been a problem, since she was a tiny child. Their mother had despaired of her. Plain, awkward, obstinate, the odd one out of the Martin sisters, she never seemed happy anywhere.

Thérèse slept little. She was up early, dressed in a simple dress that befitted her new life. Soon she would wear the plain brown dress of a postulant. How she longed for her Clothing, when she would put on the proper habit of a Carmelite nun. It was a relief to be ready to go. At any moment now she would be gone from Les Buissonets for ever.

The road to Carmel followed a route she had often taken on walks with Papa. It was with him that she had first entered the big church there with its grille behind which the nuns sang. When she had been a tiny girl, Papa, on their afternoon walks, had liked to enter churches where the Blessed Sacrament – the consecrated bread and wine – was kept behind its little curtain. There, in the presence of Jesus, he would pray intently. When they left the Carmel church he had explained to her about the nuns and how they devoted their lives to God in a very special way. She liked the pretty front garden of the convent with its white statue of the Virgin, and the pillars and curlicues which made the church look very grand.

When Thérèse was eight her favourite sister Pauline had entered Carmel. Pauline had been the most important person in her life then – ever since her mother had died – and she was very upset at Pauline's going. She had begged the Prioress to let her become a Carmelite at once so that she could stay with her sister. The nuns had laughed at her, and petted her, and let her join her sister sometimes inside the grille, but her sister had gone and that was all there was to it. It had upset her terribly. Later her sister Marie had entered. Now it was her turn. She was much more enthusiastic about it than Marie who had gone in mainly because her confessor told her to. Thérèse could not imagine how you could be so lukewarm about it.

The procession arrived and the whole family was present at Mass and Communion at the Carmelite church. The grille door stood open waiting for her to join the community. She could hear quite loud sniffs and sobs coming from her female relations and specially from Papa. Even Uncle Isidore looked a little moist around the eyes. She was the only dry-eyed one there. What she felt was excitement, her heart beating so fast she felt ready to faint. Soon she would get the signal to move to the convent door and she was so overjoyed it was almost unbearable. She usually did get what she wanted, she noticed, as if God intended it.

One by one her relatives kissed her and then she knelt for a blessing from her father. It was like Papa that he instantly knelt down too, saying 'O little queen!', as he blessed her. She thought the angels would be pleased to see an old man give up his daughter, and the daughter herself give up her freedom. But the poor King of France and Navarre! (The King and Queen of France and Navarre were the pet names the two of them had for each other.) He would miss his favourite daughter.

At last the painful goodbyes came to an end, she passed through the door of the grille where Pauline, Sister Agnes as she was called now, and Marie, Sister Marie of the Sacred Heart, were the first to embrace her. To be held in Pauline's arms and kissed made her feel that she had only left one home to return to another. Then the Prioress, Mother Marie de Gonzague, a dark, fine-looking woman in her fifties, embraced her. She was, Thérèse knew, of noble family, and perhaps this gave her her unusual self-confidence and dignity. No wonder she was constantly re-elected as Superior.

The Novice Mistress, Sister Marie of the Angels, the other aristocrat of this little community, also embraced her. She had a warm, kindly face. Then all the other Sisters hugged her, some rather distantly, others affectionately, and smiled at her – they made her feel they were really glad she was there. She was not so certain of Canon Delatroette, who had made some remark about her to Mother Marie which she did not quite catch but she could tell was sarcastic. He had done everything he could to prevent her being received at such a young age, and now she knew that he hoped she would fail. Probably he thought she was a silly little girl with a crush on the religious life; he did not know how deeply she loved God, how she would do anything to please Him.

The Novice Mistress took her up the wooden stairs between white walls with texts written on them. Once again her heart beat very fast. She would see her cell at last, or rather 'our cell' as she would have to call it in the Order. None of the Sisters owned anything personally – everything was there to be shared with others. She loved the cell at once. It was the exact opposite of Les Buissonets. Les Buissonets, like the houses of her relatives, was full of heavy mahogany tables and beds and wardrobes. There were enormous chairs with embroidered backs, sofas covered in red plush, golden clocks and candelabra decorated with cherubs and nymphs, embroidered pin cushions preserved under glass cases, glittering chandeliers. Everything was decorated, coloured, stuffed, designed to attract the eye or make the body comfortable.

The cell presented an extraordinary contrast. Both the floor and walls were of bare brown wood, and nothing hung on the walls except a plain cross, a little stoup of holy water, and a portrait of Our Lord. The bed was very narrow with a plain brown cover, and consisted of a straw mattress resting upon boards. Apart from the bed all that the room contained was a stool, a table, a lantern, an hour-glass, and a shelf which held a water jug. Thérèse reflected with pleasure that it was little better than a prisoner's cell – ever since she had prayed for the conversion of the murderer Pranzini[1] she had taken a special interest in prisoners.

The Novice Mistress looked at her few possessions – a pen, a volume of St John of the Cross, a change of dress and of underwear – and said she might keep them for now. She left her for a little while she went to office guessing that Thérèse might want to get used to her new surroundings. At once she went to the window and found that it looked out on the cloister garth – she could see the big crucifix in profile, most of the pretty statue of the Blessed Virgin holding out her arms to welcome her to Carmel, the flower beds set with rose trees and geraniums, the grass, the cinder walks. This was her new home. 'I shall be here for ever and ever' she said to herself. She said it jubilantly, knowing it was exactly right for her. She gloated once again over having her very own cell at last – the fact that it was called 'our cell' made it all the more thrilling, and she quickly knelt to thank God for his goodness in bringing her here in the face of so much opposition.

The bell was sounding for the midday meal in refectory. Now was the time to start being a nun. She went down the stairs, found the line outside the refectory where the Sisters waited in twos; she joined the end of it. Inside they sat on one side only of two long wooden tables so that they faced each other across the room. There were twenty-five nuns. She was a little surprised to discover how old most of them were. The only novice was about eight years older than herself. Then came Pauline and Marie, both in their thirties, then nuns in their forties and fifties, and finally several really old nuns. Like the stairs and passages the refectory had white walls with texts written upon them. 'The bread of eternal life' was one of them. There was also a skull to remind you of your mortality. One of the Sisters wore a chipped cup on a piece of leather round her neck and Thérèse looked at her with pity knowing that she must be the culprit who broke it. She wished she could wear it herself.

In front of each Sister was a napkin, a piece of bread, a jug of water, a bowl and a knife. The Sisters, having folded back their long sleeves, arranged the napkin in a complicated way between their plate and their habit to prevent any crumb or drop falling to the floor. Thérèse tried to copy this until she saw the Novice Mistress gently shake her head. She bowed to the Sister who poured her soup, who bowed back. The soup tasted of vegetables, but also as if it had been a little burned. Now she would eat mostly fruit, vegetables and fish. Meat, eggs, and dairy foods were forbidden for most of the year except when the Sisters were sick. When she had finished she cleaned the bowl with her bread as she saw the others do, then wiped it with the napkin.

After the midday meal there was a period of silent prayer. Thérèse prayed joyfully, her heart full of gratitude. Then she was sent out into the garden to do some weeding. She had never cared for weeding at home – Papa or the gardener did that – and enthusiastic as she was, she still found it rather boring, but it gave her a chance to see more of the garden. She worked near the chestnut walk, a pretty avenue between two rows of tall chestnut trees where the Sisters took their recreation on warm summer afternoons.

Later that evening the feelings of homesickness came. About now – on the other side of Lisieux – Papa, Céline and Léonie would be sitting down to supper, doubtless shedding a few tears as they spoke of her. God asked hard things of those who loved Him. But on the other hand she had sat beside Pauline at recreation as the Sisters sat around with their sewing and it had been wonderful to have her so close, to be able to tell her what she was thinking, instead of having to write her a letter or mumble it through the grille. It was lovely too to be back with Marie – her sister/godmother – Marie always gave you a feeling of confidence.

Thérèse could see that her sisters were respected in the convent. She still felt shy of the other twenty-four nuns – she had always been nervous of strangers and known that she seemed quaint and odd to them however hard she tried to be normal – but they had talked so nicely at recreation and everyone had made a point of welcoming her so kindly that she thought that in this holy place maybe her old problems would not recur.

She loved the quietness of the Great Silence, the time when, according to monastic custom, silence was kept from Vespers until after Mass the next morning. Even the name of it had always appealed to her and sometimes she and Céline had practised having a great silence at home just for the pleasure of it, going speechless to bed and not saying a word until Papa returned from Mass next morning. She went to bed in the dusk, lying down at last on a pallet, rustling, narrow and hard. She liked the smell of the straw. There were no sheets, just woollen blankets, a woollen pillow, and a heavy blanket of felt. She said her final prayers, thanking God for bringing her here, and folded her arms in a cross across her breasts.

She woke once or twice that night, because of the hardness of the bed and because she was so excited. It was half-light again when she heard an extraordinary sound – the clatter of castanets up and down the passages outside. She knew that she was supposed to get up at once and she did so with only a little struggle; she would have preferred to stay in bed and think about the pleasure of being where she was. She washed in the cold water, dressed herself, and went out into the corridor which was full of the shuffle of sandals as the nuns made their way down to choir. She sat in the seat indicated by the Novice Mistress and tried to wake herself up enough to concentrate on the office. Again she thought joyfully 'I am here for always, always' and felt sorry for those in the world outside who could not know such joy.

After breakfast she was set to do some sweeping. She swept the passages and the stairs, slowly – she had never done any sweeping at home and she thought how amused the Martin maid, Victoire, would be to see her now. In the middle of it Reverend Mother came along and said 'Hurry up, child. You'll never get it done at that rate. You look as if you've never swept a floor before in your life!' With a feeling of excitement that this was mortification at last Thérèse knelt and kissed the stair.

Reverend Mother sent for Thérèse later in the day. Thérèse thought she looked unwell.

'You are very young to be here,' she said in her usual sharp voice, 'but you showed a determination beyond your years. However, you will find it much harder than you expect. I notice that your sisters still tend to treat you very much as a child – as the baby of the family. That is not how I shall treat you. If you are old enough to test your vocation here, and if we find that you have a vocation, then you are old enough to be treated like everyone else.'

The words stung a little. Others had said that she was a

spoiled child, but she had never thought so. All the same, she nodded her head. She did want to be treated like everyone else.

When she saw Pauline and Marie later in the day she noticed that they did tend to fuss. Had she slept well? Was she tired by all the excitement? Did she find the work difficult? Was she hungry? It was irksome to be treated like a piece of porcelain.

Much of her day was spent with the Novice Mistress who was going through the Rule with her, teaching her what a nun was supposed to do with her eyes, feet, hands. She had found out all about the Rule when Pauline had gone to the Carmel, and she and Céline had played at things like 'custody of the eyes' – keeping one's eyes directed to the ground, ignoring interesting sights as a form of detachment – so it was not very new to her. It was hard to remember so many things at once, though, especially as Reverend Mother or the Novice Mistress rebuked you sharply if you got it wrong.

Then there were all the complications of the office book. 'It will take a while to work that out,' the Sister said. Since about four hours a day were spent singing offices, in addition to Mass, she felt bewildered quite a lot of the time.

She suspected that work would turn out to be a bigger problem than the Rule or being in choir, however. Sister Marie of the Angels checked that she really had weeded the flower-bed, and really had swept the stairs. 'Good, but slow' was her verdict. 'You'll have to speed up quite a lot.' Then she took her to the linen room and introduced her to the Sister in charge there.

'Can you sew well, child?' she wanted to know.

'I can hardly sew at all!' Thérèse replied faintly. The Sister was furious.

'Why do they always send me completely useless people?' she wanted to know.

'I am sorry I am useless,' Thérèse said. 'I will try hard,' but this didn't seem to mollify Sister, who had a big pile of torn linen beside her. She made Thérèse do some hemming. She did her very best, but when she had finished Sister said the stitches were far too big and made her unpick it and start again.

'Didn't your mother teach you anything?' she asked unkindly.

Then, it must have occurred to her that Thérèse had no mother, and she looked sorry, but Thérèse felt hurt at the implied criticism of her sisters. Why hadn't they taught her to sew? Probably because she had complained so much that it bored her. The Novice Mistress had also told her that she had not made her bed properly and had made her go back to do it again. At home Céline nearly always made the bed for her. When, on rare occasions, she did it herself, she expected thanks and praise from her sisters for this extraordinary feat. Times had changed!

She found the Novice Mistress Sister Marie of the Angels a bit of a puzzle. Since she had to spend much of her day with her she was the sister she was beginning to know the best, apart from Marie and Pauline, and she noticed that Sister Marie was, there was no other word for it, a bit of a chatterbox. Once she had begun to talk about something she went on and on, slipping in asides and ideas that had just popped into her head. It was as if being silent for most of her waking days gave her an irrepressible need to talk once she had started. Thérèse didn't mind being scolded by her – she just kissed the floor and that was that. What she found much more painful was being expected to be open about her spiritual life. Sister would ask some question about her prayers, what she did in the silence, how she thought about God or Jesus or the Blessed Virgin, and she would listen in a kind of unbelieving astonishment to what Thérèse said in reply. Thérèse knew that Sister probably thought her affected, or that she had made the answers up, and as a result she got more and more shy of talking about her religious feelings and would blush and stammer as soon as the questions began. It was really torture.

Her life was full of consolations, however. Papa wrote every day to his queen, and sometimes Céline and Léonie wrote too. In any case they all came once a week to talk to her through the grille. Papa was always bringing presents and when he did not come himself he sent them – wonderful fish, cherries, apples, plums, pears, vegetables and flowers. The Sister who operated the tourière, the revolving hatch through which objects were passed in and out of the convent, complained jokingly of overwork.

No doubt Papa feared that the convent food would not tempt the fussy palate of his youngest little girl. In truth she was suffering from indigestion and did not feel like eating very much. She wished he wouldn't send the food. It was very loving of him, but it made her feel rather silly.

In May the Jesuit Père Pichon[2] came to the convent for the profession of her sister Marie, Sister Marie of the Sacred Heart, and it turned out to be a very important meeting for Thérèse, as he seemed to be a rare twin soul. They had a long conversation during which he heard her confession. She told him a great deal, though with difficulty since recently she had become so tongue-tied in talking about her inner life. She told of her old problems with scruples (the obsessional worries about her sinfulness), of how she had always felt afraid that she would somehow disgrace her baptism and disappoint her Lord; she explained about her problem with the Novice Mistress.

She found it very consoling that he really listened to her, that he told her that he believed God was doing a remarkable work with her soul – he had watched her praying the previous evening in the choir and had been struck by the simplicity of her childlike fervour. He solemnly assured her that she had never committed a mortal sin, that although she had it in her to be a 'little demon' God's mercy had kept her on the path of love. Finally he reminded her that novice masters, and mistresses, were fallible creatures but that she had only to remember there was one supreme Novice Master, Jesus, and she needed only to please Him. She went away feeling deeply reassured, as if she had spoken to Jesus himself.

Another reassurance came from one of the old nuns whom she sat beside one day at recreation. 'Dear child, I can't imagine you have a great deal to confide to your superiors,' she said. Knowing how hard she found it to confide in Mother Marie of the Angels, Thérèse was intrigued.

'What makes you say that, Mother?'

'There's such a simplicity about your soul . . . The nearer you approach perfection, the simpler you will become; nearness to God always makes us simple.'[3]

It was comforting to feel herself understood by others, but it did not help her much when once again, having been commanded to talk about her feelings towards God, she was tongue-tied and scarlet with embarrassment.

Sometimes she went to Reverend Mother for spiritual direction. Not very often, because Mother was often ill. Thérèse was puzzled by Reverend Mother's attitude to her. She would hear her being kindness itself to other sisters, and if, say, a priest visited the community she would always say nice things about their little postulant in Thérèse's hearing. Yet whenever they met she would find fault and speak sharply to her, though Thérèse tried very hard to please her. She could not understand it.

She mentioned it to Pauline, whose wary, concerned expression did not help her much. She could talk to Pauline, however, as she had always talked since a tiny child, about her religious feelings. Pauline always understood what she meant – she was someone who knew about deep mysteries, in particular the mystery of the Holy Face of Jesus.

She encouraged Thérèse, in some of her free moments, to stand in front of the great crucifix in the cloister garth and look up into the face of the Lord, clouded with suffering, yet so deeply compassionate. Another of Thérèse's devotions was to the little statue of the Child Jesus in the cloister. She felt an immediate attachment to it. With permission she picked flowers, the sort of flowers a child would like – daisies, buttercups and roses – and arranged them in front of the statue. Once she made a daisy chain, just as she and Céline used to do.

She was exploring the nooks and crannies of her new home. There was not very much of it, but then she was allowed very little time to herself. She enjoyed the white candles of the chestnut trees, the red and white tiles of the cloister floor, the long grass of the orchard with its wild flowers and blossoming trees. She was in a beautiful place, so full of peace and quietness. Sometimes all she could hear was a bee buzzing in a flower. But even if it had been noisy and ugly she knew that it was the place where she wanted to be. Uncle Isidore had said that she had a dream of what being a nun would be like and that the reality would be very different. The odd thing was that it was exactly what she expected.

Chapter Two

THE LITTLE QUEEN

Thérèse's mother, Zélie (Azélie-Marie) Guérin had had a wretch-ed childhood. The daughter of a cavalry soldier, she was the second of three children. Neither of her parents showed her any affection – this was reserved entirely for the boy and baby of the family, Isidore – and she became a sort of scapegoat for her mother, in whose eyes she could never do right. Not particularly given to self-pity she complained that her childhood had been 'as sad as a shroud'. She was frequently ill and continually suffered from migraine.

At nineteen she tried to enter the convent of the Sisters of St Vincent de Paul at Alençon. Possibly because of her mother's secret intervention, they refused her.

Frustrated in this first ambition she decided to learn lace-making, a craft which she had enjoyed at school, in the famous lace-making school of Alençon. *Point d'Alençon* was manu-factured by embroidering over a netted base, an elaborate process that made the lace beautiful but costly. After two years' training Zélie set herself up as a professional lacemaker.

Her sister Élise had joined the Poor Clares but became so ill from recurrent pneumonia that she was obliged to leave. Eventually she joined the less rigorous convent of the Visitation nuns at Le Mans. Dosithée, as she was known at Le Mans, would play a very important part in the life of Zélie's family, advising and admonishing her sister about the upbringing of her children, instructing and disciplining the children themselves.

When Zélie was refused by the order of St Vincent de Paul she had at once begun to dream of a different sort of life – of having a big family of children, all so carefully brought up that many of them would choose to be priests, nuns, monks or missionaries.

Her husband-to-be, Louis Martin, was also the child of a soldier, an army captain who had fought in the Russian campaign. Bullied by his father, spoiled by his mother, Louis grew up as a melancholy dreamer, timid and indecisive. Without any inclination to be a soldier, and lacking the brains to be a scholar, he found it hard to find a niche in the world. He was pious, and at twenty he had made the long journey to the Swiss border in the hope of being accepted by the monks of the Great St Bernard. They had gently turned him away for lack of educational accomplishments. Suffering from the set-back he had gone to Strasbourg and studied for two years as a clockmaker, a slow, silent trade that suited his temperament rather well. Back in Alençon again he continued to dream of monastic life, and began studying in an attempt to improve his education, but the result of his studies was a nervous breakdown. He went to Paris where, living with his grandmother, he continued his clock-making studies. Years later he was to speak of the 'terrible temptations' of Paris, temptations from which he felt he had been saved by his piety. Perhaps too by his timidity. Returning from Paris he opened a clockmaking and jewellery shop in Alençon.

One day Zélie saw Louis crossing the Pont St Leonard over the Sarthe in Alençon and the Lord put it into her mind that this was the man she would marry. Louis's mother was learning lacemaking, and was able to effect an introduction. She approved of Zélie and she thought it time that her thirty-five-year-old son was married. So, without so far as we know any strong wish for marriage, Louis was promised to Zélie. Marriage was expected of those not sworn to the religious life, and this unlikely couple, both of whom had had other plans for themselves, got married in July, 1858 in Notre Dame d'Alençon. Zélie was twenty-six.

Zélie's dreams of children had become very real to her, so it must have been a shock to her when, so legend has it, Louis informed her on their wedding night (driven by what state of panic we can only guess) that he proposed they should live together as brother and sister. A 'Josephite marriage' was the term for it in those days, a reference to the tradition that Joseph and Mary never had sexual intercourse.

It was not a marriage entered into with very high expectations of personal happiness on either side yet despite Zélie's initial disappointment the couple continued together in apparent harmony. They were seen daily at Mass in the very early dawn before their respective businesses demanded their attention, they read pious books together and observed the feasts and fasts of the Church's year. The next year, 1859, Josephite marriage or not, Zélie was pregnant with the first of her children, Marie (Marie-Louise) and after this eight children came quickly one after another. Marie was followed by Marie-Pauline (Pauline), Pauline by Marie-Léonie (Léonie), and Léonie by Marie-Hélène, who was to die of consumption at the age of five. Special prayers to St Joseph produced two boys in succession, Marie-Joseph-Louis and Marie-Joseph-Jean Baptiste. Both died before their first birthdays. Then came Marie-Céline, who survived, and Marie-Melanie-Thérèse who died before she was a year old. Infant deaths were common enough at the time. All the same, Zélie felt the pain of her children's deaths bitterly but took comfort in the thought that she would see them again in heaven.

All Zélie's children, even the survivors, suffered acutely in their early years, in particular from enteritis. How far her own state of health contributed to the children's sickliness it is hard to say. For some years Zélie had had a secret, a cancer in her breast, which, though it seemed to grow slowly, was gradually undermining her health.

In 1871, whether because of prosperity or because he always found the world a strain, Louis Martin gave up his clockmaking business and the family went to live at a pretty little house with a small garden in the rue Saint-Blaise which Zélie had inherited from her father. Zélie ran her business from there – preparing designs for outworkers who then brought the work back to her for her to approve – and supervised the household. She was chronically overworked. Louis, though still in middle age, entered into a kind of retirement which would last for the rest of his life. The sale of his business, Zélie's thriving trade, and some inherited money meant that they were fairly well-to-do.

In 1872, forty-one by now, and once again pregnant, Zélie wrote to tell her brother that she was expecting another baby – a boy she felt sure – and that she thought it might come at the end of the year. She was anxious about the delivery, dreading another difficult confinement. Marie-Françoise-Thérèse was born at 11.30 at night on Thursday 2 January. She was a fine child, weighing around eight pounds, whom her mother described as 'gentille'. The birth had been easy and quick. The baby would be baptised the next day, Saturday, and the oldest Martin child, Marie, would be her godmother.[4]

It was a happy and hopeful beginning – the birth of a last, cherished child – but within a month Thérèse was showing signs of gastric illness and was soon near to death. 'The little one is suffering horribly' her distraught mother wrote, agonised that yet another child seemed to be going from her. The sick mother's milk, the doctor thought, was poisoning the baby.

In March, when the baby was around eight weeks old, Zélie sought a wet-nurse, Rose Taillé, who had nursed one of their other sick children. Rose lived at Semallé, a village within easy travelling distance of Alençon. Since she had her own family to care for and the farm to run, she could not go to live with the Martins as Zélie had hoped at first, but offered to take Thérèse under her own roof. For most of the first year of her life, therefore, the baby lived at a farm on the Bocage with her surrogate-mother, seeing her mother and sisters only on Thursdays when Rose came into Alençon to go to market. Thérèse's biographers tend to find this a charming note, imagining the baby girl surrounded by chickens and flowers. The damage to the bonding of mother and baby, now thought to be so important, the trauma of separation to be succeeded by yet another separation when the baby was returned, the intensity of inexpressible feeling, all suggest to a modern reader that this was the first of a series of tragedies that beset Thérèse's childhood, one certainly relevant to some of the psychological pain she suffered later. Thérèse returned home to Alençon in April 1874. She was fifteen months old.

Soon after Thérèse had returned, Zélie painted a poignant picture of 'Baby' in a letter written to Pauline, who was away at school.

Here's Baby coming to stroke my face with her tiny hand and give me a hug. The poor little thing stays with me all the time, and hates being parted from me. She's very fond of going into the garden, but if I'm not there she won't stay in it; she cries till she's brought back to me.[5]

Thérèse could not bear her mother to leave her sight.

Yet the baby Thérèse already showed signs both of determined character and of a lack of physical fear. 'Your father has just put up a swing, and Céline couldn't be happier. But you ought to see Baby swinging: it's so amusing, the grown-up way she sits there, and you can be quite sure that she will hang on to the rope. But soon she starts yelling because it isn't going fast enough, and then she has to be strapped down with another rope in front – even so, it makes me nervous to see her perched up there.'[5]

It was a loving family in which to live. Zélie, although weakened by her illness, and spending more time on the couch or in her chair working on lace designs, was still well enough to enjoy her life and her children. Céline, three and a half years older than Thérèse, and a source of boundless admiration for her, was a useful companion. Marie and Pauline, aged thirteen and twelve, played a very active part in looking after the younger children in their holidays from school. The odd one out, then as later, was Léonie. Not as pretty as her sisters, physically awkward and slow at lessons, she had a kind of obstinacy which Zélie felt to be a challenge to her authority. Léonie, although a religious child who loved Bible stories and had a real faith of her own, would not spend the time in private prayer that her mother prescribed, nor follow little disciplines designed to make her a 'good child'. Overreacting, Zélie seemed to fear that Léonie might be damned, and openly wondered once whether it would have been better if she had died during one of her childhood illnesses. Taking their note from her, the rest of the family, so emotionally involved with one another, seemed always to leave Léonie out, or to ridicule her clumsy comments, or to speak of her only in tones of exasperation as 'poor Léonie' without even noticing they did it. Her loneliness must have been intense, and the more intense because of the patent 'goodness' of everyone connected with her. If they were good then she must be bad.

Thérèse clung to Zélie, but her special passion was for Papa. Louis, who was given to extravagant names for his daughters – Marie was his diamond, Pauline his pearl – gave the most extravagant of all to his youngest. Thérèse was 'the little queen', or 'the queen of France and Navarre' (to which she riposted by always calling him 'the king' or 'the king of France and Navarre'). Perhaps because she was the last child, or maybe for quite other reasons, Thérèse seemed to open wells of tenderness and love in Louis's rather repressed nature that none of his other children had discovered. When Zélie protested, with truth, that he was spoiling the child outrageously, he replied simply 'But she is the queen!' as if he half believed his own fantasy.[6] Neither Zélie nor the other children doubted that he loved Thérèse before them all, but, as sometimes happens in families, they transmuted their jealousy by themselves heaping love upon the favoured one.

Thus Thérèse was always the centre of attention, her charming babyish sayings and doings a matter of continual delight within the family, written down so that the girls away at school should know all about it. Her mother's letters tell us that Thérèse is clever and original ('perhaps the cleverest of all of you'), that she is good and sweet as an angel. 'She has a blonde head and a golden heart, and is very tender and candid.'[7] 'The dear little one is our sunshine. She is going to be wonderfully good; the germ of goodness can already be seen.'[8]

The fondest hope of Zélie and Louis was that their daughter would turn out to be a 'little saint'. 'I ask the Holy Virgin', Zélie wrote to her sister-in-law in words that seemed to acknowledge her approaching death, 'that all the little girls she has given me may become saints, and that I may be permitted to follow their destinies from close by.'[9]

So, the education of Thérèse and her sisters, though loving and tender, with many hugs and kisses, was concentrated on making them good. Good children, they soon learned, went to heaven, which was a place much better than this earth. Bad children went to hell. The first words that Thérèse was taught to recite were pious verses depicting the place above the bright blue sky. At the appropriate words Baby had learned to turn her eyes heavenwards, a trick that delighted servants and relatives. 'We never tire of having her repeat this, it's so charming! There is something so heavenly in her look that it quite carries us away.'[10]

Thérèse was a very precocious child, bright, lively, funny and touching. She is described alternately as an imp, an urchin, and a monkey. She was bravely obstinate, particularly perhaps in the face of the insensitive punishments visited upon children of the period. 'When she says "no" nothing can make her change, and she can be terribly obstinate. You could keep her down in the cellar all day without getting a "yes" out of her; she would rather sleep there.'[11] This suggests a considerable conflict between Thérèse and her mother, one which Thérèse was winning.

The child was truthful, almost excessively so. Picking up the family's enthusiasm for penitence and for asking for forgiveness, she managed almost to caricature it, pushing and smacking Céline and then insisting on instant confession, tearing the wallpaper and making sure her father was informed the minute he got home.

Quite soon, however, there was fear beneath all this struggle for goodness, fear of losing Zélie's love, and fear of having committed a mortal sin. Thérèse, acutely observant, noticed how sharp and unkind Zélie could be with Léonie who had difficulty in joining the family's taste for penitence. Zélie gave Léonie a number of cork pieces, one of which she was supposed to put in a drawer every time she did something wrong; Léonie refused to play this game and Zélie was distraught at her refusal, imagining that it revealed sinful pride or worse. Zélie also worried whether her dead daughter Marie-Hélène, who had told some little fib before she died at the age of five, would be damned for it. Thérèse was so awed by all of this that, according to her mother, she would not tell a fib to save her life.

Thérèse had other faults, though, which her family treated half seriously, half with amusement. They noted that she was quite vain about her appearance and loved to admire herself in the glass in a pretty dress as little girls do. After this they took care never to tell her she was pretty, but on the contrary said she was ugly, presumably regarding this as a lie in a good cause.

She was given to tantrums and tears of rage and sometimes she 'back-answered' her father whom her sisters thought was far too lenient in letting his little queen order him about. She had a strong sense of her own dignity. Once Zélie said she would give her a sou if she would kiss the floor the way nuns did when they committed a fault in the convent. (This, like so much else in Zélie's way of managing her family, reveals her ambition to make life in the home as much like life in a convent as possible. Not surprisingly, it was around this age that Thérèse first declared that she would be a nun when she grew up.) A sou was a small fortune to the little girl, but Thérèse refused indignantly. It would be good to think that Zélie felt rebuked by the child's integrity, but there is no evidence that she did. She tells the story with some amusement in one of her letters.

Thérèse and Céline had become inseparable friends. Rose Taillé had presented the children with a couple of white bantams – a cock and a hen – and Thérèse remarked that she and Céline could no more bear to be parted than could the cock and the hen. The children would bring the chickens indoors and sit cuddling them before the fire for hours.

When Céline was six she had a string of movable beads that Marie had brought home from her convent school – a special sort of rosary – on which she was taught to move a bead every time she made a 'sacrifice'. 'Sacrifices' meant letting others win games, or doing small jobs around the house when you would rather be playing. Thérèse, then three, had to have one too. She kept it in the pocket of her apron and Zélie delighted to see her little hand go into the pocket to move a bead when she thought she was being unselfish.

At three years old, a time of chaotic emotion in most children, the practice seems forced and unnatural. Thérèse's priest biographers were full of enthusiasm. 'From the beginning there was a happy tendency towards restraint, reticence, renunciation, recollection in all senses.'[12] Thérèse herself believed that her iron self-control came naturally to her. Yet her mother's letters paint quite a different picture, a much more normal one.

Baby, when things aren't going well for her, gets pitiably worked up, so that I have to talk her round; she seems to think that all is lost, and sometimes the feeling is too much for her, and she chokes with indignation. She's such a very excitable child . . .[13]

The weapon used against her natural wishes – that God would be displeased with her – was an overwhelmingly powerful one in a household in which God was the only thing that mattered. 'When she was still very small', her sister Marie remembered, 'it was necessary only to say to her . . . "That offends God." '[14] 'Since the age of three,' said Thérèse of herself, 'I have refused God nothing.'

Soon she developed a rather pitiable habit of asking, whenever she did anything at all, whether it would please Jesus or displease him, the thought of displeasing him being a source of boundless anxiety to her. At five she had a habit of asking when Pauline put her to bed whether she had been good that day, and whether God was pleased with her. 'I always got the answer "Yes". I would have cried all night otherwise.'[15] Sleep was impossible if she had neglected to say her prayers.

If a childhood lived so remorselessly in the atmosphere of 'sin', and 'being good' imposed heavy anxieties, it also provided its own poetry. Louise and Zélie went out at 5.30 every morning to Mass and the children longed to be old enough to share the privilege too. The family dressed itself for the pleasure of Sunday and of going to Mass, and, unusually among the townspeople, Zélie and Louis both refused to do business on Sundays, so that the day could be entirely devoted to God and to the family. They walked together, sang, visited relatives. The seasons of the Church's year brought their own especial joys, with flowers and processions and special prayers and hymns.

In May, the month of Mary, she for whom all of the children were named, they built an altar in the home right up to the ceiling with fruit blossoms and greenery. Zélie was very particular about how this was done, as she was about all else. 'Mama is very hard to satisfy', Thérèse significantly sighed once. 'Much harder than God's Mother!' On Sundays, when Thérèse was still tiny, she was left at home with Louise the maid while the others went to church. They would return with some 'pain bénit' (consecrated bread) for the stay-at-homes, which was received by Thérèse with rapturous excitement. Once when Céline left it behind at church, the two children consecrated a bit of home-made bread themselves and found, mysteriously, that it tasted just the same.

In Thérèse's earliest years Marie and Pauline were away at school – at the Convent of the Visitation at Le Mans. Once Thérèse and Zélie travelled there by train, just the two of them, partly to visit the girls, partly to visit Aunt Dosithée. Aunt had prepared a white sugar mouse as a treat, and a little basket of sweets which included two rings made of sugar, one, Thérèse decided, for herself, and one for Céline. To her distress the sweets, including one of the rings, dropped out of the basket on the way home, an accident that caused her a lot of distress.

The highlights of the younger children's lives were when the big girls returned for the holidays. Pauline, Thérèse's favourite, always brought a stick of chocolate for her, sweeping the little girl up in her arms for hugs. Thérèse loved to play with Pauline's long plaits.

Marie, the oldest of the sisters, suffered terribly from scruples, partly from her mother's continually questioning her as to whether she had committed any 'fault' and thus driven God from her heart. At eight, when she went as a boarder to the Visitation convent, Aunt Dosithée noted that she was 'melancholy'. She cannot have been made any more cheerful by Aunt Dosithée's methods. Seeing that the little girl wept a lot from homesickness, she refused to cuddle or kiss her until she stopped crying. Marie loved her aunt and was devastated by this punishment. Soon after Thérèse was born Marie fell into a severe, mysterious fever, probably hysterical in origin. A mixture of envy of the baby coupled with despair at her own tormented existence may have been responsible.

Pauline, the second of the Martin daughters, was Zélie's favourite, and the one who most closely resembled her. Pauline was a strong, practical, assertive person, whom her sisters often called 'Paulin', as if she was the boy of the family. More extravert than Marie her youthful problems had more to do with social adjustment than with self-doubt. It troubled Pauline that, unlike most of her schoolmates at the Visitation, she was not nobly born, that the Martins did not live as luxuriously as others, and that she was rather small for her age.

Léonie, uncooperative and given to fits of rage, was Zélie's despair. The maid Louise was taken on with the express purpose of controlling the rebellious and unhappy little girl, and succeeded at the cost of terrorising poor Léonie. Aunt Dosithée had made two attempts at taking over the care of Léonie, perhaps as much to give Zélie a rest as anything. Desperately sick in infancy, given to accidents in which she hurt herself badly, painfully slow at learning anything, driven to fury by all attempts at discipline, Léonie was a continual source of worry and grievance to Zélie.

Céline, by contrast, was a sunny, physically active, perhaps rather unimaginative child, seemingly without problems, the most stable of the Martin children.

From when Thérèse was about three her mother's long illness began to take a turn for the worse. Perhaps because of this Marie stayed home from school and began to take over some of the duties of the household, including teaching Céline. Thérèse, who hated to be parted from Céline, sat in on these lessons, often bored, sleepy and tearful but determined not to miss anything. Perhaps because she was brighter than Céline she quite quickly began to learn herself.

Léonie decided one day that she was too old to play with dolls any longer and she produced a basket of dolls' clothes with stuff for making other little dresses and told the two little girls that they might choose whatever they liked. Céline, like a well brought up child, chose some pretty braid, but Thérèse, whole-heartedly, said 'I choose the whole lot!', a story which would often be retold in the Martin family. Writing about this rather charming act of greed nearly twenty years later Thérèse saw it as the key to her whole life. She was one who wanted everything, and because she wanted everything she wanted God, and the total surrender of self which she saw as the road to God.

Even at three or four she thought and talked of God continually, picking up the habit of the Martin household. When Céline asked how God could fit into something as tiny as the Host Thérèse was heard to explain that since He was Almighty he could do anything. With the sort of precocity that Zélie and the big girls fostered in them the two children worked out a 'Rule of Life' for themselves (a plan about prayer, mortification and attendance at the Mass) to the amazement of a local shop-keeper who overheard them talking about it in the grocer's.

'What *are* they talking about?' she exclaimed in astonishment.

They were also encouraged to give money to beggars they met on the road – Thérèse was dismayed one day when a man on crutches she thought she was being kind to refused her offer with some indignation. She realised that she had hurt his feelings.

There was something more than a little precious about all this self-conscious practice of religion. Thérèse, recalling her three-to four-year-old self, says that 'I always made a point of not complaining when things were taken away from me and when I was blamed for something I hadn't done, I held my tongue instead of making excuses.'[16] Already at three she is living in the atmosphere of the convent.

Not surprisingly she was finding it hard to mix with children outside the family. Sometimes she and Céline played with the *préfet's* daughter, a wealthy child with lovely toys and a big garden. But Thérèse preferred it when she and Céline stayed at home and played with each other, scraping bits of shiny stone off the garden walls, pretending they were valuable, and selling them to Papa.

Her life was an odd mixture of security in a home in which everyone was devoted to her (it obviously rankled a bit, though, that the maid, Louise, frankly preferred Céline) and deeper feelings of the utmost terror. These centred upon hell, and she suffered at least one bad dream in which she saw demons dancing in the garden.

Some of Thérèse's distress came from her child's perception that her mother was desperately ill. With iron self-control Zélie carried on with life as usual for as long as she could, but during the last eighteen months of her life she was in too much pain to run her business or her family. Marie and Pauline took over the reins of the household, teaching and caring for the little ones.

A comment of Thérèse to her mother when aged about three and a half, 'I wish you would die so that you could go to heaven', has been hailed as a sign of the future saint's otherworldly vision. It is possible to think of much more mundane explanations – that the child was, rather archly, parroting back the underlying statement of her family's way of life, or, more tragically, that she was, tentatively, asking whether her mother was going to live, in the oblique, frightened way that children do sometimes ask such important questions. Or it might be that the sight of her mother's long-drawn out suffering, even when partly concealed from the child, was a potent source of distress and what she meant was 'If you are going to die, die, because I cannot bear seeing you suffer, nor the suspense of wondering whether I am going to lose you.'

Certainly for two years before she died of cancer Zélie Martin was seriously ill. She had discussed her symptoms with her brother, the chemist, Isidore Guérin, as long before her death as 1864. With enormous determination she had carried on life as usual for as long as she possibly could, but eventually she moved to a room away from the rest of the family – where any cries could not be heard. She continued to go regularly to early Mass and Sunday Mass, though often she needed to be physically supported. In June 1877 she made a pilgrimage to Lourdes with the three older girls hoping for a miracle but came home to begin the final stage of her illness. Even then she did not expect to die soon, maybe feeling that her iron will would keep her alive. It took Isidore to inform her rather bravely one night at dinner that she would be dead within the month and that she needed to prepare herself. Towards the end she became acutely, agonisingly sensitive to sound, movement and loud voices, probably because she was in terrible pain, pain too great to allow her to lie in bed. She continually dragged herself up to walk about the room.

Little children are not usually as ignorant of painful facts as grown-ups choose to believe, though they may pretend to know less than they do, but a child of Thérèse's intelligence must have observed much and feared acutely what was coming. She was kept away from her mother in a way that she was not used to, and when she was with her she could perceive all too clearly how changed she was, how she could no longer take her in her arms, or even smile, except with difficulty.

Thérèse, who had suffered two dislocations in her young life – one from her mother soon after birth, the other from her surrogate-mother of a year – was broken by the shock of her mother's death when it came.

Days before the death, the two youngest children were kept away from Zélie, sent off to stay with neighbours and play with their children while knowing about the crisis that waited at home. Once Céline took home an apricot that a neighbour had given her, having kept it as a present for her mother, but Zélie was too ill to eat it. All five of the daughters knelt in Zélie's bedroom when she received Extreme Unction, Louis weeping as loudly as any of them. On 28 August 1877, Zélie Martin died.

When she was dead Louis picked up Thérèse in his arms so that she could kiss the cold forehead. A great loneliness came upon the child. She crept away to crouch in a lonely corridor and found herself overshadowed by a gigantic piece of wood – the lid of the coffin, as she gradually realised. 'I hated the size of it,' she says. A kind of hopelessness about life seized her. She consoled her four-year-old self by thinking of a heaven 'so joyful, with all my trials over, the winter of my soul for ever past.' In the spring of that year Zélie had written to Pauline of Thérèse, 'Her disposition is so good. She is a chosen spirit.'[17]

Chapter Three

BORN FOR GREATNESS

Thérèse was deeply affected by Zélie's death. The child who had shown a merry, outgoing disposition changed overnight.

I, who had been so lively, so communicative, was now a shy and quiet little girl, and over-sensitive. Merely to be looked at made me burst into tears; I was only happy when nobody paid any attention to me; I hated having strange people about, and could only recover my good spirits when I was alone with the family.[18]

A very moving scene followed Zélie's funeral. Upon Louise making some sentimental remark that the poor little mites no longer had a mother, Céline threw herself into the arms of Marie saying 'Then you've got to be Mamma.' Thérèse immediately followed suit with the sister she loved most dearly – 'My Mamma's going to be Pauline.' Léonie, caught between the older and younger children, as usual stood alone.

Zélie's death brought about another marked change in the life of the children. Uncle Isidore and Aunt Céline lived at Lisieux, and feeling that his children would need the guiding hand of a woman, Louis moved to Lisieux, to a house called Les Buissonets. It was a delightful house for a growing family, bigger than the one in Alençon and surrounded by a pleasant garden with many trees (the name of the house means 'little shrubbery'). In spite of their grief the children were excited by the change. The whole family set off for Lisieux, arriving at the Guérin household at nightfall where their cousins Jeanne and Marie were standing at the door looking out for them. The Martins' brief stay with the Guérins while their own house was got ready made Thérèse very fond of her cousins and enchanted by their prettiness, though a little frightened of Uncle Isidore.

At Les Buissonets a whole new life began for the stricken family, as they drew together to comfort themselves for the loss of Zélie. Léonie, as usual, was cut out of the charmed circle, going off as a boarder to the Benedictine school which later Céline and Thérèse would attend as day-girls. Doubtless grieving herself for the loss of her mother she had to do her grieving among strangers while her sisters drew ever closer together without her.

Pauline really did take over the role of Thérèse's mother, inheriting some of the formidable strength of character that Zélie had shown. She dressed Thérèse in the morning, helping her say her prayers. Then Marie and Pauline alternately taught the two little girls – reading, catechism, bible history. Thérèse was a good reader, but tended to grow tearful over the mechanics of grammar. Pauline often showed her pictures, usually of a pious kind, and one of these, significantly, was called 'A little flower at the door of the Tabernacle.' Somehow she identified with this flower, so patiently offering itself to Jesus.

She loved romantic tales, particularly if they had a religious tinge. She was particularly fired by the story of Joan of Arc. She was very excited at the idea of glory – 'gloire'. 'I felt that I was born for greatness.' She decided that the only way she was likely to achieve this was by becoming 'a great saint'.

In this she and Pauline were in accord. Moulding a saint was very much to the taste of Zélie's daughter. Surrogate-motherhood was, in many ways, an onerous job for a seventeen-year-old, one which Pauline's natural capability and undoubted gift for teaching made light of. Although a good teacher she does seem to have been rather doctrinaire, more so than Zélie would have been, maybe from a wish not to betray Zélie's dying trust in her.

It also seems likely that, alongside her warm love for her little sister, Pauline found it fascinating to try out her theories on religion and upbringing on a real child. Thérèse, so bright, so obliging, was treated as a mixture of pet and doll. When she came to write her autobiography she seemed so excessively grateful to Pauline, so lavish in her praise, so incapable of entertaining even a breath of criticism, that after a while the reader begins to wonder whether Thérèse is suppressing doubts that she might, in part, have been a victim. But when a sister has sacrificed precious years of her youth to standing in for a lost mother, and when love is, in a sense, the only permitted attitude, it is difficult to admit resentment, in this case resentment at an education that made Thérèse quaint, unchildlike, and painfully anxious about her sins.

Pauline worked out an educational system in which she gave Thérèse 'marks' – wooden tokens – for each piece of work properly done. Sometimes she gave 'special marks' for outstanding work and enough of these entitled Thérèse to a whole holiday. On an ordinary day she went off to show Papa her five marks in his room at the top of the house and that meant that the two of them were free to go for an outing in the afternoon. If she didn't get the five marks then Pauline would not let her go.

Papa's idea of a walk was not to visit swings or other places of childish delight but to go and pray quietly in one of the town's churches. That way Thérèse got to know most of the local churches. But he remembered to buy a tiny present for the 'little queen' on the way home, a cake or some sweets.

After the walk she played in the garden, mixing 'tisanes' of her own invention from seeds and bits of bark which she then made Papa drink from a doll's cup. Gardening, of the busy kind which makes it hard for anything to grow, was another of her pleasures. She also liked arranging flowers on tiny altars she had built around the garden. Dolls did not figure much in her playing. Ida Görres, one of Thérèse's more perceptive biographers, makes the interesting suggestion that maybe mothering was too painful now that Thérèse lacked her own mother. She did not wish to be reminded.

Occasionally she and her father went fishing together, carrying jam sandwiches cut by Pauline. Thérèse didn't much enjoy the actual fishing, but preferred sinking into a sort of meditative trance, among the flowers and birds. 'Earth', she says, in a most unchildlike way, 'seemed a place of exile, and I could dream of heaven.' Maybe it was a plan to rejoin Zélie.

Pauline worked hard at being a substitute-mother. She not only looked like Zélie but she had her firmness of character, and her steadfastness. Thérèse knew exactly where she stood with her; if she forbad something it remained forbidden. Thérèse had become frightened of the dark, but Pauline devised a sort of aversion therapy getting the little girl by degrees to go and fetch things from dark rooms until her fear gradually evaporated.

Once Thérèse was very rude to the servant Victoire and hurt her feelings by calling her 'une petite mioche' (a little brat) which was what Victoire was fond of calling her. Under pressure Thérèse apologised but twenty years later she remembered that she had not really been sorry because she felt Victoire had deserved it.

At six Thérèse made her first confession to a curate called M. Ducellier. Pauline had prepared her very carefully for it, making sure she understood that it was God to whom she was confessing her sins. Well-primed, Thérèse went into the confessional only to discover that she was so small that the priest did not notice she was there. At his suggestion she made her confession standing up and he then gave her a little talk about devotion to the Blessed Virgin, to which she listened with great care.

Once M. Ducellier came on a visit when only Thérèse and Victoire were at home, so he came into the kitchen and had a chat with Thérèse and a look at her school-books, which made her feel very pleased with herself.

Pauline was good at explaining the Christian mysteries as the various feasts came round. Thérèse's favourite was Corpus Christi when she could throw rose petals at the altar. The best day of all was Sunday, however. It began with Pauline bringing her her chocolate in bed as a treat, and then she was beautifully dressed up and her hair was curled with the curling tongs. 'It was a very happy little girl who went downstairs to put her hand in Papa's and be greeted with a specially loving kiss in honour of the day; and then we all went off to High Mass.'[19]

The king and queen of France and Navarre held hands all the

way to the cathedral and then insisted on sitting together once they had got there. Maybe Thérèse, who had quite a lot of the actress in her, found something sentimentally romantic in the occasion. 'People seemed so impressed by the sight of this fine old man and his tiny daughter . . .'[20]

Thérèse tried hard to understand the sermons. If ever her namesake, Teresa of Avila, was mentioned, Papa used to admonish, 'Listen carefully, little queen; this is about your patron saint.'[21] Thérèse did listen carefully.

Except when he was playing with Thérèse Louis seemed very melancholy these days. She noticed that his eyes were quite often filled with tears.

Sundays were such a delight that she began to feel sad towards the end of the afternoon walks, reflecting that the day would soon be over and tomorrow it would be back to boring lessons again. Marie or Pauline often spent Sunday evenings at the Guérins. Occasionally Thérèse did too, but she was still quite scared of Uncle Isidore, of his habit of asking her a lot of questions, or of sitting her on his knee while he sang a song about Bluebeard.

Going home in the starry night she found a constellation that looked like a T, and rather coyly insisted to Louis that her name was written in heaven. Even more tiresomely she resolved that she 'wasn't going to waste any more time looking at an ugly thing like the earth'.

The winter evenings were great fun – there were games of draughts, and Papa singing to the little ones in a fine voice, or reciting poetry to them. Thérèse was impressed at Louis's appearance at family prayers – 'you had only to watch him to see what Saints are like when they pray.' The sisters kissed him goodnight formally, starting with the oldest and working down to the youngest. In order for Thérèse to be kissed he had to lift her up by the elbows and she would be so excited that she would shout goodnight at him.

In bed on winter nights she often felt afraid of the dark, but thanks to Pauline's cure she gradually got over this and the dark never frightened her again. During winter colds and summer fevers Pauline nursed her very devotedly. Once when Thérèse was in bed and feeling ill Pauline gave her her own prized mother-of-pearl pocket-knife to cheer her up. 'If I was dying,' Thérèse once asked Pauline dramatically, 'would you give me your watch to save me?' 'Save your life? I'd give it to you at once if it just made you feel better!' Such remarks gave Thérèse deep reassurance.

Pauline received her confidences and her doubts and resolved the most complicated theological questions that Thérèse could think up. Thérèse, rather revealingly, wondered why God did not give the same amount of glory to all the elect when they got to heaven. Didn't it make some of them unhappy to be less glorious than others? (Shades of childhood envy.) Pauline filled a drinking-mug and Thérèse's little thimble with water and asked which was the fuller? Thérèse had to admit that they were both full, and Pauline explained that each soul was given as much of God's glory as it could contain.

Not all Pauline's teaching methods were quite so straight-forward. Ida Görres quotes a hot and tired little Thérèse begging Pauline for a drink.

And Pauline would reply: 'How would you like to save a poor sinner by giving up your drink?' With a heavy sigh the child nods. The big sister is so touched by this willingness that after a while she comes to Thérèse with a glass full of water. Puzzled, Thérèse asks whether she will not harm the sinner if she drinks after all. No, Pauline suggests; first you gave him the merit of your sacrifice; now you can help him by your obedience.[22]

On the surface the child has been taught a lesson in self-control. Behind that, however, is a whole doctrine of substitutive suffering, one that it is impossible for Thérèse to check in any way. If she suffers, so the admired Pauline claims, then some one else will be saved. How can she be such a monster as to choose *not* to suffer? The blow to her self-esteem would be too great. It is only a short step from this to choosing to suffer in *every* situation with a vague feeling that this is what love demands. Zélie and Pauline might have felt that this was the end-result they sought to produce; in a child as willing and sensitive as Thérèse, who had seen the way Léonie was punished for *not* accepting this harsh regime, it was not very difficult to train her in this way. But it produced bewilderment in Thérèse. Since she must drink and eat and have her own way sometimes, how could she know when those times were? And since it was painful to have needs which were not met, it was easier to learn to repress the needs themselves. From there it was but a short step to losing touch with the needs altogether, simply not knowing any more whether one was thirsty or hungry or tired. Simultaneously this brought a loss of contact with the inner self and its requirements. Thus, the 'higher self', as Pauline might have thought of it, the self that insists on rigid self-control, becomes the enemy of the 'lower self' with its insistence on survival. The higher self begins to see the body, with its natural appetites, as 'the enemy', to which the body responds with mute rage and, sooner or later, with symptoms. Pauline, however innocently, was, we may think, embarking on a dangerous game.

'I cannot remember,' says Pauline (Mère Agnes) in her deposition at Thérèse's canonisation, 'that she was disobedient to me a single time. In all things she asked for permission, and when I refused she sometimes cried, but she obeyed without ever insisting on having her way.' The obedient nun was well on her way to being formed.

Fortunately there were more childlike episodes. When Thérèse was seven or eight her father took the family to the seaside, to Trouville. Thérèse had never seen the sea before and was immensely excited by it. She was running about on the sand when a couple asked M. Martin if that pretty little girl was his daughter. Thérèse, always self-conscious, and more than a little fascinated by the picture she made, was secretly delighted, though Louis frowned and made it clear that he did not want them showering compliments upon her. For Thérèse it was confirmation of a secret belief she already held about herself, that she was pretty, if not actually beautiful. Having carefully regaled the incident in *The Story of a Soul* she goes on to say that she wasn't really interested in the admiring looks the lady gave her, because she 'never took any notice of what other people said, except you (Pauline) and Papa'. It is a piece of disingenuousness. What the grown-up Thérèse thought she ought to have felt does not tally with what the little girl so plainly felt.

The sheltered life of the Martin household, and the extraordinary regard in which all her relatives held her, did not, on any except an academic level, prepare Thérèse very well for school. At eight and a half she was sent as a day-girl to the Abbey school,[23] where Léonie was a boarder and Céline already a day-girl. 'I've often heard it said that one's school-days are the best and the happiest days of one's life,' says Thérèse ruefully 'but I can't say I found them so . . . I was like some little flower that has always been accustomed to put out its frail roots in a soil specially prepared for it; such a flower does not take kindly to a garden which it shares with a variety of others, many of them hardier than itself, which also draw, from a common soil, the vitality it needs.'[24] The unconscious narcissism and snobbery of this remark does not detract from its truth. Thérèse's upbringing *had* made her into an exotic, a hothouse bloom, one very poorly adapted to holding its own in normal life.

Part of Thérèse's school problem was that she was much further advanced in school work than her contemporaries which meant that she was in a class with girls much bigger than herself. Then, she appeared to invite the spite of one of the girls in the class who teased her continually. Nothing in Thérèse's previous experience showed her any way to deal with this except to cry about it. Her cleverness, or her old-fashioned way of talking, seemed to put off her classmates, and she was unable to make a friend. If she had not been able to join Céline in the breaks from the classroom she thought that she would not have survived the humiliation of being always alone.

The irony was that in some ways she was a great success at school; she was doing very well in her lessons, and she loved going home, announcing her good marks to Papa and showing him the badge she had been given. Papa usually gave her a shining threepenny bit which she immediately put into a box she

kept for charitable donations. Pauline, on the other hand, gave
her a hoop, perfect for playing in the long alley outside Les
Buissonets.

Thursday afternoons, as is usual in French schools, was a
holiday, but Thérèse was dismayed to discover she was not
allowed to spend it as she liked. She was obliged to play games
'not just with Céline . . . but with my Guérin cousins and the
Maudelonde girls. I looked on it as a penance.'[25] Little Thérèse
was becoming very precious indeed, though she does say that it
must have been pretty boring for the other children having her
around. The trouble was that she had forgotten how to behave
like a child. Try as she would she no longer had the knack of it.

Other Thursday afternoons were spent dancing, usually
quadrilles which she hated as much as she hated playing games.
Just occasionally the children were taken to a local park instead,
where Thérèse showed an unexpected skill in finding the prettiest flowers and picking them faster than anyone else.

Only once did Thérèse shine at playing which was when she
hit on the idea of playing hermits. Several of the children pretended they lived in rude huts with a few vegetables and a small
cornfield. They took it in turns to be 'active' or to pray, both
parts of the hermit life being carried out in complete silence. So
fascinated did she and Marie Guérin become by this play that
when her aunt arrived to take them home they insisted on telling
imaginary beads as they walked along the street, making ostenta-
tious signs of the cross over the buns that they were given for tea.

One good thing that happened was that she and her cousin
Marie became very close – twin souls, Thérèse says. There were,
fortunately, a lot of jokes and some shared games, including the
one where they walked along a crowded pavement keeping their
eyes shut until they fell into an array of open boxes arranged outside a shop and got a telling-off from the shopkeeper.

The old affection for Céline did not diminish. Céline was much
more robustly disobedient than Thérèse, and generally a much
bolder child. When Thérèse was teased and bullied at school
Céline stood up for her. Like the big girls, she seemed inordi-
nately anxious over Thérèse's health. Céline's carefulness of

Thérèse was so great that the family called Thérèse 'Céline's little daughter'. Mothering Thérèse had become a general occupation for the Martin sisters.

When Céline was prepared for her First Communion by Marie, Thérèse listened carefully, longing to be eleven and have her turn. For three days before the great event, Céline went away to a retreat, and Thérèse was inconsolable at her absence.

A much worse loss was about to strike her. Pauline, at twenty-three, felt the call to a Carmelite vocation, and visits to the Carmel in Lisieux established that they would be prepared to accept her as a postulant. Thérèse overheard Pauline telling Marie about this decision.

It was a terrible way to learn such news, and it cut Thérèse to the heart. 'I was going to lose my mother all over again,' she says pitiably. 'I can't tell you what misery I went through at that moment; this was life . . . when you saw it as it really was [it] just meant continual suffering, continual separation.'[26] Apart from anything else she felt betrayed by Pauline. Playfully in the past, when Thérèse had announced her ambition to become an anchoress (a hermit who lived a solitary life enclosed in a cell), Pauline had said that they would go off and become anchoresses together one day. Unknown to her Thérèse had fantasised about this glorious future.

Now Thérèse, always prone to crying, wept uncontrollably. Pauline very gently took her on her knee and began to tell her about life in the Carmel. Thérèse, only nine, went away and brooded about it and came up with an extraordinary response. 'I came to the conclusion that this must be the desert in which God meant me, too, to take refuge. So strong was my feeling about this that it left no shadow of doubt in my mind; it wasn't just the dream of an impressionable child, it was certain with all the certainty of a divine vocation.'[27] It is true that from this time on Thérèse never wavered in her determination to become a Carmelite nun until she in fact became one.

The next day she told Pauline of this new development and Pauline, humouring her, said that she would take her to the Carmel to see Mother Marie de Gonzague, the Prioress, and

Thérèse could tell her the news of her vocation herself. A Sunday was fixed for the visit, though to Thérèse's annoyance her cousin Marie was invited to come too. Because they were still children they were to be allowed into the enclosure instead of kept outside the grille. Thérèse was concerned that, with her cousin there, she would have no chance to confide that she, no less than Pauline, had a vocation. Insisting that she had private matters to discuss with the Prioress, and rather touchingly believing that she would be accepted as a postulant along with Pauline, Thérèse went into the parlour with Reverend Mother and told her the great news.

Reverend Mother received the confidence calmly and then pointed out that she couldn't receive a nine-year-old into Carmel. Thérèse must wait until she was at least sixteen. Thérèse, who might have had all this made clear to her by her own family, was heartbroken, since she could not face losing Pauline.

There were still several weeks before her sister was due to enter Carmel during which time Thérèse, pathetically, stuck to her like a limpet, endlessly buying her cakes and sweets. On 2 October Pauline entered, as Thérèse poetically puts it, 'the day when Our Lord picked the first flower in this garden of his.' The whole family wept, as usual. Poor little Thérèse 'looked up at the clear sky, and wondered how the sun could shine so brightly when my own heart was plunged in sorrow'.[28]

As ill luck would have it 2 October was also the day she had to return to hated school. After school she went back to Carmel, and for the first time went through the pain of talking to Pauline through the grille. It was the beginning of a period of desperate unhappiness. Although members of the family went frequently for visits they always went as a group. Thérèse, who had been used to having Pauline to herself, now had just a few snatched minutes which she was usually too tearful to make use of. It seemed to her that Pauline ignored her in favour of others. 'Deep in my heart I felt: "Pauline is lost to me." '[29]

During that winter she got more and more depressed and began to suffer from continual headaches, sleeplessness and skin trouble. At Easter, Louis took Marie and Léonie to Paris, leaving the younger children with the Guérins. Sensing that something was very wrong with Thérèse, Uncle Isidore spent time alone with the little girl, talking gently of her dead mother and telling her of plans that she and Céline should have lots of treats that Easter holiday. After this Thérèse looked so worn out that her aunt put her to bed, but Thérèse was seized with a fit of trembling, and despite blankets and hotwater bottles she shook all night, and suffered hallucinations.

The next day the doctor was called who said, rather enigmatically, that it was 'a very serious complaint'. When the rest of the family returned from Paris, Marie came to the Guérins to nurse Thérèse. The child continued very ill until, dramatically, on the day of Pauline's clothing as a nun, she got up seemingly perfectly well. Once again she had the opportunity to be held in Pauline's arms, of hugging and kissing her and sitting on her lap. 'I did get the chance of seeing her, looking so lovely, in her wedding dress.'[30]

This brief episode over, Thérèse returned to Les Buissonets and immediately became as ill as ever, suffering from delirium, rambling in her speech, sometimes unable to open her eyes, sometimes frenzied in her movements. She could not bear Marie out of her sight, and when she left the room to take meals or sleep and Victoire took over, Thérèse began calling hysterically for 'Mama'. Léonie too tried to help but was rejected by Thérèse, though Céline was permitted, in words used later by Thérèse, to 'shut herself up for hours with a sister who to all appearances was a lunatic'.[31]

The Martin family, reflecting on this illness in later years, decided quite simply that it was a visitation from the devil, a revenge for the attack Pauline had launched on him by going into the Carmel. In fact it seems to bear all the marks of hysteria, not least the dramatic recovery that lasted a day. Thérèse, deeply disturbed and angry at her desertion by a series of mothers, yet unable freely to admit her rage against God for taking her Pauline, had no alternative to falling ill, an attention-getting device which had the whole family continually tending to her.

Thérèse, though she repeats the story of the devil, seems to have some doubt about it, and reports her worry at the time about whether she was *really* ill or whether she was 'playing the invalid'. It continued to worry her so much that when she entered Carmel years later she asked her confessor whether he thought she had been shamming. She was comforted by his insistence that this could not be possible.

In the intervals of delirium Thérèse cut pictures out of cardboard to send to Pauline, or made daisy and forget-me-not wreaths to place on the statue of the Virgin which stood in the bedroom. It was May, the month of Our Lady, and while the sun blazed outside and the flowers bloomed, Thérèse was doomed to stay in bed. Pauline sent her 'child' presents – an hour-glass, and a doll dressed as a Carmelite, a present which Uncle Isidore, with rare insight as to the cause of Thérèse's illness, regarded as unnecessarily tactless. Louis paid for Masses for Thérèse's recovery at the Church of Our Lady of Victories in Paris.

One Sunday morning, 13 May, and the feast of Pentecost, a strange incident happened. Marie, who had nursed Thérèse during most of her illness, went out into the garden, leaving Thérèse with Léonie who was reading by the window. Thérèse, as usual, began her cry of 'Mama, mama!' Eventually Marie came back.

I was quite conscious of her entering the room, but I couldn't recognise with any certainty who it was, so I went on calling for 'Mama' louder than ever. It was very painful to me, to have this unnatural conflict going on in my mind, and it must have been still more painful for Marie. When she found she couldn't convince me that she was really there, she knelt down beside my bed, with Léonie and Céline, turned towards Our Lady's statue and prayed for me like a mother praying for her child's life.[32]

Thérèse too turned towards the statue and prayed, asking for pity from 'her Mother in heaven'. Suddenly she had a vision of the Virgin smiling upon her and looking at her with infinite kindness. Thérèse burst into a flood of tears and from that moment her illness was over.

Chapter Four

A DROP LOST
IN THE OCEAN

In the moment when she saw the Virgin smile Thérèse had found a mother who would not die or go away. The wound of her mother's death, reopened by Pauline's departure, was healed.

Although Thérèse began to resume normal life at once, a peculiarly painful circumstance surrounded the whole event. Without knowing quite what had happened Marie and the other two sisters realised that Thérèse had had some 'supernatural' experience, and Marie persisted in making her talk about it.

Thérèse was reluctant to do so. The experience had a feeling of extraordinary intimacy about it and like all such experiences, it was impossible to describe it accurately or even truthfully in words. But the child was accustomed to obeying her sisters and when Marie would not leave the subject alone she did her best to explain what had happened. At once she sensed that in some way she had spoiled, or betrayed, the trust and favour shown her by the Virgin and felt deep shame. That was bad enough, but then Marie, delighted with her description, passed the story on to Carmel and when Thérèse went there on a visit she found the convent was agog with it. There was no end to the questions. Was the Blessed Virgin carrying the infant Jesus in her arms, the nuns wanted to know. What did her face look like? Was she surrounded by light?

The questions muddled Thérèse who became unsure of what it was she had seen. Once again she wondered if she had made the whole thing up. The more they questioned her the more she contradicted herself, and the sillier and more miserable she began to feel. She knew, much too late, that she should have kept her vision to herself.

Her piety deepened. She had romantic fantasies of herself as a Carmelite and decided she would like to be called Thérèse of the Child Jesus, because of her special devotion to the divine child. She knew herself now as one marked out by God.

She still missed Pauline badly, although the old desperation was gone. She found one ingenious way to keep in touch with her. She took over her sister's old studio, an attic, and furnished it to her own taste, with odds and ends she found around the house. There was a picture of Pauline, some of her old drawings, a hanging basket of grasses and flowers, a big black crucifix, an aviary full of birds – canaries and linnets – to whom Thérèse was devoted, a bookcase full of her school-books upon which stood a statue of our Lady, with fresh flowers and candles. There were other holy statues, including one of St Joseph, and various pious knicknacks. On her 'desk' by the window – a table with a green cloth on it – stood an hour-glass, a watch-case, some flower vases and an inkstand. There were some chairs and a doll's cot which had been Pauline's. She also had a 'hanging garden' outside the window, pots and window-boxes full of the flowers she loved to grow. The room satisfied her taste for pretty things.

Maybe to take her out of herself a little, or at least to provide a little healthy convalescence, Louis took Thérèse back to Alençon for a stay during the school holidays. There she was made much of, and the pair of them were continually invited out by friends and neighbours. She says that she was 'entertained, petted and admired'. It is difficult to imagine that Alençon was a very sophisticated town or that the entertainment of a ten-year-old consisted of much more than picnics, rides, meals, and visits, but in writing about it Thérèse manages to make it sound more than a little decadent and her hosts intolerably worldly and frivolous when they were only trying to give the little girl a good time.

Whether Thérèse had the puritan reaction at the time or only when she came to write her story in the convent is not really clear. Perhaps she just needs the story to point up the superiority of Carmel. One of the troubles of choosing to live 'out of the world' as Thérèse was to do, is that it seems to encourage a ludicrously melodramatic view of 'the world' and its failings as a way of heightening the wisdom of the choice to leave it. What annoys Thérèse, in retrospect, about their friends at Alençon is that they 'had the knack of serving God and at the same time enjoying, to the full, the good things of earth', a trick Thérèse was never really to learn.

Soon, however, she was back home again, preparing for an event she had longed for – her First Communion. This was a great step in the life of Catholic children, a sign that they had become adults in the faith and were allowed to join in the most important rite of the Church. It was painful that Pauline could not be the one to prepare Thérèse for it, as she had prepared Céline, but Pauline did write her a special little treatise of preparation, prettily decorated with roses, violets, bluebells and daisies. There were spaces in which Thérèse had to write down 'sacrifices' and 'acts', so that when the notebook was returned to Pauline she would be able to observe her progress.

Meanwhile Marie took her on her knee every night and talked to her about what her future life would be like and what a consolation her religion would be. Marie was warm, and comforting, much less exacting than Pauline. Maybe she had learned a sense of balance from her own acute religious struggles. It was a time of great closeness between the two sisters – Thérèse says, simply and beautifully, 'the great generosity of her heart passed into mine.'

Marie had not at this time decided what her own future was to be, whether she would enter the Carmel like Pauline or perhaps marry; she had Pauline's gift for teaching. She told Thérèse that what mattered most was fidelity over little things, a remark important for her sister's future development.

Thérèse, all by herself, had begun to work out a process of mental prayer, climbing into a private little space between the wall and her bedcurtain, and dwelling slowly and deeply on thoughts of God and eternity. Neither Marie nor her teachers realised that this was what she was doing, and they continued to teach her vocal prayers to say.

In addition to Marie's preparation Thérèse was taught her catechism at school at which, as in most subjects, she was top of the class; success mattered desperately to her and she used to burst into tears if someone else briefly took the top place from her, to the dismay of Abbé Domin who took the class. In happier moments he called her his little Doctor which gave her tremendous pleasure. Her other gifts were for writing and history. She could also sometimes command the admiration of the other girls by being a good story-teller, something which her autobiography bears out. She was one who naturally saw life in dramatic colours . . .

She was still a strange, even morbid, child, picking up dead birds from the school grounds and burying them in a bird cemetery she had started. As before she made tentative overtures of friendship with other children and for a time thought that two of them really cared for her, but was dismayed to discover that her feelings were much more intense than theirs, and 'I wasn't prepared to go about asking for affection when there was no disposition to give it', she says tartly.

Céline had developed a crush on one of the mistresses, a 'special friendship' as Thérèse calls it, and her sentimental feelings were returned. Thérèse timidly tried to follow her example, but without success. Looking back on this she says that it was just as well that she had 'so little gift for making myself agreeable' since human love makes the love of God impossible. The trouble with human love, she goes on to surmise out of her narrow experience, is that to love a human being is inevitably to love 'immoderately'. Certainly she had loved Pauline 'immoderately' and it is not surprising that human love had come to seem dangerous to her.

In one of those melodramatic flights which reveal how little she knew of the world, she claims that if God had not cut her off from human relationships she might have 'fallen as low as St Mary Magdalen', a fate rather difficult for us to believe in. No doubt she imagines the life of the prostitute as one of unbridled lust, a fate that no conceivable set of circumstances would have seemed likely to impose on Thérèse Martin. Yet she may be telling us something important about herself, that she perceives within her rather sad struggles to obtain human love – from schoolmates and a teacher – something insatiable that she knows in advance can never be satisfied. The repeated losses of her infancy and childhood have left her with a legacy of longing and fear so great that to live with love means to evoke the terrible danger of loss. The risk is intolerable. The love of God, though it lacks precisely 'the human touch', has the total advantage in that it can never be lost except perhaps by one's own wilful choice. Already, on the threshold of adolescence, she had decided that loving relationships outside her own family were too difficult and painful to be attempted. So far as we know she was only to deny this decision once.

Soon Thérèse, like Céline before her, went for her First Communion retreat at the Abbey, which meant becoming a boarder for a week. It was a rite of passage by which you passed from being a child to being one of the big girls. Now bigger and stronger – eleven years old – she felt much better able to cope with separation from the family than in the past. She loved being part of a religious community for a few days and rather ostentatiously wore a huge cross when she attended the offices. The mistresses and girls were rather startled to find that she did not know how to dress herself without help, nor to comb her own hair, and she had to be helped out by a kind teacher. It poses the question 'Did the Martin sisters need Thérèse to remain as a baby, or maybe a live dolly whom they dressed and cared for?' It suggests that she had become very passive, letting the control of her life and of herself pass entirely into the hands of her sisters.

Predictably, she enjoyed the retreat tremendously. She had daily visits from Papa, Marie and Léonie, she listened with enormous pleasure to the addresses, and worked hard at her meditations. She made her confession on the eve of her Communion and received absolution, and then on the great day itself, 8 May, she and the other girls put on their dresses 'white

as snowflakes'. It was the happiest day of her life, so happy that
she could not stop crying, something which baffled her fellow-
Communicants. She was selected to say a prayer of consecration
on behalf of all the other children.

By an odd chance it was also the day of Pauline's Profession
(the taking of life-vows), and that evening Louis took Thérèse,
dressed in the lovely dress that Marie had made her, to Carmel
where she saw Pauline wearing the crown of roses. Papa gave
Thérèse a watch as a present.

First Communion had been a much more profound experience than her relatives guessed, or than many of her schoolmates
can have known themselves. It seemed to her that the 'first kiss
of the Lord [was] imprinted on my soul! A lover's kiss; I knew
that I was loved, and I, in my turn, told him that I loved him,
and was giving myself to him for all eternity.' It also seemed to
her that 'Thérèse had simply disappeared, like a drop lost in the
ocean'.[33]

Alongside this act of self-surrender Thérèse's long fascination
with suffering had become manifest. Talking with her about her
spiritual life, as Marie frequently did, Marie said to her one day
that suffering was a path that she probably would not have to
tread, that she 'would always be carried like a little child in the
arms of God's mercy'. Almost at once Thérèse felt a great
attraction to suffering. She had already entered the strange
tortured world of Thomas à Kempis and at Communion used to
repeat the words from the *Imitation*, 'Jesus, sweet to the taste
beyond all our telling, turn all earthly consolations into bitterness for me.'[34] Marie had little idea of Thérèse's new ambition.

A lonely little girl who cannot find acceptance among her
peers, who has endured repeated experiences of bereavement,
who has been encouraged in a scrupulous and perhaps morbid
environment, already knows a lot about suffering. Suddenly a
new path offers itself which seems to offer a degree of control
lacking before. If suffering is embraced instead of avoided some
of the sting is taken out of it. If it is also true, as Pauline had
seemed to suggest to her, that it has positive usefulness in
bringing God's love to others by actually bearing the pain in

their place (what is called substitutive suffering), in itself an imitation of Jesus bearing the sin and suffering of the world upon the cross, then she can find glory in her ignominious pain, though it is necessarily a somewhat secret glory. She has found a pathway through the insoluble problem of being helpless Thérèse, though it is a tragic one.

Her spirits were cheered by her Confirmation and by picking enormous quantities of marguerites for Corpus Christi. 'Dear little Léonie stood godmother' to her at her Confirmation. Léonie was twenty-one, and the adjectives seem contemptuous.

At school Thérèse found her schoolfellows more 'worldly' than ever and they found her still more insufferable. They believed her impossibly spoilt by her family – noting the gifts Louis lavished on the little queen and the way he insisted, amusingly in view of the family ideas about modesty, that her hair must be freshly curled every night.

The annual retreat brought a problem that had been threatening for many a year – scruples. 'My lightest thoughts, my simplest actions, troubled my conscience afterwards.'[35] She would report these torturing thoughts to Marie, obtain reassurance from her, only to feel the excruciating pangs of guilt return. The misery of 'scruples' coincided, not altogether surprisingly, with the onset of adolescence.

Meanwhile Céline, now sixteen, had finished her schooling at the Abbey and left. Unable to continue without the support of her sister, Thérèse broke down, with continual blinding headaches, and Louis, by now thoroughly anxious about her health, allowed her to leave school too. Instead of school, she took lessons at the house of a widow, Madame Papinau. Madame Papinau's mother lived with her, and received a string of visitors, many of whom made complimentary remarks about the prettiness of the teenage girl and the beauty of her fair hair. With her usual ambivalence Thérèse tells us both how much people admired her and how this would have made her vain if God had not snatched her away from the world in time.

No doubt Thérèse's shaky self-esteem needed a boost, but

perhaps we may wonder whether she was quite as pretty as she
would later have liked to believe. (If you are going to renounce
the pleasures of your youth and beauty for Jesus the better the
looks the greater the renunciation. If you are plain, it suggests
you have only embraced Jesus *faute de mieux*.)

How attractive was Thérèse at this stage of her life? Photographs of Thérèse in her teens show her as vivacious and attractive, with bright eyes, but with over-full cheeks and the small
mouth that seemed peculiar to the Martin sisters.

Leaving the Abbey school before she had finished her education created a special problem for Thérèse. The school, like
many Catholic schools, had a special pious society the girls were
allowed to join called the Association of the Holy Angels. In
their mid-teens, if they were known for leading devout lives,
they were allowed to join a club for older girls called The
Children of Mary. Thérèse very much wanted to join this.
Leaving the Abbey school, however, made her no longer eligible. She braved the headmistress who, obviously piqued by
her leaving early, said that she would decide whether Thérèse
was a suitable candidate if, for the time being, she spent two
afternoons a week at the Abbey. So, twice a week, Thérèse
drifted in and out of classes, ignored by everybody, until she
finished up praying in front of the Blessed Sacrament until Papa
arrived to take her home. 'Our Lord was my only real Friend,
the only Person I could really talk to.' Then, with a touch of
sour grapes she adds 'What more could I want?'[36]

But the bitter loneliness of her schooldays still haunted her.
She wandered about the Abbey feeling, as she says 'depressed
and ill', punished by nuns and girls alike for evading a school life
that had become intolerable. Once again she began to yearn for
eternity.

The Guérins took Thérèse and Céline to the seaside and did
their best to give them a lighthearted holiday at Trouville where
they stayed at the Chalet des Lilas. They rode on donkeys and
went paddling and shrimping. Aunt Céline gave Thérèse some
pretty blue hair ribbon, which thrilled her until scruples set in
and she felt obliged to go to confession about it.

Marie Guérin was going through a hypochondriacal fit, continually crying and complaining of headaches. Marie was a pretty child, if anything more spoiled than Thérèse, and her aunt made an endless fuss of her. Thérèse, who suffered quite a lot from headaches herself, decided to copy Marie's attention-getting methods, but found to her dismay that nobody believed her headaches were the problem and that they started probing for some deeper cause for her malaise. Ashamed of herself and humiliated at her cry for love and attention she decided that, for reasons mysterious to her except in terms of the will of God, she was not intended to be cherished in that sort of way.

A further blow was about to fall on her – her sister Marie's decision to enter Carmel. Marie had never had Pauline's clear sense of vocation, and she only made the decision now because her confessor told her that it was what God wanted her to do. Thérèse had given up her dependency on Pauline with the greatest difficulty and only because she really had no alternative. 'It had been terrible', she says, 'trying to get accustomed to living without her, but there was a barrier between us you couldn't cross, and you had to admit it, Pauline was lost to me as if she'd been dead.'[37] For Thérèse her relationship with her big sisters was partly a matter of physical contact – sitting on their knees, even as a big girl, embracing them or having her hair done – partly a matter of long, luxurious conversations in which she confided all her feelings. Carmel, with its grille and its supervised conversations, made such relationships impossible, at great cost to Thérèse.

She had lost Pauline, her beloved 'petite mère' in this fashion and now, she was told, she was to lose Marie. Her immediate response was reminiscent of her behaviour when Pauline prepared to leave. She followed Marie about, continually knocked at her door and covered her with kisses, and burst into tears at the least provocation. Louis, with a wan hope of distraction, took her to Alençon, but there she broke down and wept hopelessly at Zélie's grave, distraught, it seemed, simply because she had forgotten to bring the flowers she had picked specially. Remembering the occasion years later, when she no longer broke down nor needed anyone, she also remembered the sting of what people in Alençon had said about her. 'A weak character.' Emotional adolescent girls were nothing unusual, but the youngest Martin girl seemed to be continually in tears as well as being too pious for her own good.

Piety was in the air that summer. Léonie, perhaps not wanting to be outdone by Marie, desperate to carve a niche for herself in a family where only piety counted, went off to the Poor Clares in Lisieux while the family were on holiday in Alençon and got herself accepted as a postulant without telling anybody. Perhaps it was an unspoken rebuke to her sisters for the method of their melodramatic departures from 'the world'. It certainly has the feeling of a dash for freedom and a longing to count in a family where she seemed scarcely to exist. Significantly, her going did not seem to trouble Thérèse very much in itself, though she was hurt that Léonie was prepared to go without saying goodbye, and, like all the Martins, she thought it 'very odd'. Louis, and the three girls at home, found it somehow embarrassing. They all went to see Léonie in her new habit, who said that they must be sure of taking a good look at her eyes – after this she would always have to lower them in public.

Alas for Léonie's bid for escape, after two months she was back home again not having made a success of life as a Poor Clare. 'We saw those blue eyes of hers again', Thérèse tells us, 'often wet with tears.'[38]

On 15 October Marie joined Pauline at the Carmel, and the usual heartbreaking ritual was enacted once again. The first effect of losing yet another deeply-loved person was a recurrence of Thérèse's torturing scruples. This time there was no one to turn to. On an inspiration Thérèse prayed to her brothers and the sister who had died in infancy asking them to intercede for her, 'reminding them that I'd always been the darling, the spoilt child of the family, because I was the youngest, and if they'd lived they'd have been as kind to me as the rest.'[39]

As if trying to grow up Thérèse now began to do a few – a very few – household chores. Just before her fourteenth birthday there was to be another milestone in her growing up. On

Christmas Eve the Martin children, like other French children, placed their boots in the chimney corner, and returned from Midnight Mass to find them filled with sweets and little presents. Devoted to family rituals and still very much a little girl, Thérèse loved this treat and looked forward to it. Dashing upstairs to take off their hats before starting on the delights of their 'boots' Thérèse and Céline overheard Louis say, 'Well thank goodness, it's the last year we shall have to do this!' Depressed, beset with strong-minded daughters who went their own way, Louis had had a difficult year.

Thérèse was stricken by the coldness of this, as Céline saw at once. 'Don't go down yet,' Céline advised, 'it'll only make you miserable.' But in a gesture that felt of great importance to Thérèse, a moment of self-victory, she dried her tears, and went downstairs, smiling, to unpack the boots with every appearance of unalloyed pleasure. It is a story which opens a window on a strange world, one in which self-conquest mattered more than truthfulness in relationship (why *should* Louis be deceived in this way?). But the incident gave Thérèse a new sense of strength – it was, she says, as if she'd recovered the self she lost at four and a half when her mother died.

Another reassuring thing happened. Thérèse had become very interested in stories of a criminal called Pranzini who had murdered two women and a child in the course of committing a robbery; she prayed diligently for his repentance and arranged to have a Mass said for him. Then she asked Our Lord for a sign that her efforts for Pranzini had been rewarded. Sure enough, as she discovered when she broke Papa's injunction against reading newspapers and followed up the story of the execution, she learned that Pranzini, about to lay his head on the block beneath the guillotine, had wept and kissed a crucifix three times. The knowledge of Pranzini's repentance was very important to Thérèse. Through it, she had discovered, as it were, a vocation within a vocation.

Thérèse's formal education was now over. She was fourteen and she now had little to do except pray and read, both of which she did a great deal. She knew the *Imitation* so thoroughly that her aunt used to tease her by opening it at random, giving her a line or two's prompt, and then letting her recite it from memory from there. In the summer she carried it always in her pocket; in winter in her muff. Céline had, in some measure, become her confidante now, and they sat up late at night talking of their aspirations – the incident over the 'souliers' at Christmas had brought them very close.

When she was little Thérèse had longed for Céline to confide in her and Céline, in the cruel manner of children, had refused to do so, saying that she was a 'baby'. Now Thérèse had suddenly grown tall, and seemed so much more mature that it seemed as if the two girls were the same age, or even perhaps that Thérèse had overtaken Céline and become the leader.

The fact that soon became very clear to both of them was that Thérèse was simply filling in time until she was received into Carmel. She had no other ambition than this, no thought of marriage or of 'having a good time', no real duties or interests. Not surprisingly, her rather scheming character began to revolve plots as to how this cherished plan could be achieved.

There was a formidable line-up of obstacles. The first of them was her age – sixteen was the minimum age, and a wait of eighteen months seemed out of the question to her. Marie, who probably understood Thérèse better than anyone, said simply that she was too young. Pauline, on the other hand, subtly encouraged her, and Céline found the whole idea too thrillingly heroic for words and was her sister's staunch ally.

Thérèse knew, all along, that the worst person to tell would be Papa, since to lose his 'little queen' would cost him far more than losing Pauline and Marie to Carmel. While the two girls were plotting, Louis, who may well have understood more than they imagined, had a stroke which left him temporarily paralysed. He recovered from the worst of it fairly quickly, suffering only a weakness of the legs and the depression which was more or less habitual to him. One of the oddest features of the Martin story, though, is that within less than a month of the stroke, Thérèse, well knowing how Louis doted on her, informed him of her wish to enter Carmel at fifteen and asked for his permission.

Did she fear to see her father die, as her mother had done, or worry that he was about to become an invalid, so that she would be stuck with the role of sick-nurse and would have to postpone her entry to Carmel indefinitely? Only the sense that she needed to get away for her very survival would seem to justify the apparent cruelty of informing a sick man that he was about to lose the person he loved most on earth for reasons of no greater urgency than Pauline's abrupt departure when Thérèse had badly needed her.

On the feast of Pentecost, 29 May, at sunset, when Louis was sitting in the garden by the well, Thérèse went and sat beside him, and told him of her ambition. He wept as she told him of her desire to enter Carmel, but said no word to discourage her except to suggest that she was very young. They walked up and down the garden while he tried to take in the enormity of it, tried to say that God was doing him an immense honour in taking one daughter after another.

At one point he pulled some tiny white lilies from a wall and gave them to Thérèse as a sort of analogy of her own life. She noticed that he had plucked the flower root and all, and thought that, like it, her roots were about to be transplanted. She pressed the little plant between the leaves of the *Imitation*, and there it remained; 'only the stalk has broken off now, close to the roots, as if God meant to tell me that he's going to sever my connection with this earth before long.'[40]

Chapter Five

A TOY OF NO VALUE

After Marie's departure Céline and Thérèse had enjoyed a
liberty unusual for young women in the nineteenth century.
Louis was too depressed and too lost in otherworldly pursuits to
play the interfering parent, and in any case Thérèse's wish was
his command. Léonie, in another attempt at the religious life,
had entered the convent of the Visitation at Caen. In marked
contrast to her distress at the loss of her other sisters Thérèse
does not even mention it in her writing. With all three of the big
sisters out of the way, Céline and Thérèse could do as they liked.

Some teenage girls might have used this opportunity to chase
boys, to take up artistic pursuits (the sisters did, in fact,
attempt a little drawing), or to fall into romantic daydreams, but
the Martin girls were single-mindedly set on the religious life –
this *was* their romance. Or at least it was Thérèse's.

Suddenly all her immense energy and determination became
constellated around this single aim, and all the people who
might have been considered her natural allies became foes, or
anyhow opponents to be won round. Uncle Isidore was one of
them. Regarded as the head of the Guérin/Martin clan and in
some ways more of a father to Thérèse than Louis because less
infatuated and more perceptive, he was plainly horrified when
she told him of her ambition to become a Carmelite and flatly
refused his permission. What was more he told her that she was
not to raise the issue again until she was at least seventeen. He
said it nicely, but he also pointed out, correctly, that she had no
experience of the world, and that it would be 'the height of
imprudence' for her to be admitted so young.

Thérèse's immediate response to this rebuff was to go into a three-day depression which she compared, excessively, to the agony of Jesus in the garden. It poured with rain for the whole three days, about which Thérèse remarked naively that she had often found that at critical moments in her life the weather behaved in appropriate fashion. For the rest of her life she had the annoying habit of speaking as if the weather was somehow attendant on her moods and private catastrophes.

On the fourth day she went back to see Uncle Isidore; sensing that he was beaten he wearily remarked that she was a flower God had decided to pick while it was in bud. He, like her aunt, was plainly distressed by her decision, but Thérèse cared little for that. She had won, and 'light of heart', as she said, she made her way home; the rain had ceased.

If Thérèse was untouched by the grief of her uncle and aunt she was still more oblivious to the pain of her father, who became more irritable and emotional than before. The pain of losing the child he had loved more than anyone, almost certainly including his wife (it was, after all, Thérèse, not Zélie, who was the 'queen') had begun to destroy him, but as in the case of Thérèse, when Pauline had left home, he could not argue with God, and the inner rage had to be ruthlessly suppressed. Determinedly oblivious that her actions might be relevant to her father's suffering, as Pauline had once been determinedly oblivious of hers, a few years later she was to write with a wonderful egotism of this time, 'It's a time of great suffering, but I feel that I've got the strength to bear worse trials than this.'

Louis's frailty did not prevent Thérèse pressing him into service when she took the next step on the road to achieving her object and went to see the Father Superior of the male Carmelite house whom the Bishop of Bayeux, Monsignor Hugonin, had delegated to attend to her request. He was cold and silently disapproving. Despite Louis strongly supporting Thérèse's appeal, as he would have supported almost anything she asked him to do, Father said that he could see no reason for hurry. If the child wanted to lead a Carmelite life she could start by

practising at home. If the Bishop personally took her part of
course he would not oppose him, but really he didn't feel. . . .

Thérèse burst into floods of tears, and father and daughter
left; it was pouring with rain. Louis, desperate at her distress,
offered to accompany her on a visit to the Bishop himself, and
Thérèse replied that she 'was so determined to carry my point
that I'd go to the Holy Father if the Bishop wouldn't let me
enter Carmel at fifteen'.

Some respite from these endeavours was gained by an act of
charity. Thérèse and Céline offered to take temporary care of
two little girls whose mother was dying. Thérèse talked so
glowingly to them of the Child Jesus that the elder child, aged
six, was much impressed. It struck Thérèse how easy it was to
influence children. Like Pauline before her, it seemed to her
that children were 'like wax to receive impressions for better or
worse', and like Pauline again, she had no uncertainties, or
hesitations, about what those impressions should be. What one
ought to do was 'train them from the very start'.

Soon, however, it was time for Louis and Thérèse to keep
their appointment with the Bishop of Bayeux. Thérèse put her
hair up for the occasion, and wore a pretty dress, in order to
seem as old as possible; the photograph of her taken for the
occasion has a faintly mischievous quality. Despite all the tears
and dramatics occasionally one suspects that Thérèse found the
process of getting herself into Carmel something of a lark.

The visit to Bayeux was not much fun, however. It was
obligingly pouring with rain yet again, and the father and
daughter went into Bayeux on the omnibus and had lunch at a
grand hotel to fortify themselves for the ordeal ahead. (The
special meal was Louis's idea, of course. Never very interested
in food, Thérèse did not do justice to the lunch, but she could
see Papa was trying his very best.)

They were still much too early for their appointment, and the
rain was still lashing down, so they hung about the Cathedral,
getting themselves embarrassingly mixed up with a funeral
party, though Thérèse said some lengthy prayers in an empty
chapel.

She was desperately nervous, realising that she had to give a good account of herself to get her own way. Louis, who could not imagine anyone refusing her anything, said that the Bishop was bound to give way. He was all set to send a telegram to Carmel the minute the meeting was over. M. Reverony, the clergyman they had been told to ask for, swept them up, asked her a few questions, and seeing the unshed tears beginning to gather in her eyes said, 'Now then, no diamonds, please. His Lordship wouldn't like it.' Thereupon they were whisked through several vast rooms into a study with a blazing fire and three large armchairs.

Louis and Thérèse knelt to receive the Bishop's blessing, the Bishop and Louis took the two chairs by the fireplace and Thérèse, with some difficulty, was persuaded to take the seat in the middle.

Giving her reasons was just as difficult as she had feared. As her shy observations fell one by one into the silence she could see that Mgr Hugonin was not impressed at all.

'Had she wanted to be a Carmelite for a long time?' he enquired at last.

'Oh yes,' she replied from the vantage point of her fifteen years, 'a long, long time.' She went on to explain how ever since the age of reason she had planned to be a nun, and that more lately Carmel had seemed just the right place to fulfil her longing.

'What about her father?' the Bishop asked. 'Should she not stay and be a comfort to him for a few years yet?' Louis loyally interrupted at this point to say that *of course* Thérèse must be allowed to go into Carmel if that was what she wanted. Thérèse thought the Bishop must be very surprised and impressed by this.

The Bishop stalled by saying that he would have to talk some more with the Father Superior, and remembering how disapproving of her he had seemed Thérèse broke the interdict on tears and cried freely. This softened the Bishop, who put a comforting arm round her, at which she leant her head on his shoulder and sobbed uncontrollably. When he had had enough of this he saw them out into the garden, and Louis told him artlessly about Thérèse having put her hair up specially. Perhaps he thought it would make him realise the strength of her resolution. Thérèse, not surprisingly, cried all the way home. Only a visit to Pauline at Carmel comforted her.

Desperate to lighten the atmosphere, Louis had prepared a tremendous treat for her, though like all his treats, it was rather damply received. Maybe with some intention of distracting her, either temporarily or permanently, or maybe just because he had always liked travelling, he proposed to take Céline and Thérèse for a grand tour of Europe. Knowing very well that no holiday would succeed with Thérèse if presented simply as fun, he chose a pilgrimage which would include a visit to Rome and an audience with the Pope in the itinerary. A number of people from Lisieux were going and as it turned out M. Reverony was of the company.

The pilgrimage began in Paris, but Louis took the two girls there a few days beforehand so that they could see the sights. He was, for once, in tremendous spirits, humming old tunes to himself, and showing off his favourite places. Thérèse only really came to life in the church of Our Lady of Victories, a place she had wanted to see ever since her miracle cure. The pilgrims set off from Montmartre, offering their intention to God at Sacré Coeur. Thérèse, who had been shy at first of the society ladies and priests who were fellow-pilgrims, began to be more sociable. She noticed M. Reverony's eye on her several times, and thought he was watching to see whether she would make a good Carmelite.

She was tremendously excited as the train passed through the Swiss countryside, rushing from one side of the railway carriage to the other, gasping at the beauty of the mountains. The combination of majesty and prettiness in the little villages appealed to her enormously. 'That God should have seen fit to squander such masterpieces on a world of exile!' she exclaimed rather pompously. In fact, the splendour of the landscape may have threatened her resolve to become a Carmelite in a way that made her very uncomfortable. The thought that it might be a great pity to give up such a beautiful world, and that there might not even be a very good reason for doing so, was ruthlessly suppressed. She dealt with the overwhelming experience of natural beauty by promising herself that when she was 'shut up' she would use these sights to recall the greatness and power of God. 'No attraction for me about the puppet-shows of earth, now that I've had this foretaste of what our Lord has in store for those who love him.' The priggishness of this is somehow pathetic.

When they got to Milan Thérèse and Céline proved themselves indefatigable sightseers, inspecting every statue in the cathedral, dogging the Bishop's footsteps as he showed the relics, climbing the marble towers, examining the Campo Santo grave by grave.

Then there was Venice, Padua and Bologna, which was quite spoiled for Thérèse because a forward university student lifted her down from the train to the platform. Eventually the train drew into Rome and the sleeping travellers were woken by the porters shouting 'Roma, Roma'.

They 'did' all the sights. Predictably for Thérèse and Céline the high spot was the Colosseum – 'the arena in which so many martyrs had shed their blood for Christ – at last I should be able to kneel and kiss that holy ground.' But a cruel disappointment was in store for her. The arena turned out to be a litter of fallen masonry which visitors were expected to contemplate from behind a distant barrier. There, far below, was the special bit of paving on which so many martyrs had suffered, and Thérèse could barely see it. She looked vainly round for a ladder, and seeing no other hope for it, climbed over the barrier, shouting to Céline to do the same and started plunging down into the ruins, the ground crumbling beneath her at every step.

Louis and the guide were at first too thunderstruck to make any sound. Then Louis started feebly issuing orders to them to return, orders Thérèse, with her usual wilfulness, had not the slightest intention of obeying. Bruised and filthy, the two girls reached the bit of pavement, sank on their knees before it, and kissed the dust of the place where the martyrs had died. 'I asked for the grace to bear a martyr's witness to our Lord,' says

Thérèse, 'and felt deep in my heart that the prayer had been granted.'

The two girls snatched up a stone or two and returned by the perilous way they had come. It was naughty, but undeniably brave. In the Catacombs too they filched some earth from St Cecilia's church, and in the Church of St Agnes Thérèse worked loose a little red stone in the mosaic to present to the saint's namesake, Pauline, Sister Agnes, on her return. The two girls were high on the excitement and the fervid emotion of the pilgrimage.

The high spot of the tour was, of course, the audience with Pope Leo XIII. Frantic with nervousness they put on their black dresses, their lace mantillas, and the papal medal with its blue and white ribbon, and set off for the Pope's chapel in the Vatican. After Mass the Pope sat down in an armchair and the pilgrims approached one by one, kissing first his foot, then his hand, and finally receiving his benediction. Then the members of the papal guard touched each kneeling pilgrim on the shoulder and it was time to get up and make way for the next pilgrim.

Thérèse and Céline, like the naughty self-willed girls they were, had hatched a rather bold plan. When it was time for Thérèse to kneel down, instead of crouching dumbly there, she would speak up and ask the Pope's permission to enter Carmel early. It had been one thing to think this idea up in an hotel room; it was a resolve that became terrifying as her turn in the line approaching the Holy Father grew nearer. A number of priests stood round the Papal chair, among them M. Reverony. With shrewd insight into the girl with whom he had to deal M. Reverony remarked to the pilgrims in general that they must not speak to the Pope since there was not enough time.

Alarmed by this, perhaps wanting to give up her wild resolve, Thérèse turned anxiously to Céline, who immediately said 'Speak out!' With the air of one brave enough to dare all for the cause Thérèse kissed the Pope's foot, and then clasped her hands together, tears swimming into her eyes, and informed the Holy Father that she had a favour to ask of him. 'Most Holy

Thérèse as an eight-year-old

Thérèse aged three

Les Buissonnets

The interior of Les Buissonnets

Thérèse aged fifteen, with her hair up to impress the Bishop

Thérèse as a novice, aged sixteen

The Carmelite cloister and garden

The Carmelite Church

The refectory at Carmel

Thérèse's cell

Thérèse in 1894, the year she
started to write her autobiography

Thérèse three months before her
death

A typical statue of Thérèse in a village church

Father,' she went on while Pope Leo's great dark eyes stared into hers, 'in honour of your jubilee, I want you to let me enter the Carmelite order at fifteen.'

The Pope seemed stunned by this approach and turned questioningly to M. Reverony, who explained that Thérèse was known to him, that she wanted to enter Carmel, and that the case was being looked into.

'Very well, my child,' said the Pope, 'do what your superiors tell you.'

This wouldn't do for Thérèse at all, so she clutched the Pope's knees and continued, 'Yes, but if you'd say the word, Most Holy Father, everybody would agree.'[41]

To which the Pope replied slowly and with conviction, 'All's well, all's well; if God wants you to enter, you will.'

Thérèse was just about to start debating this with him, and Céline was also chipping in to vouch for the strength of Thérèse's vocation when the Papal guards, helped by M. Reverony, lifted her bodily to her feet. 'I kept my arms on the Pope's knees,' says Thérèse without shame, 'and they had to carry me away by main force.'[42] They carried her to the exit where she and Céline and Louis were soon reunited, the two girls in tears, and Louis as usual more upset at Thérèse's distress than at her bad behaviour. The skies of Rome had clouded over for the occasion.

Describing this in her autobiography Thérèse begins to expound her fantasy of herself as an idle plaything of the Child Jesus, a 'toy of no value', say a ball. 'He can throw it on the ground, kick it about, make a hole in it, leave it lying in a corner, or press it to his heart if he feels that way about it.'[43] In Rome, she fantasised, he made a hole in the ball to see what was inside it, and then abandoned it.

The grand tour continued with visits to Pompeii and Naples, Assisi, Florence, Pisa and Genoa, with the Martins always staying at the best hotels and seeing marvellous scenery. Thérèse says, with adolescent grandiosity, that there was no balm for a bruised heart in gilded ceilings, marble staircases and silk hangings. All she wanted to make her happy was Carmel. In

Florence she touched one of the nails used in the crucifixion.

She returned to Lisieux at the beginning of December, half expecting, for no very good reason, that she would be safely inside Carmel by Christmas. She went to the Carmel as soon as they returned to Lisieux, to take the little piece of filched mosaic to Pauline and to pour out all her adventures. Pauline was sympathetic as usual, and suggested another letter to the Bishop. Christmas came without further sign, though Thérèse had haunted the post office for days for the Bishop's reply.

On her return from Midnight Mass, the time when once Thérèse had looked so eagerly at the contents of the 'souliers', Thérèse found a bowl in which Céline had arranged a floating ship. The name of the ship was 'Self-Abandonment'. On this tiny ship the Child Jesus lay asleep with a ball close beside him.

Despite Céline's love Thérèse wept her way through Christmas Day till afternoon came and it was time to go off and visit Pauline at Carmel. The Carmelites, by now fully aware of the drama Thérèse had created around herself, had prepared a gift for her – a statue of the Child Jesus holding a ball in his hand with the name of Thérèse written upon it. Thérèse's fantasy of being a plaything of Jesus, perhaps confided to Pauline, had taken the fancy of the nuns. When she had got over this surprise the nuns sang a hymn about Jesus written specially by Pauline.

New Year's Day brought a mixed blessing. She learned that the Bishop had given his consent to her entry to Carmel, but that Carmel itself in the person of the Prioress, Mother Marie de Gonzague, had decided to postpone admitting her until Easter. It seems likely that they did this to spare the postulant the rigours of Lent and of winter cold right at the beginning of her time in the religious life, but Thérèse, with her usual fierce determination to have things her way, raged and wept about it, almost as if they had rejected her altogether. How could she possibly wait so long – a whole three months?

In the end she reconciled herself to the disappointment by devising small acts of renunciation and discipline for herself: 'to repress the rejoinder which sometimes came to my lips; to do little acts of kindness without attracting any attention to them;

to sit upright instead of leaning back in my chair.'[44] She seemed to feel this would make her 'less unworthy of a heavenly Bridegroom'. Once she had discovered that, rail as she might, nothing was going to get her into Carmel before Easter, she settled down to using this last three months 'in the world' as well as she could.

Chapter Six

THE LITTLE BRIDE

On the Feast of the Annunciation, 9 April 1888, Thérèse at last entered Carmel. She had found her way into one of the most austere of the religious orders. The Carmelite Order, for men, was founded in Palestine by St Berthold around 1154. By 1250 a 'Rule', a system of practice, had been laid down of extreme asceticism. In 1452 an Order of Carmelite Sisters was founded. In the earliest centuries of the Church, before there were religious orders, there had been many who had chosen, as individuals, to live as hermits in deserts and caves, giving up their lives to the contemplation of God. For some this had been a wonderfully fruitful experience. Others had lost themselves in loneliness and madness, and it was in an attempt to provide a more structured life in which to worship God that founders like St Benedict in the sixth century had collected communities together and drawn up sets of guidelines – Rules – to govern their behaviour.

The Benedictines were not primarily interested in solitude, but in a life of communal prayer, study, and manual work. The Carmelites attempted something different, a system which provided a kind of communal solitude. Living together mainly in silence, groups of friars or of nuns devoted their time to reciting a cycle of prayers, usually composed of fragments of scripture (the Office), to performing the manual duties of the house, and to private 'mental prayer' (as opposed to 'vocal' or spoken prayer). Carmelite friars undertook preaching, hearing confessions, and the giving of retreats, occupations which gave them contact with the outside world. The nuns never left their houses, not even for such events as family funerals, and their contact with the outside world was extremely limited, usually to fairly brief conversations through an iron grating – 'the grille' – a system not unlike some kinds of prison visiting.

The Carmelite Order, the Order of Our Lady of Mount Carmel, had an eventful history. By the sixteenth century, the period of the Counter Reformation, its austerities had become relaxed and the way of life easy-going. The great Teresa (little Thérèse's namesake as Louis Martin had often pointed out), entering a convent in Avila as a young girl, found that it was a sort of gossip-shop for the town, with young men coming regularly to sit in the parlour to chat with the prettiest nuns. There were outings and visits to friends' houses, and a very leisurely programme of prayer. The atmosphere was rather like that of a high-class girls' boarding school.

Teresa, though naturally sociable, soon felt dissatisfied with a life that had neither the freedom of 'the world' nor any real devotion to prayer. As her own mystical genius flowered she set about reforming the Carmelite houses, travelling all over Spain to set up houses with a very different attitude to life and prayer. The reform was extensive, covering every detail of the life of a nun or friar.

Teresa restored the Office, the great twenty-four-hour cycle of prayer, which meant rising in the night to recite Matins and Lauds in choir, returning to bed for another three hours and then rising again at five to say Prime and Terce, to have an hour's mental prayer which in turn led up to the conventual Mass. This was spoken on ordinary days, sung upon Sundays and Feast days. After breakfast there was work until mid-morning when Sext and None were recited. Dinner followed and after dinner recreation, a period in which all sat together and talked – in the case of nuns they usually sewed or drew at the same time. Then Vespers, more work, another hour of mental prayer, supper, a short recreation, Compline, and bed.

Teresa worked out exactly what the reformed Carmelites should eat: they should have no meat, they should have no milk or eggs on fast days or on Fridays, they should fast from Holy

Cross Day, 14 September until Easter. They should have no linen but their blankets, sheets and underclothing should be of wool, and they should lie on a straw palliasse. Winter and summer, instead of shoes or boots, they should wear a pair of straw Spanish sandals known as alpargatas – it was this latter detail that gave the Reformed Carmelites the nickname of Discalced Carmelites, meaning 'Carmelites without shoes'. The houses were without heating in winter except in one room where the Carmelites might go for brief periods to warm themselves.

Unlike the nuns in the easy-going convent of Teresa's youth the Discalced were bent on finding out their own and each other's frailties and doing penance for them. In the daily Chapter of Faults they 'proclaimed' themselves and one another, and performed penances, often of a fairly humiliating kind. To be 'mortified' was thought to be good for one's own soul and for the souls of others – it was a sort of death in life that reminded you that you were dust. When rebuked by your superior you prostrated yourself and kissed the floor in a sort of gratitude.

The Rule of the Discalced was drawn up by Teresa not with an air of misery but with a passionate enthusiasm for the cause, an enthusiasm congruent with the Carmelite device 'Zelo zelatus sum pro Domino Deo exercituum' (With zeal have I been zealous for the Lord God of Hosts). It was a call to a life of heroism, a call often answered by those who otherwise might have had little opportunity to be heroes or heroines. Suffering otherwise endured by the poor because they had no alternative was chosen readily by men and women often of upper- or middle-class backgrounds as a sign of their devotion to God. It was part of the paradox of Christianity, the way it turned the standards of the world upside down, so that things there thought good (riches, material possessions) became meaningless in the light of eternity, and that things there thought bad (pain, hunger, discomfort, cold) were transformed by faith into joyful obedience.

What the Carmelite life was about, according to Teresa of Avila, was, first, the contemplation of God. It was for this freedom that women and men detached themselves from the life of the family and commerce. Having herself charted the degrees and modes of prayer with an almost clinical accuracy, Teresa set up a system whereby men and women, not necessarily as gifted as herself, had space and time for exploring the relationship with God.

Out of that relationship sprang other religious practices and forms. Intercessory prayer through which the Carmelites prayed for the conversion of the world, 'the zeal for souls' as they called it, were one such form, a form which appealed to Teresa particularly in an age when 'heretics' were seen as a dreadful threat to the Catholic Church. Thérèse had been following in the same tradition when she prayed for the murderer Pranzini.

The act of intercessory prayer led to a concern for the outside world, if not always a very realistic understanding of what was going on in it, and a deep wish to relieve some of its suffering and redeem some of its evil. Deprived of other contact with the world the Carmelite nun offered not only her prayers, but her penances and mortifications for the good of others. Hunger and cold, sickness and frustration, the snubs and rebukes and disappointments and humiliations of her life were her 'work' for the world as much as her prayer.

It is not difficult to see some of the features of Carmelite life which had drawn young Thérèse as she had watched and studied it over the years, going to sit in the parlour to talk to her sisters and to Mother Marie de Gonzague, praying in the Carmelite Church, receiving letters from Pauline telling of her deep joy in the life and recommending 'practices' to her little sister. The deep respect with which the Martin family regarded religion, the frustrated ambition of both parents to join religious orders, the visits with her father to the reserved sacrament in the Carmelite church, the drama of her beloved Pauline 'giving up everything' to enter Carmel (accompanied as it was with deep pain for Thérèse) had all combined to make the life desirable.

Thérèse had a feeling for high drama, with herself at the centre of it, earning 'gloire' in one way or another. Of the two careers open to her, as wife and mother or as nun, not a great deal of 'gloire' seemed at first sight to be available, but at least the second offered a kind of hidden 'gloire'. Her yearning for the heroic, for self-sacrifice, for something bigger and more exciting than the humdrum realities of life in a provincial French town, meshed with the wilful self-abandon, the high ideals, the element of 'noblesse' in Carmelite spirituality. By shutting herself away in such a spectacular way, by surrendering the normal small joys and pleasures of life as well as the bigger ones such as freedom, sexuality, and childbearing, she changed from being an ordinary girl into being, in a paradoxical way, somebody. It was as if she had become the heroine of a novel.

The life suited Thérèse, of course, on far more than this romantic level. Already deeply involved in a sense of relationship with God, in particular with Jesus, now she felt that she would at last have time to know God better, to deepen the love she felt, as well as to pray for the conversion of more souls. She had always enjoyed liturgical practices, was never happier than when at Mass or reciting prayers. She had had little interest in men, and none, so far as we know, in the idea of sex or of bearing children. If ever a girl was suited to being a nun, Thérèse seemed to be that girl.

It is not easy to work out from her autobiography quite what the experience of Carmel was like for her once she had settled into the routine. After all her dreaming about it, it would be rather surprising if the reality had not come as something of a disappointment. She, however, insists that this was not so, that she had had no illusions about it, and that the life was exactly what she had expected. Almost in the next breath she speaks of suffering, of how 'those first footsteps of mine brought me up against more thorns than roses', a circumstance which seems much more likely than that an idealistic girl should have her illusions all preserved.

What is striking about the Carmelite timetable to the eyes of any outsider is how lacking in variety it is. Long hours of prayer relieved only by work, sleep, and a minimum of conversation, seem an odd regime for anyone, but particularly for a teenage girl. It is one in which the volatile emotions of adolescence, the need for inner exploration and the discovery of personal identity can have little place except in relation to God, or in limited relationship with other nuns. Similarly the adolescent growth into independence, limited as this was for nineteenth-century girls, is also made impossible by the enclosed environment which Thérèse was never again to leave, as well as by the emphasis on obedience.

Perhaps her desperate need for security, for a home from which important figures could not go away and leave her as successive mothers had done, more than compensated for her losses, at least at the beginning. There was the great pleasure of settling down to what she was quite sure was her life's work – loving God in as direct a way as possible. Then too, the life, despite, or maybe because of, its austerity, had great beauty, with its silence and its contrasts, with the feasts of the Christian year passing in splendid procession, with its intimate knowledge of the seasons, of heat and cold, of darkness and light. It was nobler, if only because so much simpler and, in a sense, more natural, than life in a cluttered and heated drawing-room. The clothes, the ritual, the 'stability' of being always in one place, the simple order of it all, had an undeniable grace.

Thérèse responded to the life as to the one thing she had always been waiting for. She does not complain of boredom, nor of resentment of her chosen imprisonment, though she does, rather pathetically, say how much she misses seeing wild flowers grow in the fields. Once the first exciting newness of it all has worn off, however, she will complain, as so many religious before and since, of *accidie*, a sort of depression in which life is drained of meaning. For her this bears no relation to the constrictions of the life, nor the anger that on some level she may feel about them. She insists that it comes, like all her feelings, directly from God.

What, we wonder, constituted the 'thorns', the suffering at the beginning of her life in Carmel of which she speaks so poignantly? Certainly manual work formed one of her early problems. The Carmelite choir sisters (the more educated women who sang the Office) did not do the hardest forms of work, scrubbing, digging, etc. – they had lay sisters, peasant women of little education, who performed those – but they washed clothes, swept floors, laid tables and sewed. Thérèse, so ill-prepared by her sisters to deal with the practical chores of life, suffered a lot over her incompetence at such tasks, and at the impatient and cutting remarks made by other nuns about her awkwardness. She had been brought up to be helpless, and now suddenly, just when she longed so much to be a good nun, she could not manage simple tasks that others performed easily. It was humiliating.

Then again it was difficult for her having a Novice Mistress, Sister Marie of the Angels, who, while being thoroughly kind, was not in the least *simpático* and who could make almost nothing of Thérèse's form of spirituality. Thérèse throve on intuitive understanding and withered in the cold blast of incomprehension. The Rule obliged her to speak daily of her spiritual concerns to Sister Marie of the Angels, and daily she blushed and stuttered and struggled, unwilling to speak of her experiences, and knowing in advance that the advice she was given was not what she needed.

It seems possible that even Pauline, yearned over from afar during the long years she had been in the convent and no longer available to her little sister, may have been a bit of a disappointment, now that, to a degree, she was permanently accessible. She still tended to see Thérèse as a little girl, as if their relationship was fixed for ever at the point when she had left home, whereas for Thérèse becoming a Carmelite was synonymous with being grown-up, or at least trying to be.

There was certainly one person in the convent who had the intelligence and the spiritual knowledge to respond to Thérèse in the way she wished – the Prioress, Mother Marie de Gonzague. Her position in the convent, to which she had been elected, automatically endowed her with total authority since the nuns had taken vows of obedience. But her influence went far beyond the importance of her office. Of aristocratic background, attractive and educated, Reverend Mother was a strong and autocratic personality who commanded enormous attention. In the restricted emotional life of the enclosure it is clear that some of the nuns were more than a little in love with her. In spite of the general fears about 'special friendships' which were such a feature of the religious orders of the time, and in spite of teachings about 'detachment', it seemed to be natural and allowable to be emotionally fixated on 'Mother'; at any rate Mother herself did little to discourage the process, in fact in subtle ways she encouraged it, picking certain nuns to take care of her during her numerous illnesses, making it clear, in arbitrary fashion, that she preferred some to others. No doubt many of the feelings held by the nuns about their actual mothers, both good and bad, got projected onto Mother Marie.

It would have taken a far more mature personality than Thérèse's not to get drawn into the emotional web that surrounded Reverend Mother. Scarcely out of the period of the schoolgirl crush, possibly still searching for her lost mother, lacking others with whom to share her peculiar kind of spiritual intensity, it was inevitable that she would share in the ardent love that a group of the nuns felt for the Prioress.

If the Prioress had responded straightforwardly to Thérèse's feelings, showing gentle encouragement in her struggles, interest in her spiritual preoccupations, and quietly suggesting the ways in which she was going wrong, Thérèse might have grown in the relationship and been spared much of the suffering of the first years.

As it was, Mother Marie, pleading, of course, that everything she did was for the nuns' spiritual good, made a capricious and sometimes cruel use of power. She showed favouritism to some nuns and took pleasure in making others feel rejected by her. Among those rejected was Thérèse. Reverend Mother was harsh with her, rebuking her frequently, often with sarcasm; Thérèse said ironically that she had only to see Reverend Mother to find herself kissing the floor. Naive, sensitive, idealistic, coming from a home where she had been much petted and admired, Thérèse suffered acutely.

Reverend Mother's excuse was precisely that Thérèse had been spoiled at home. Point was given to this observation by the fact that Pauline and Marie, always accustomed to take care of

Thérèse, and convinced of her 'delicacy' since her childhood illness, could not stop fussing over her, and frequently requested special dispensations for her. In her first winter at Carmel, before she had taken the habit, they arranged for fur boots to be sent in for her ('Thérèse feels the cold so badly'), an annoying intervention for one trying to practise austerity.

Then, too, the precious way Thérèse had been brought up probably made her more than a little hypochondriacal, not least because she suffered a good deal from illness. Thérèse continually reported stomachaches to the Prioress (the Rule did, in fact, require her to report illness to her superiors) until she was crushingly rebuked for being so interested in herself.

Mother Marie had got a little princess on her hands which was not an easy situation to deal with, especially as Pauline, who was obliquely critical of Reverend Mother's way of handling Thérèse, was emerging as the leader of a rival group in Carmel. Mother was beginning to wonder, as well she might, at the wisdom of taking three sisters from one family; the Martin family had a way of sticking together.

But the very real difficulties of being Prioress do not excuse the misery she inflicted on Thérèse who, it was plain for anyone to see, was in love with her. Much later Thérèse wrote painfully of her days as a postulant, of how she would think of excuses (permissions to do this or that) to go into Reverend Mother's office just to see her and talk to her for a moment – 'a crumb of comfort' as she puts it. She fought her longing, sometimes clinging to the banisters to prevent herself from following her inclination.

Another novice, who had followed her into the convent, was soundly rebuked by Thérèse for her affection for Reverend Mother with a degree of righteous indignation that speaks volumes for her own bitter struggles with her feelings.

Her ingenuous habit of pointing out other people's faults to them, even outside the Chapter of Faults, did not make people like Thérèse any better. She came across as a goody-goody, her daddy and sisters' darling, and a religious know-all who seemed to feel she had a hot line to Jesus. It was very irritating. What seems to emerge is that, after the first welcome, Thérèse was not really very popular with her Sisters in religion. As a result of her loneliness and wretchedness as a schoolgirl she had never grown confident in the art of getting along with people outside her family. Knowing that she was an oddity she was sharp and defensive in relations to others. Other girls had never seemed to like her much, for reasons that were not entirely clear to her, and she had resigned herself to a certain sort of loneliness, a habit which stood her in quite good stead in the loneliness of life in a Carmelite convent. But whatever her problems in relationship, and however unfortunate her family's interventions, there was something that impressed the nuns about Thérèse in spite of themselves. Her commitment was greater than most of theirs, something to which they gave their respect, if somewhat grudgingly.

One faithful friend to her was old Mother Geneviève. In her very first half hour in Carmel Thérèse had been aware of Mother Geneviève kneeling in the choir praying for her. Again and again the aged nun showed her that she cared and understood about her struggles, as if she saw her own youthful self in the anguished young novice.

Mother Geneviève's maturity and balance seem to have been unusual. Most descriptions of the life of Carmel and its relationships at this period suggest an emotional hothouse in which tiny incidents were inflated beyond all reason, or in which nerves were frayed to breaking point and beyond.

Reverend Mother was the emotional centre of many people's lives. For Mother to be too unwell to come to Recreation caused her, Thérèse tells us, the most acute disappointment. What she continually longed for was to be able to spend time talking to Reverend Mother and best of all to be able to talk about her spiritual concerns with her – spiritual direction, as it was called. Some nuns had this privilege. Thérèse had to make do with a sharp yes or no when she formally asked for a permission, or a stinging criticism of the way she was cleaning the stairs or weeding the garden. Once she had the job of returning the keys of the grille to Reverend Mother's room. Looking forward to the brief exchange of words when she got there she was disappointed to find another nun there. Thérèse insisted she must hand over the keys to Reverend Mother herself. The other nun said that was impossible since Reverend Mother was ill and asleep. Thérèse wrangled over the matter, using the excuse of obedience to get her own way, until at last Reverend Mother emerged from her sickbed to claim the keys in person. It is impossible to read this without feeling the emotional poverty of Thérèse's life at the time, the desperate longing for warm human contact, and the consequent sadness and loneliness when this was denied and she returned to her silent cell.

It was, of course, in being 'Alone with the Alone', in experiencing the moment of pain or joy as they detached themselves from earthly loves, that the Carmelites were supposed to fulfil their vocation. Remembering, years later, her longing for love in the early days, Thérèse was inclined to say that it was good that she had been treated so harshly, that she had had to endure the 'firm discipline' of Mother, that her 'little flower' had seen no sunshine to speak of, but had been watered by the 'waters of humiliation'. She had learned to live – without praise, encouragement, sympathy or love.

What Thérèse writes suggests that although at the beginning of her time in Carmel, she was obsessed with Mother (as with her history she might well have been), later, from sheer necessity, she worked to a position of emotional independence. Certainly in the pages addressed to Mother Marie towards the end of the autobiography we catch a glimpse of a mature Thérèse who can offer both affection and cool criticism to the adored superior with an even hand. But before that we may guess there was a long period when the lonely and emotionally smitten little girl suffered a great deal from Reverend Mother's treatment of her, and that in this she found the thorns she so poignantly describes. Even after Thérèse had learned detachment Mother Marie still behaved towards her in a punitive and unsympathetic way.

Given Thérèse's total dedication to the religious life, her passionate attempt to be a good nun with every fibre of her being, we may wonder why Mother Marie behaved as she did. No doubt if we could ask her she would say that it was a method of training, and that because Thérèse's vocation was a remarkable one there was all the more reason to be exacting and stern with her, to be sure of bringing her to a state of perfection.

At the same time she must often have been irritated at the intervention of Thérèse's sisters on her behalf, at their pleas for special treatment and dispensations for a child who had freely chosen to enter Carmel and was perfectly fit and well. Maybe she thought Thérèse had put them up to it, maybe she worked her exasperation at them off on Thérèse. It later emerged that she was very jealous of Pauline's status in the community, and it also seems likely that in a community of around twenty-five, three sisters from one family, later to be followed by another sister and a cousin, may have seemed a threat to the balance of power.

Her fears and moods are understandable enough, but it is impossible to forget that, once elected, a Reverend Mother had absolute power. Nuns are not exempt from the danger of absolute power corrupting absolutely and reading of the almost flirtatious way Mother Marie alternately approached and neglected Thérèse, and her extraordinary talent for doing or saying the hurtful thing, it is impossible for a modern reader not to observe a sado-masochistic pattern at work. It is to Thérèse's credit that instead of being drawn further and further into this hateful game, she grew to a place in which Mother's torments could no longer touch her. But not quickly, or easily. Easily depressed, she was sometimes wretched to the point of melancholia. On one such occasion she went to visit old Mother Geneviève as she lay on her sickbed, Thérèse in such deep spiritual darkness that she even doubted the love of God. The old woman drew her to her, gazed deeply at her and said 'Serve God with peace and with joy; remember, always, that our God is a God of peace.' Thérèse went away deeply comforted.

She often needed this sort of personal attention, rarely as it was forthcoming. In the unheated rooms she suffered terribly from the cold, and in winter was often unable to sleep because of it. Her nerves, unstrung by tiredness and silence, were often irritated past endurance by the small noises – the shufflings, fidgetings and throat-clearings – made repeatedly by Sisters in choir. At the big communal washtub where nuns stood round in a circle scrubbing the sheets, she suffered, as they all did, from the hot noonday sun beating down on her thickly-clad body, and she had the conviction that other nuns splashed her with dirty water on purpose. She suffered too under the castigations of a crippled old nun, Mother Peter, whom she had to help make the painful journey from choir to refectory, leaning heavily on Thérèse who always went too slow or too fast. Once in the refectory she settled her with difficulty at the table, and cut up her food for her. The old nun, often in pain, was sharp with her, though she gradually became fond of her and dependent on her.

There were many good moments, moments of luminous prayer, of transparent joy, of almost lightheaded happiness. In May, a month after she had joined the community, her sister Marie made her profession, taking the name of Sister Marie of the Sacred Heart. Thérèse herself crowned her with the traditional bridal wreath. The following January, the Chapter 'received' Thérèse, permitting her to become 'clothed', that is to wear the dress of a Carmelite novice. A photograph was taken of her on this day of days wearing the long brown habit of wool with the rosary at the waist, and the white veil of those who have not yet taken life vows. She looks plump and rather jolly, still very much the schoolgirl hiding an irrepressible grin.

The clothing ceremony had very nearly had to be postponed. Soon after Marie's profession, and only a few months after Thérèse had left him, Louis had had some kind of seizure, perhaps a second stroke, or possibly a fit that presaged a mental breakdown. Whichever it was he had been seriously confused, at times mad, a fact which brought the Martin sisters grief and, it would seem, embarrassment. He had borne the loss of the beloved Thérèse with extreme nobility, writing to friends that 'that little queen of mine, Thérèse, entered Carmel yesterday. It's the sort of sacrifice only God could ask of one. No, don't offer me any sympathy; my heart is overflowing with happiness.' The collapse in his health does not seem the likely outcome of extreme joy but rather of emotions repressed and denied. A cruel twist was that while the daughter he loved so passionately had disappeared forever into Carmel, Léonie, such a trial to her parents, had returned from her unsuccessful stay with the Visitation nuns. The daughter he wanted was gone, and the daughter he didn't want had returned.

With the extraordinary capacity to pull themselves together in times of need – a feature of the Martin family – Louis managed to gather his wandering wits in time for his daughter's clothing and to appear on the day looking composed and handsome, although he was reeling under yet another blow. Céline, who had been his nurse during his recent illness, had now informed him that, like her sisters, she intended to join the Carmelite order.

Thérèse was tremendously excited to have reached 'clothing'. To her delight there was an unexpected shower of snowflakes as white as her veil. Born in January she liked to think of herself as a white winter flower.

At the end of the ceremonies she kissed her father and went back to the snow-covered cloister garth and the little statue of the Child Jesus amid its flowers and lights. She decided that the snow was a betrothal present from Jesus. The Bishop of Bayeux, who had come for the ceremony, stayed to talk with her in obvious admiration for her sense of vocation.

A month later Louis Martin had a more serious attack, and seemed not to know who he was. Thérèse reports it as 'such a wretched, such a humiliating experience' for him. He was confined for a time in an asylum at Caen where Céline and Léonie went to look after him. His health improved after a while – there is a photograph of him in an invalid carriage surrounded by relatives and his two remaining daughters – but from then until his death in 1894 he was to move, with temporary remissions, into deeper states of darkness and helplessness. The chief burden of caring for him was borne by Céline and Léonie, but the three sisters in the convent seemed to feel, oddly, that they were the ones marked out for suffering. Mental illness, whatever the cause, carried a stigma which was uncomfortable.

Thérèse says that 'words couldn't do justice to our feelings', though, of course, 'those three years of Papa's cruel torment were years of great value, of great spiritual profit to his family.'[45] Mother Geneviève, loving as ever, seemed to be the only Sister who fully understood and sympathised.

Meanwhile convent life continued as usual. After taking the habit Thérèse had begun work in the refectory, where Pauline was also working. She tidied, cleaned, laid and cleared tables, distributed water, bread and beer. She claimed that the refectory was a good place for trampling self-love under foot. She tried hard to do that in other ways too.

She struggled with her disappointment when a favourite water jug she had been allowed to keep in her cell was allocated to someone else and she got an old chipped one in its place. She was rebuked for the breaking of a jug which she had not broken at all, and kissed the ground without making an excuse. She tried to inflict various kinds of penances or mortifications on herself, like not leaning back in her chair, but if these were noticed she got rebuked for them.

On one level all the examples she gives of her struggles seem rather foolish, the minutiae of a life so narrow that trifles assumed a vast importance. There was something disconcertingly out of perspective about much that happened at the Lisieux Carmel – it is tempting to wonder how these Sisters would have coped with a job or a family – yet there is a sense in which Thérèse is right. It is the details of life which hurt or which give us joy, which are the straws which tell us what is really going on in our hearts and our souls. With a childlike candour and her usual thin-skinned sensitivity Thérèse notes painfully that 'you got no thanks for doing your duty, unless you were prepared to stick up for yourself, whereas the mistakes you made became public property at once!'[46] She was not without a childish lust for the sort of revenge in which the grown-ups would feel sorry. 'All these things', she pondered, 'would come out on the Day of Judgement.'

Thérèse, like her Sisters in religion, saw this period between 'taking the habit' and her profession as a betrothal period. Few of them can perhaps have pursued this idea as literally as she did. When she was told that her profession – the 'wedding' – which was due to take place a year after her taking the habit, would be postponed (maybe because of her youth, or maybe because of Louis's illness) she was very upset but told Jesus that she would not ask him to change this arrangement. 'I'm ready to wait just as long as you want me to; only it mustn't be through any fault of mine that this union between us has to be put off . . . I know quite well that nothing in heaven or earth will prevent you from coming to me, and making me, once and forever, your bride.' In what she believes to be the correct attitude of a bride-to-be she says, of Jesus, 'After all, I'd given myself over to our Lord for his pleasure, his satisfaction, not mine.'[47]

She consoled herself, in the long wait for profession, in preparing what she called her 'wedding dress'. Nuns making their profession did approach the altar in a white dress with a gauzy wedding-veil and a bridal wreath made of roses. Thérèse's dress would be made of white silk trimmed with swansdown, and her long fair hair would be curled for the occasion. It is not this dress she had in mind when preparing for her 'wedding' however, but one 'all set with jewels'. By jewels, she says, she means 'trials' – Papa's illness, the disappointment that he could not come to see her make her profession, the emotional dryness of the retreat she made before the great day.

A striking thing happened on the eve of her profession. Making the Stations of the Cross she suddenly, and for the first time, had a clear vision (which she ascribed to the Devil) that her vocation was 'a mere illusion. I still saw life at Carmel as a desirable thing, but the devil gave me the clear impression that it wasn't for me . . . Darkness everywhere; I could see nothing and think of nothing beyond this one fact, that I'd no vocation. I was in an agony of mind.'

She did what a nun should do and reported the feeling to her Novice Mistress. Even as she began to describe it it vanished. Still worried perhaps, Thérèse rehearsed it all again for Reverend Mother who 'only laughed'. Only Mother Geneviève was to tell the girl later, that she too had had similar torturing doubts before taking her final vows.

The next morning, 8 September, Thérèse walked up the aisle to take her vows. As was the custom she had written out her 'billet de profession', and wore it under her dress against her heart. A sort of declaration of purpose, it read:

Jesus, my heavenly Bridegroom, never may I lose this second robe of baptismal innocence; take me to yourself before I commit any wilful fault, however slight. May I look for nothing and find nothing but you and you only; may creatures mean nothing to me, nor I to them – you, Jesus, are to be everything to me. May earthly things have no power to disturb the peace of my soul; that peace is all I ask of you, except love; love that is as infinite as you are, love that has no eyes for myself, but for Jesus, only for you. Jesus, I would like to die a martyr for your sake, a martyr in soul or in body; better still, in both. Give me the grace to keep my vows in their entirety; make me understand what is expected of one who is your bride. Let me never be a burden to the community, never claim anybody's attention; I want them all to think of me as no better than a grain of sand, trampled under foot and forgotten, Jesus, for your sake. May your will be perfectly accomplished in me, till I reach the place you have gone to prepare for me. Jesus, may I be the means of saving many souls; today, in particular, may no soul be lost, may all those detained in Purgatory win release. Pardon me, Jesus, if I'm saying more than I've any right to; I'm thinking only of your pleasure, of your contentment.[48]

The ceremony passed happily. Thérèse seemed to be carried along on a tide of interior peace. The long curls were cut and she made her vows. When the ceremony was over she laid the bridal wreath at the foot of Our Lady's statue. She made the present of a flower in bud to the statue of the Child Jesus. When it grew dark she gazed up at the stars promising herself that soon she would join her heavenly Bridegroom in joy everlasting.

The day appointed for the final ceremony of 'taking the veil', of exchanging the white headdress of the novice for the black one of the professed nun, and of assuming her full name in religion – Thérèse de l'Enfant Jésus et de la Sainte Face – was

24 September. (Like her sister, Pauline, she had started to spend much time gazing and meditating upon the face of the dying Jesus.) On this occasion she felt very tearful and orphaned. Papa could not come, the Bishop who had become a kind of surrogate father and who had promised to come was ill, and Père Pichon was in Canada. A few days after Thérèse took the veil, her cousin Jeanne Guérin got married. With a rather sickening coyness Thérèse tells us that, on Jeanne's visit to the convent, she studied her well to learn 'all the little attentions which a bride ought to lavish on her bridegroom'. She also used Jeanne's wedding invitation as a model for a mock invitation of her own.

Almighty God, Creator of heaven and earth, Lord of the whole world, and the glorious Virgin Mary, queen of the heavenly court, invite you to take part in the wedding of their son Jesus Christ, King of Kings and Lord of Lords, to Thérèse Martin, now invested by right of dowry with two freedoms, those of the Sacred Infancy and of the Passion.[49]

It is not a modest exercise.

Very soon after Thérèse's profession Mother Geneviève died. It was the first death-bed Thérèse had attended and she watched with interest, noting with surprise her own inability to have any feelings about it at all until the very moment when Mother Geneviève died, when she was filled with joy. Believing Mother Geneviève a saint the Sisters were eager to preserve relics of her. Thérèse removed a teardrop from the dead woman's cheek on to a piece of fine linen and forever afterwards carried it round her neck in the locket in which she kept her vows. Soon afterwards she dreamed that Mother Geneviève was making her will, that she had given everything she had away to the Sisters and there was nothing left for Thérèse. But suddenly the old woman had raised herself in bed and repeated three times, in a penetrating voice, 'To you, I leave my heart.'

Chapter Seven

THE LITTLE WAY

Thérèse was now approaching her nineteenth birthday. At the beginning of 1892 she was put in charge of the sacristy, the job she liked best of all the jobs in the convent, since she loved to touch the sacred vessels and prepare the altar linen 'for our Lord's coming'. But suddenly the convent was hit with the scourge of influenza and several nuns died – no doubt the poor diet and the bitter cold of the unheated rooms scarcely helped recovery. Thérèse, with a couple of other nuns, alone escaped the plague. With a new strength and aplomb she found herself nursing the sick, organising funerals, and laying out the dead. Thérèse's birthday was marked by the death of one nun, and two more followed in quick succession. One day Thérèse had a presentiment that Sister Madeleine had died, and going into her room found her lying dead on her pallet fully dressed. Sisters already in a state of desperate weakness dragged themselves up to help others worse off. There was one funeral after another.

It is difficult not to feel that Thérèse enjoyed the drama of all this in what was otherwise a very uneventful life. She enjoyed the sense of being useful and practical, someone to whom others turned for help for a change. On a different level she was pleased that because of the danger to life she could receive Communion every day – something unusual in those days.

She noticed at about this time that her old scruples were much less troublesome. She cheerfully admits to her thoughts often wandering during her prayers and to occasional periods of nodding off. The religious life had loosened her up in this important respect.

She had also been lucky in finding a priest who understood her and to whom she felt she could really open her heart. She had been going through one of her bad times, even to the point of doubting whether heaven actually existed, but knew from of old that no one would listen to her fears. Going into the confessional at a retreat (a period of withdrawal from the common life for private recollection), however, she found to her surprise that she could open her heart and felt herself understood 'with an insight that was surprising, almost uncanny'. Pouring out her fears and scruples, her terror of somehow dropping out of the sight of God and being lost (as she had been lost when Zélie died, and when Pauline had left her?) she received a response that totally reassured her. Speaking as a representative of God, the priest said, using every ounce of his authority to comfort her, 'I assure you that He is well satisfied with what you are doing for Him.' The loneliness of convent life with the carping criticism of Reverend Mother and the abrasiveness of daily contact with her fellow-nuns suddenly fell away. Thérèse felt appreciated, loved, caressed, in the way that she needed so badly.

Nowadays she was allowed to do more congenial work in the convent. She redecorated the chapel, she acted as an assistant store-keeper, she became 'Tourière' – the sister who operated the revolving hatch through which presents and communications of all kinds entered Carmel from the outside world, a job which gave her a little external contact. In her spare time she began writing poetry and doing some painting. The poetry lacked originality of expression and when it was not a purely pious theme tended to be a nostalgic recollection of life in the old days at Les Buissonets. Her painting, like every other form of self-expression, was pressed into religious service. She painted a coat of arms to be shared between herself and Jesus, a *jeu d'esprit* of heavy solemnity and humourlessness. The life of Carmel did not seem to encourage great art.

In 1893, to Thérèse's great delight, her sister Pauline, Sister Agnes, was elected Reverend Mother in Mother Marie de Gonzague's place. It was, says Thérèse, a golden day 'that

Pauline should stand, in my life, for our Lord's earthly representative'. The election in fact had nearly split the convent in
two with factions rooting for each of the two powerful leaders,
and Mother Marie de Gonzague openly sulking when she failed
to be re-elected. Thérèse was appointed assistant to the Novice
Mistress.

In 1894, Céline, released by the sudden death of Louis in
July, entered Carmel as Thérèse had all along been determined
that she should. Any attempt by Céline to choose another life for
herself was circumvented by Thérèse's formidable determination. When Céline tried to go to a dance Thérèse 'wept in
torrents' and prayed vigorously against the undertaking, so
much so, Thérèse reports with smug satisfaction, that the young
man who accompanied her 'simply couldn't get her to take the
floor. There was nothing for it but to take her back to her place.'
Thérèse is serenely unworried by any thought of moral black-
mail over this episode, as she quite cheerfully admits to having
foiled a plan of Père Pichon that Céline should join his mission
in Canada. (She is also shameless about having 'prayed down' a
sister who, not without reason, thought that three Martin sisters
in one community were quite enough.) Thérèse had, as she says,
'this cherished dream . . . that Céline should enter Carmel, our
Carmel. It seemed like a dream too good to be true, that I should
ever be able to live under the same roof again with my childhood's playmate . . .' What she would do, Thérèse decided, was
to offer 'dear Céline, fresh and graceful as a nosegay of flowers,
to the same Master's service'.[50] Nothing, not Céline's own
wishes, those of a cherished priest or a fellow-sister, counted
beside such a dream. Thérèse had a will of iron. By September
Céline was safely in Carmel.

As always the contradictions of Thérèse's nature strike us, the
extraordinary egotism buried in the claims of self-abandonment.
Like a wife who might hesitate to demand something for herself
but will do it unhesitatingly if she feels it is for her husband,
Thérèse has no qualms about manipulating other people if she can
persuade herself that it is what her husband Jesus would like. The
self-deception of this – the hidden will to power – is distasteful.

To read Thérèse's writing is to feel that Carmel gave an inadequate outlet for her energies and her intelligence. It lacked stimulus, challenge, the opportunity for physical exercise and virtually all opportunity for what might be called 'play'. Life was solemn, dull, uneventful, silent, a kind of middle age imposed on an ardent girl. Naturally enough Thérèse, always an imaginative child, turned to fantasy as consolation.

In addition to fantasies of herself as the 'little wife' of Jesus or as his childhood plaything, she had always been given to fantasies of herself as crusader or martyr. Now these day-dreams returned, together with poignant pictures of herself as priest, apostle, missionary traveller, Pontifical Zouave dying on the battlefield in defence of the Church. In these intense dreams she represses entirely her knowledge of what it is that debars her from a rich active life – being born a woman with its disappointing weight of social disability – and fancies herself truly eligible, as a man would be, for the adventure she craves.

She feels as if 'she could never satisfy the needs of my nature without performing . . . every kind of heroic action at once'. If she were a priest

how lovingly I'd carry you in my hands when you came down from heaven at my call; how lovingly I'd bestow you upon men's souls . . . I long to enlighten men's minds as the prophets and doctors did; I feel the call of an Apostle. I'd live to travel all over the world, making your name known and planting your cross on heathen soil.'[51]

But more than all these ambitions she longed to die for Jesus, to shed her blood to the last drop.

Martyrdom was the dream of my youth, and this dream has grown in the sheltered world of Carmel . . . A single form of martyrdom would never be enough for me, I should want to experience them all. I should want to be scourged and crucified as you were; to be flayed alive like St Bartholomew, to be dipped in boiling oil like St John . . . offering my neck to the executioner like St Agnes and St Cecily, and, like my favourite Joan of Arc, whispering your name as I was tied to the stake.[52]

The drama of martyrdom, the masochism and orgasmic

excitement of total abandonment, the siren call of death, all beckon the young woman away from the sombre reality of life towards the lurid colours of imagination. Eventually the frustration of disappointed imagination pushes her back again towards another struggle with reality, and it is one which rewards her greatly.

Reading St Paul she dwells on the famous saying that the purpose of life is love (not heroics), and it is as if Jesus himself has spoken to her telling her that her vocation is love and that it can be realised right here and right now. In a transformation of her masochism she evolves her 'Little Way' or 'Little Doctrine' as her sister Marie liked to call it, a path as straightforward and liveable as her fantasies of being boiled in oil were perverse and fantastic.

The Little Way meant trying to get on with life as it actually was, living it with kindness, unselfishness, detailed care – 'always doing the tiniest thing right, and doing it for love'. It was, in some curious way, the reversal of everything she had been taught, the inflated form of Christianity with its dreams of sanctity and martyrdom. Now she saw that all you were asked to do was to follow the will of God, whatever it might be, and to give yourself unreservedly to *that* life and to no other. In a moment of revelation she realised that instead of trying to be something she was not – a crusader or an Apostle – she was now free to be Thérèse with all her little problems, including the babyishness which she had begun to recognise in herself as a kind of permanent imprint. It was as if she had scraped away years of nonsense and found a fundamental truth which had eluded her by its very simplicity. 'It's love I ask for, love is all the skill I have.' It struck her that her very poverty of gifts and of opportunities might make her a kind of representative of all who were poor and inadequate in the world, but who strove to love God. 'I implore you', she says to Jesus, 'to look down in mercy on a whole multitude of souls that share my littleness.' Praying for those souls, working out the 'Little Way' in her own life were, she saw now, her true vocation, and it was one that filled her with joy. She no longer dreamed of dreadful martyrdoms because she saw that, in the present, without manipulations on her part, her life was already a 'burnt offering' for a purpose she could only dimly understand but knew that she had chosen.

Thérèse's spiritual coming of age had important consequences for the convent since, on becoming Prioress, Pauline had appointed Mother Marie de Gonzague as Mistress of Novices, with Thérèse as her assistant. For the first time Thérèse had a job that made use of her abilities and which forced upon her the human contact she had dodged most of her life. There were not many novices, one or two at a time, one of whom was Céline, but Thérèse had to help instruct them, listen patiently to their spiritual and personal difficulties, point out to them the self-deceptions and motions of false pride which motivated them, and generally act with a maturity that had never been required of her before.

It would have been easier to perform the task without being the underling of the sarcastic and fault-finding Mother Marie de Gonzague – the novices, Thérèse felt, took advantage of this situation to play her up a bit, but she was pleased and touchingly proud at finding she could do the job. She realised that her long apprenticeship in the art of unpopularity stood her in good stead; she could point out faults and endure the pique of the novices without worrying too much about being disliked. Perhaps this very fact made them begin to trust her and she found to her delight that they seemed glad to confide in her (maybe because they found Mother Marie too formidable). She was warmed by this human contact and astonished to find herself, for the first time in her life, perceptive about others, sometimes astonishing the novices by strokes of insight about their states of mind. She began to develop a kind of psychological interest in them, as well as a human and spiritual one. 'One thing I've noticed is this,' she says. 'All souls, more or less, have to put up the same sort of fight, but on the other hand no two souls are alike.'[53]

She discovered that different techniques worked with different Sisters. For some of them it was important to know that she too had her fair share of human weakness, so that they could become bold enough to admit their own humiliating defects. Others needed to believe her perfect for a while, and she saw that there was a sort of upside-down humility in bearing with their projections while they found themselves in the religious life. Some needed enormous gentleness, and others strictness and firmness. All of them needed to find her a good example, in that she led the religious life joyfully and with integrity.

She needed to be available for conversation, to know when to be unyielding with a novice who was looking for a loophole to let herself off the recognition of her own pride, to know when to scold and when to let something go.

So much wisdom and good sense in a very young woman shows how much Thérèse had grown up at Carmel, what a long way she had come from Les Buissonets. She was growing to be an important figure in the little community.

In 1894 she wrote a play in verse about her favourite Joan of Arc, not then a saint (she was canonised in 1920, only five years before Thérèse herself) but a much loved French figure with the improbable title of Venerable. On two or three days in the year Carmel discipline was slightly relaxed and on one such day Thérèse's patriotic and pious piece was enacted, with herself playing the part of the saint. Rather surprisingly she was permitted to wear home-made armour over a skirt for the occasion and wear her hair, now grown quite long again, in flowing locks round her shoulders. Céline, wearing her habit, played St Margaret.

During Pauline's term of office as Prioress she suggested that Thérèse start a correspondence with a young seminarian who had written to the convent asking for a Sister to pray for him as he approached ordination and prepared to go out to the mission field. Thérèse had always thought she would like to have a brother who was a priest and she accepted eagerly the task of praying for the young man and writing letters to him. Such requests were not unusual and when Mother Marie de Gonzague received a similar request and invited Thérèse to respond to it, she felt that she now had two brothers, a sort of substitute for the two brothers who had died in infancy.

In December of 1894 Thérèse was launched in an undertaking that was to have tremendous consequences. Sitting chatting with Pauline and Marie one evening, Thérèse was going over some of her favourite memories of childhood. Marie casually suggested that she should write them down. Pauline, momentarily taken with the idea, but knowing that Thérèse would probably never find the time for it, suddenly assumed her official mantle as Prioress, and said 'I order you to write down the memories of your childhood.' Thérèse, obviously surprised, had no choice but to obey.

Her life made little provision for uninterrupted bouts of concentration, but at night when she could have been sleeping she began to write in a school exercise book, keeping the pages in a wooden writing desk.

It is not easy to imagine quite why Pauline had issued the order – perhaps merely on a whim – but she had unwittingly given an extraordinary source of pleasure to her sister. With unconcealed enjoyment, and no little literary talent, Thérèse, always so locked in her childhood experience, describes in vivid detail the life of her pious bourgeois French family, first at Alençon, then at Lisieux. She evokes days in the kitchen with her mother and Victoire, games played with Céline, outings with Papa, moments when her big sisters returned from school, the appalling pain of the loss of her mother and of Pauline, the joys and excitements of religion, the pain of school and the pleasures of the family. There is sentimentality and false piety (some of it inserted after her death), moments of sheer silliness and a pervading lack of humour, but nevertheless it is a literary *tour de force*, a piece of writing which carries the reader along fascinated except where it slides into religiosity. Thérèse is, as always, deeply fascinated by herself and her own story, and, unexpectedly, this makes her a wonderful *raconteuse*. We remember that her only success among her playmates at school was her ability to tell a story.

It is difficult to imagine what she felt as she worked at this recapitulation of the family life of the Martins. Her pleasure in writing it suggests that it was a wholesome holiday from 'being religious' – a chance to be simply and naturally herself and to remember happy times. The book took her about a year to write, presumably because she had very little time or energy to work on it, though the style is one of rapt literary concentration. In January 1896, Thérèse carried the completed manuscript into chapel with her, bowed before the stall of the Prioress, her sister Pauline, and laid the sheets down before her, her task completed 'under obedience'.

As it happened Pauline's three-year term as Prioress was completed a week or two later, and by a curious swinging of the pendulum of convent politics which was to make both women alternate leaders of the community for a number of years to come, Mother Marie was restored to the office of Prioress and Pauline had to stand down. In the work of handing over office she did not get a chance to read her sister's manuscript until a couple of months later – one sees her storing it up as a sort of treat at a time of greater leisure. She recognised its quality at once, and thought about the possibility of circulating it among friends of the convent as an exercise of evangelism, but found herself in a dilemma. In this part of her memoirs (Thérèse started a new manuscript soon after, this time addressed to her sister Marie) she had concentrated almost entirely upon the domestic life of the Martins and said very little about the life of the convent. Maybe if Pauline had still been Prioress, as she had probably expected to be, she would have added a few religious conceits to the book and sent it out to friends. But she could not imagine that Mother Marie, wary of the Martin sisters in general and of Mother Agnes in particular, would look kindly upon any scheme that gave them greater publicity. So the manuscript began to gather dust.

Whether Thérèse felt disappointed about this we do not know – like any author she enjoyed her own work and felt secretly that others would like it too. But she had other things on her mind that spring. She kept the full fast of Lent in all its rigour, suffering acutely as always from the cold, but feeling unusually well. On the night of Maundy Thursday, however, she retired to her cell at midnight, after long hours watching in front of the altar of repose, lay down in bed, and at once felt her mouth fill with a warm, sticky substance which she guessed to be blood. She had a longing to light her lamp to verify the fact, but feeling this would be an indulgence, she disciplined herself to wait until morning. The morning light confirmed her guess; her handkerchief was covered in blood. Haemorrhaging from the lungs, she knew very well, was a symptom of disease that was probably mortal. For a long time Thérèse had been half, or more than half, 'in love with easeful death'. Her response was in keeping. The bleeding from her lungs was, she says, a present from Jesus, 'nothing less than the hope of seeing him, quite soon, in heaven'.

When she woke on the fateful Good Friday it was with a sense that good news was coming to her, and in the morning light she 'realised that there was no mistake'. The Bridegroom was on his way.

She was, she says, longing to tell Mother Marie de Gonzague of the event and could scarcely wait until Prime and Chapter of Faults were over. She told Reverend Mother the news, adding that she was in no pain and wanted no special treatment, only to keep the Good Friday fasts and austerities like everybody else. Incredibly Mother Marie saw no reason to argue with this. Already weakened by bleeding, Thérèse went without food and spent the working part of the day washing windows. A novice seeing her at this task and noticing at once that she was ill, without, of course, knowing what had happened, begged her to rest. She did not do so. That night she haemorrhaged once more.

Convent life continued as normal with no mitigation of the Rule for Thérèse. If she had thought that Mother Marie might begin to show the face of love to her in her physical distress she was mistaken. In this the old sado-masochistic pattern between them continued unchanged. Thérèse fell into a severe depression. Heaven no longer seemed a delightfully close possibility but a source of 'conflict and torment', because she could not possibly be worthy of it. The physical exhaustion that accompanies bleeding, the loneliness of facing death without the loving sympathy of others, the hurt of 'Mother's' cruelty, all filled her with despair. Thérèse was only twenty-two and her youth fought hard against the fate prepared for it. She comforted herself as best she could by identifying with all those millions with no torch of faith to guide them in similar suffering. Like Columbus divining the unseen New World and finding his way to it so she, with only intuition left to her, would find her way to heaven and Jesus. Yet the fear that her doubts were blasphemous troubled her dreadfully. She took comfort in the simplicity of the 'Little Way'.

Within a few weeks of the Good Friday discovery Thérèse had a dream of great significance that lifted her out of the 'dark tunnel' of despair. She was not given to dreaming as a rule, except about flowers or fields, and was therefore astonished to see three Carmelite sisters in the dream, one of them the Venerable Mother Anne of Jesus who brought the reformed Carmelite order to France. Her face conveyed an extraordinary beauty and sense of eternity as well as a deep love. Thérèse felt emboldened to ask an important question – Would God come and fetch her soon? Yes, said Mother Anne, very soon. Then, bringing out the other deep, childlike question that always occupied her heart (it was the night-time question of her childhood – 'Was I a good girl?'), Thérèse painfully asked whether God was really satisfied with her 'unimportant little sacrifices', or did he wish something else from her. With a look of deep love, Mother Anne told her that God asked no more. 'He is content with you, well content.' The old sense of the closeness of heaven returned with its comforting reassurance.

But the suffering was very great. Photographs of Thérèse in this phase of her life are disturbing. Unlike the picture of the plump-faced young novice with the eyes of a merry schoolgirl which was taken on the day of her clothing, the later photographs show her with dark shadows under her eyes and a look of inexpressible sadness. Although only six years have passed since the first picture, she looks like a woman twenty years older.

It is not clear exactly when Thérèse contracted tuberculosis. Despite her sisters' fears she had been a strong girl when she entered the convent, and had been one of only two Sisters left on her feet during the great influenza epidemic. Yet just over four years later she was gravely ill. In June 1894, she had suffered from a persistent soreness of the throat which had been treated by cauterisation with silver nitrate. Convent gossip attributed this malaise to too much talking to the novices rather than to anything remotely dangerous.

Institutions such as schools, convents and seminaries were notorious for the high number of deaths from pulmonary tuberculosis; in some institutions, such as the school where two of the Brontë children died, infected milk and water supplies and poor food seem to have both carried infection and weakened resistance. Such deaths were a tragic commonplace.

Knowledge of the essential hygiene to prevent the spread of the disease was not advanced. Patients used the same cups, plates, napkins and towels as healthy people, and no one suspected the dangers of sputum brought up in coughing attacks. On the other hand in France in the late nineteenth century something was known of the importance of rest (it seemed a natural response to the terrible exhaustion of tuberculous patients), of fresh air and of nourishing food. Yet despite the seriousness of her symptoms no particular care was taken of Thérèse. She continued with the rigorous fasting (in itself, perhaps, one of the culprits which had undermined her resistance), with hard physical work and interrupted sleep. In the curious game that she and Mother Marie played with one another there was a kind of grim satisfaction on both sides in not giving way and recognising a special need. Reverend Mother would make special concessions to Thérèse if she would come to her and beg for them. Thérèse, who had learned not to beg for anything from Mother Marie and who had a stubborn determination to live as if she was not ill, would not ask for them. Even though the bone over which they fought was Thérèse's life, two determined people were not going to give way.

The dreadful details of Thérèse's decline were meticulously

charted by a French priest, Etienne Robo, in 1955. His sister had died of tuberculosis in an Ursuline convent in 1904 where she was similarly deprived of necessary care, and in crusading zeal he wrote about the scandal of Thérèse's final illness (a labour which, not surprisingly, angered the Carmelites considerably).

Reminding us that it was the duty of a Prioress to care for her nuns physically as well as spiritually, he asks the question, 'How is it that for twelve months, from March 1896 to April 1897 [Thérèse] received no care, no treatment worth mentioning and was allowed to keep all the Rules without any relaxation?'[54] One of the Sisters during the process of Thérèse's canonisation made the situation perfectly clear. 'In spite of her illness she never exempted herself from devotions in common, nor failed to attend any of the public devotions, nor did she seek exemption from heavy tasks.' She went on without complaining to the end of her strength. 'I can still go about,' she would say, 'I must stay at my post.' It was, of course, seen as an example of heroism, with the question of why she must stay at her post instead of going to bed until she felt better never asked.

When her cough became worse the local doctor prescribed a bottle of tonic. Whether he also prescribed leaving the window open at night we do not know. Fr. Robo says that in his sister's case this practice was disallowed on the grounds that 'it was not proper for nuns to keep their windows open at night'.

By September 1896 she was sleeping scarcely at all, kept awake by violent fits of coughing that forced her to sit upright in bed. She felt herself fortunate in that her cell stood by itself, next to the Chapter House so that she did not disturb her Sisters. Yet after these sleepless nights she got up unfailingly at five or six in the morning to go to Mass, and would follow this with a day of strenuous chores, doing the washing, maybe, cleaning, decorating, gardening.

We may wonder why Thérèse's natural sisters, always so anxious about her, did not grasp the gravity of her state sooner. The answer is that she concealed it from them (as she was not permitted by the Rule to conceal it from the Prioress). 'My poor little Mother,' Thérèse was to write about Pauline later, 'you must thank God I did not tell you, for, had you been aware of the state I was in and seen me so little cared for, it would have broken your heart.'[55] This inadvertently suggests that Thérèse felt a sense of blame towards the Prioress who did not choose to lift her heavy burden and send her to bed.

Late in 1896 Thérèse was given a mustard plaster late at night (as described by George Orwell in *Down and Out in Paris and London*, an excruciatingly painful form of treatment). She got up and went to Mass as usual. Concerned about her sister's appearance Pauline followed her back to her cell and found her sitting on her stool, leaning against the wall, as if unable to support herself. Why had she gone to choir, Pauline asked her passionately, receiving one of Thérèse's stubborn replies, 'This is not too much suffering for the privilege of Holy Communion.' Yet Communion could easily have been brought to her in her cell or in the infirmary.

So she continued through the bitter winter weather, worn out by her cough, her fever, and her haemorrhages. The infirmarian Sister Marie of the Trinity noticed her condition and went to the Prioress to suggest some mitigation of the Rule for Thérèse. The Prioress was short with her. 'I have never heard before of such young people as this who think of nothing but their health. In former times one would never have thought of missing Matins. If Sister Thérèse of the Child Jesus has come to the end of her strength, let her come and tell me so herself.' So the battle between them continued.

Thérèse justified her tragic obstinacy in terms of obedience. 'Our Mother knows very well that I am tired: it is my duty to tell her what I feel, and since in spite of it she gives me permission to keep step with the community, it must be that she is inspired by God, who wants to grant my wish to go on working to the very end.'

Behind such a statement are unspoken volumes about the relationship between Thérèse and Mother Marie de Gonzague. If Mother Marie was punishing Thérèse by ignoring her mortal illness, then she in turn may punish her by dying.

Chapter Eight

A VERY LITTLE SAINT

During the winter of 1896–7 Thérèse struggled on alone with the terrible inroads of her illness, suffering daily from high fever, bearing the bitter cold of the open cloister and the interminable hours in choir without complaint. Like her mother Zélie who had tried to carry on family life as usual in the final stages of cancer, and who had done her best to conceal her suffering from anyone, Thérèse smiled, held herself upright and lived out the Rule as it was written. Yet fever, a bad cough, pallor, extreme fatigue, are not so easily hidden, we would think, at least not from those who are with us night and day.

By April of 1897 she had become so breathless that one night it took her half an hour to climb the stairs to her cell, and another hour to undress with long pauses for recovery between each action. Beaten at last in the unequal struggle she told the Prioress that she could not carry on. As if to show how generous she could be when appealed to in a properly humble manner Mother Marie at once sent for the doctors and began to organise a succession of expensive treatments. She appointed Céline and Pauline to nurse Thérèse, with her sister Marie allowed to be in constant attendance.

Medical science was, we know now, more or less helpless to treat advanced tuberculosis until the arrival of sulphonamides in the 1940s but this did not prevent a number of measures being tried. In addition to the painful plasters of mustard and belladonna, there was cupping (a treatment which involved raising the flesh of the back here and there with a glass cup), painting of the chest with creosote, and an excruciating process of injecting dozens of needles. The purpose of most of them seems to have been a sort of stimulation – by causing the blood to rush to the afflicted place through the use of hot substances it was hoped the body would be provoked into defensive action which would also destroy the tubercle bacillus.

Meanwhile the patient suffered a terrible wasting, so familiar to us from the description of nineteenth-century deaths, a desperate cough which, as the lungs decayed and hardened, literally brought up fragments of the lung. The result of this was a growing difficulty in breathing at all, extreme fatigue and weakness. Dipping a pen in an inkpot, sewing, holding a book, were often too exhausting. There was also severe pain.

The Prioress who had watched, apparently unmoved, through so many months while Thérèse gradually declined, was now all concern, describing Thérèse as 'the angel of the community', fulsomely praising her on every occasion, weeping freely in chapel when Thérèse was prayed for. Her cruelty had swung into its opposite – sentimentality. For Thérèse, however, it was a matter of great joy that she was once again apparently in favour with 'Mother' – she was touchingly pleased. She saw this as a special gift from Jesus. In the person of Mother Marie he now smiled upon her.

Her lapse into weakness and the official change in the treatment of her made a big difference. The Guérin family now knew of Thérèse's condition and they charged Marie, who had just that year been admitted to Carmel as Sister Marie of the Eucharist, to send them daily reports, in itself a sort of check on the treatment received by her.

For Thérèse the chief comfort of the new state of affairs was the constant attendance of her sisters and the freedom to chat to them as freely as she had done in childhood. Her days were spent in bed, or sitting in a little white armchair, or, when the summer drew on, outside in the cloister or the chestnut walk in the invalid carriage which Louis had used in his last years. The last photograph of Thérèse shows her reclining in this carriage in the cloister, her emaciated face tiny in its starched cap.

Thérèse had not the smallest doubt that she was dying – in

the spring of 1897 she told Céline that she would die 'this very year'. She was impatient for it. 'I am like a small child at the railway station, waiting for its parents to place it on the train. But, alas, they do not come, and the train is leaving. Still, there are other trains . . .' She also compared herself to a child who is longing for a piece of cake and keeps holding out its hand for it, only to find the cake withheld. Picturing death with her usual vivid imagination she wanted to get on with the process. It was to be much more protracted and horrific than even she could possibly guess.

At first, however, there was the relief from the intolerable struggle to live as if she was well, the lift of spirits that came from resting, eating better food, simply giving way to the disease that had her in its power. The beauty of the spring, the release from the dreadful cold of a Carmelite winter buoyed her up for a little. With her sisters she reconstructed some of the precious memories of Les Buissonets.

In June, lying out in the chestnut walk in her chair, she embarked on the final section of her autobiography which she addressed to Mother Marie de Gonzague, perhaps the only human being apart from her own relatives whom she had ever deeply loved. This, like the earlier exercises in autobiography, she wrote under obedience. In the change of climate that had occurred since Thérèse had succumbed to the ravages of her disease Pauline had felt it possible to go to Mother Marie de Gonzague, tell her about the earlier autobiographical writings, and to suggest that Thérèse might now occupy her idle hands writing something about her life as a nun. Pauline knew that it was touch and go whether the Superior would agree or refuse. She immediately agreed.

Thérèse was so weak that she was forced to write in pencil, and even then her handwriting, usually neat, like that of a young schoolgirl, was hard to read. There were other difficulties too. The other nuns, passing her on the way to haymaking and other summer duties, continually interrupted her with friendly conversation and gifts of flowers. Thérèse rather churlishly complains about this in the midst of her writing, objecting that the flowers would be better still waving on their stalks. Inept as always in the ways of friendship she misses the point of their kindness, their oblique attempt to tell her that they love her.

The writing that they interrupted, however, was her own attempt to express love for Mother Marie, and on page after page it charts their difficult relationship, hinting at the deep emotions below the surface, and placing the whole in the context of Thérèse's life in the convent, and her overwhelming love for Jesus. It is a difficult terrain, especially for one like Thérèse who had no aptitude for tact. If she left out the pain Reverend Mother had dealt her over the years she would distort their whole history. Yet a diatribe of accusation would be un-Christian. Besides, the warmth of emotion she feels for this surrogate-mother often wipes out the resentment and the pain, particularly in a phase, like her present one, when the face of love is being turned upon her.

Thérèse solves the problem rather neatly by writing down many of the incidents in her life with Mother Marie, but offering fulsome gratitude for the pain involved by suggesting how much they helped her to grow – which, it might be argued, they did. Whether all of this material is written quite 'straight', whether the skilled novice mistress is practising her skill to get a lesson home without too much loss of face, whether she is engaged on a self-consciously Christian effort to suppress her angry feelings, or has just 'smoothed over' her pain is hard to know.

What she claims to feel is an enormous 'gratitude' towards Mother Marie, as well as a sense of her heart being 'knitted' to hers. She says that she treats her not at all as a Prioress but 'as a mother'. The severity she has endured at her hands she describes as 'firm, motherly discipline'. 'I thank you from the bottom of my heart for not having treated me too gently. Jesus knew well enough that the Little Flower he had planted was in need of watering; only the waters of humiliation could revive it – it was too weak a plant to take root without being helped in this way. And it was through you, Mother, that this blessing was bestowed.'[56] She remembers what happened on the unforgettable Good Friday when she woke up soaked in her own blood.

How she confided to Mother Marie what had happened and how, encouraged by Thérèse, she remitted none of the exacting duties of the day. 'Never had it appealed to me so much, the severe way of practising austerities we have in Carmel.'

Despite the months of neglect Thérèse piles on gratitude for the most recent change of heart.

I am touched by all these motherly attentions of yours; my heart really is overflowing with gratitude, and I shall never forget what I owe you, never. The most touching thing of all is the novena which you're making to Our Lady of Victories, all the Masses you're having said for my recovery. What a wealth of spiritual resources! . . . Mother, look at the life I live here! . . . all I've got to do is to carry out the work you've given me to do, such easy work! And then, all this motherly care you shower on me! I never feel the pinch of poverty; I've always got everything I want. But above all, here at Carmel I have your love and the love of all the Sisters, and it means so much to me! I see in you not merely a mother, greatly loving and greatly loved, but beyond all that Jesus himself . . . Of course, you treat me like a special case, like a spoilt child, so that obedience costs me nothing. But something deep in my heart tells me that I should act just as I do, love you as much as I do, if you saw fit to treat me harshly. I should still know that it was the will of Jesus; you would only be doing it for the good of my soul.[57]

This extraordinary recital of gratitude is difficult reading. Even when we are used to Thérèse's strange inversions so that what is bad is good and what is good is bad, and the puzzling distortions they make in the truth, it is still tempting to say bluntly 'That's a lie! She treated you abominably and you know it!' Yet we may wonder how conscious Thérèse was of the un-truthfulness involved. What is most interesting and important about these statements of hers is the way they illustrate how total the dependence of Thérèse had been upon Mother Marie. In her longing to feel loved by this Mother whom it was almost impossible to please (like Zélie?), she survives by denying neglect and harshness, the harshness which, by offering a sort of un-answerable riddle, kept Thérèse bound. There *must* be a way to make Mother Marie love her, Thérèse had felt, as helplessly as a child with a capricious mother. There must be an answer to the riddle which would make her lovable. She would try and never stop trying. Dimly she perceives that her Superior's cruelty to her indicates something special in their relationship – that the two of them are caught up together in a mutual exploration of different aspects of suffering – one of them of power and the other of pain. But in the summer of her illness the rules of this dreadful game seem to have changed, temporarily at least, and in the joy of this fact she writes rapturously of life in the convent and of the spiritual ambition which drives her. She writes with the kind of passionate intimacy, the longing to tell everything, with which another woman might write to her lover. In the sombre and lonely place where she confronts her own death she needs to feel loved and understood; maybe Mother Marie, disturbed and hurtful as she may have been, even in some sense the architect of her present misfortunes, may have seemed like the only contemporary with the intelligence and the insight to enter with her into this final struggle. At the very least it was an invitation to her to do so.

Jesus and Mother Marie are as one person now in Thérèse's mind. Once when Thérèse had felt snubbed and ignored by Mother she had felt that Jesus had decided that the waters of humiliation were what the Little Flower needed to make it grow. Now, in the bitter experience of a dreadful illness in which 'my humiliations have reached the brim', Thérèse felt that Jesus had decided that there was no longer any need for the external application of humiliation, and so he, and Mother, smiled on her, having decided that the plant needed sun to make it grow.

The disease did indeed find ever new forms to distress and to humiliate, coupling extreme weakness, the fight for breath, and the racking cough, with fits of uncontrollable vomiting and pain so severe that the patient was beside herself with agony and longed for nothing but release. She became unable to eat anything but liquid food and even that often filled her with acute nausea. One of the nuns was deeply offended when Thérèse refused a cup of broth she had brought her and stormed away saying that not only was she not a saint as rumour had it in the convent that she might be, she was not even a good nun. One of Thérèse's rare flashes of humour showed at this news. 'What a benefaction', she said, 'to hear on one's death-bed that one has not even been a proper nun!'

She who had never had much interest in food, who had seen it mainly as an opportunity for strengthening her self-control, suddenly felt she was starving, as indeed she was, and had continual fantasies of eating all kinds of delicacy, a phenomenon quite well known in the later stages of her disease. She found the experience deeply shaming, and believed that the devil was doing his best to humiliate her.

She moved in and out of periods of spiritual darkness as her body fought its fierce battle. In June she had had a sort of vision of her faith as a lighthouse beckoning into the harbour of heaven, but this was frequently obscured by her terrible sufferings.

'Oh, how I pity myself', she remarked movingly. 'Nevertheless I would not suffer less.'

She told the Prioress that she had never asked God for suffering, and that therefore it was up to Him to give her the strength to endure it.

'It seems to me you are made for suffering,' Mother Marie replied, truthfully enough. 'Your soul is tempered for it.'

'Oh, for spiritual suffering, yes; I can take a great deal of that . . . But as for physical pain, I am like a little child, a very little child. I cannot think at all, I only suffer, minute after minute.'

Thérèse was not unusual in regressing to the state of 'a little child' in sickness – it had always been a favourite recourse of hers, in any case. More than once the thought of suicide occurred to her and she warned Pauline about the dangers of leaving poisonous medicine within reach of patients in great pain.

Not knowing how long the agony must go on, but only that it would be terminal, made it worse. In July when she was so much worse that she was moved to the infirmary the chaplain tried to jolly her along by decrying all her talk of entering heaven, an infuriating sort of patronism. Her 'crown' was far from finished, he told her. She replied that although she had not finished it, God had finished it for her.

It occurred to her that death was really much like all the other events in her life that she had looked forward to. Like First Communion, or entering Carmel, or being clothed or professed, it seemed like a longed-for place that she had no idea how to reach. And yet, after all, she *had* reached those other peaks. But in the meantime she had the very human feeling that she did not know how dying was done.

Just as Bunyan's Christian had been much haunted by hobgoblins in the Valley of the Shadow of Death, so poor Thérèse was troubled by the whispering in the darkness, by the sense of supernatural threat and the temptation to despair. A candle burned all night in her room and her bed was sprinkled with holy water. It seemed to her that, like Job, she was being tried by extreme suffering, driven towards the blasphemy of denying her faith. She clung to the thought that God was, and would be, present in the suffering however bad it was. In the heart of the suffering, she claimed, she felt a core of peace, or maybe it was that suffering and joy were, on some deeply mysterious level, the same thing, the two faces of love.

'What do you say to God?' she was asked.

'I say nothing – I just love Him.'

The weariness and pain from moment to moment, the continual fighting for breath, were very terrible. Again the strange role of the Prioress emerges. In August when the usual doctor was on holiday, Dr Néele, her cousin Jeanne's husband, temporarily replaced him. Either because of their relationship, or because he perceived the gravity of Thérèse's condition more clearly, he suggested that he should come every day. The Prioress, seemingly annoyed at this, only allowed him to come three times in all. In addition to her other troubles Thérèse had developed bedsores which made any movement in bed agony. Sitting upright to breathe in attacks of coughing felt like sitting on red-hot iron. On 22 August her intestines began to be very badly affected; drinking a glass of water to assuage her raging thirst felt like throwing water into a furnace. She was beside herself with agony. Dr Néele was not sent for until 30 August.

The regular doctor, Dr de Cornières, returning from his holiday in September, was sufficiently appalled by the suffering of Thérèse to recommend hypodermic injections of morphia. This the Prioress rejected out of hand. The doctor insisted on some syrup of morphia. This too the Prioress deplored and tried to reduce to a minimum, but almost surreptitiously Pauline and Céline offered it in the worst moments. It was not very effective. Many devout writers on the life of Thérèse have excused Mother Marie on the grounds that the use of a drug mitigated the heroism of the Carmelite life. 'Soul-making' took precedence over every other consideration, even, it would appear, the virtue of compassion. It was the last, and the most terrible example, of Mother Marie's form of exercising power.

As so often in the life of Thérèse, in her dying there were puzzling failures of relationship. There is the story of the nun who liked to come and stand at the foot of the bed and laugh at her sufferings. Hagiographers have relished this detail as proving the superhuman patience of Thérèse without discussing the improbability of it or at least what degree of mental derangement it might have indicated in the nun.

Then there was the gossip among the nuns about how 'useless' Thérèse now was, how she was not 'doing' anything, how she was being 'spoiled' once again by her sisters. There was even some suggestion that she was not half as ill as she pretended. When she seemed on one occasion to be near to death her pallet, on which she would be laid for burial, was tactlessly placed outside the door where she could see it. The Sisters are shown as endlessly persecuting her with silly questions about dying, cruel demands for her attention, struggles to obtain relics, as well as envious remarks about the luxury of her present life.

No doubt some visitors stayed too long and were thoughtless, that some pointed remarks were made about how the Martin family had got it together again, and that some irritation was felt at the Martin girls' premature insistence that the youngest Martin was a saint. Anything beyond this in a small community in which one of their number was seen to be suffering acutely seems psychologically unlikely, a distortion that has more to do with a wish to show that Thérèse was perfect than with anything that is humanly probable. Unless, of course, we are to believe that Thérèse had been living in a house of monsters.

Reading between the lines of the considerable amount of material written about Thérèse's death we may wonder if one of the heavier burdens she had to bear was not the attentions of her natural sisters. With the curious spiritual ambition that had always been typical of the Martin family they were very determined that Thérèse should be seen as a saint, and many of their remarks and gestures in her dying weeks were designed to convey to her that nothing less than a sanctified death was expected of her.

Fallen back into the care of the determined big sisters who had, in the words they would have used, 'moulded' her as a child, she had little choice but to try to please. In a thousand ways their expectation was conveyed to her, an expectation which, of course, chimed with a cherished hope of her own. So that day after day between the fever and the pain, the struggle for breath and the vomiting, the question was always being silently asked 'Are we watching the last days of a saint?' It was this ambition which the rest of the community picked up from the Martin sisters, partly believed in (see their determination to obtain relics), and partly mocked.

How did it show itself? In the notebook which Pauline whipped out, time after time, to record the most artless utterances of the tormented invalid, and in the endless questioning of her designed to make pearls drop from her lips. Later in the shameless effort to collect relics – hairs, tears – from her still suffering body. The notebooks which all the sisters kept accumulated an enormous amount of evidence about Thérèse which was later used to make points in the canonisation ceremonies; it is perfectly clear that Pauline had just such a use in mind.

We may find it difficult to think of another saint who had a Boswell, whereas Thérèse had two. Pauline admitted in the canonisation ceremonies that the note-taking had been painful and inhibiting for Thérèse, although she had submitted to it out of love for Pauline. Here, as in the battles over the administration of morphine, love and compassion take second place to spiritual ambition, and Thérèse is damagingly exploited. She complained of those death-bed inquisitions that she suffered, that she felt like the Maid of Orleans before her accusers.

Her sisters wondered aloud in her hearing whether her body would decay in death or whether it would remain incorrupt as a sign of sanctity. They planned the sort of death they thought she ought to have – joyful and fearless. They seemed worried that death itself would take too long and thus detract from the interest and attention being shown her by her relatives and fellow-nuns. They asked if she thought she would be made an angel when she got to heaven. They asked, rather oddly, what she would die of. 'Death,' replied Thérèse succinctly. They asked if she had an intimation of when she was to die. She had none. They cried out that she was indeed a saint.

The question of sanctity was, as always, the unanswerable conundrum. If she said she was a saint she would be guilty of the sin of pride and therefore would not be one. If she said she was not a saint and actually was one, then, out of false modesty, she would be guilty of a lie. In practice, since sanctity is accompanied by a lack of all egotism, the saint is unlikely to spend time wondering if she or he is a saint – only if asked the cruel question do they have to struggle with the meaningless idea. Thérèse had longed so much to be a saint in her youth, and knew how greatly her sisters' hopes were pinned to the idea. The listlessness of her replies to their questions suggests that in pain and weariness the matter did not interest her as much as formerly.

She began by saying that far from being a saint she was only a very little soul upon whom God had heaped favours. Then, having given the matter more thought she said, in a very Thérèsian style, that she was only 'a very little saint'. Plainly she worried about her own humility, whether she was genuinely 'humble of heart'. In the weakness and confinement of the sickroom with her sisters' shining conviction about her continually voiced, or at least assumed, it was difficult to keep a sense of perspective.

Once, having implied to her sisters that they were looking after a saint she added 'But you are saints too!' It was as if the potentiality for sainthood was what mattered, not the human failure. She resisted, with some courage, both the affectations and the coynesses that Pauline encouraged. She refused to scatter rose petals to a group of the nuns who came to see her – that belonged to a different part of her life altogether, the intimate love she felt for Jesus. When Pauline saw her in the garden gazing at the sky she commented archly with what love she was looking towards heaven. Not at all, Thérèse said tartly. She was not thinking about the real heaven at all, a mystery that, in any case, seemed entirely closed to her, she was simply admiring the material world.

Maybe it was the cloying adulation of her relatives that made Mother Marie's naturally sardonic nature a welcome relief. In her critical eyes at least, the expectations were not high.

This attitude of Mother's chimed with Thérèse's present desire to taste humiliation 'to the brim'. It seemed to her that she needed to renounce 'the last shred of dignity', to feel like everyone's drudge, everyone's slave. Perhaps this was the genius of the 'Little Way'. To lie dying an excruciating death that took away the little privacies and forms of self-control which are precious to most of us, to endure almost unremitting pain, to have to rely upon others for the smallest services, to be an object of (not always kind) gossip in the convent, to be harried and cross-questioned by those who loved her most but who did not grant her peace, was to have 'the last shred of dignity' forcibly ripped away. What else to do then but to 'choose' it, to respond to it out of freedom rather than necessity?

Looking back over her life as a nun in that last summer she had written, interestingly, of the 'tangled undergrowth of Carmel'. Her intense idealisation of the life as an adolescent girl has given way to her mature understanding of the way good and bad are mixed up in the life there as they are everywhere else.

Humour appears now in her writing, small *aperçus* of convent conversations and conduct, full of irony.

A haymaking nun has just taken leave of me with the words: 'Poor little Sister, it must be very tiring for you to be writing like that all day.' 'Don't worry about that,' I said, 'I look as if I were writing a great deal, but there's hardly anything to show for it.' She seemed relieved at that. 'A good thing too,' she said, 'but all the same it's just as well we're getting the hay in; a bit of distraction for you.' I should think it did distract me, quite apart from the infirmarians' visits; it was no exaggeration to say that I hardly got anything written.[58]

This is Thérèse's form of grumbling.

Spending most of her days and nights in bed she pondered deeply about questions that had always interested her. She thinks about acts of charity, how it is easy to do them to create an impression or not to annoy somebody who has asked for help, and how the only kind of love that is really any good is the sort that is a free gift of oneself. Yet the more she thinks about it the more mysterious it all becomes and she feels that instead of writing any more she would like to 'throw away my pen'.

An interesting form of indignation emerges in these last writings of Thérèse, a sense of outrage that she has tried to swallow down and will now ignore no longer. Tiny vignettes of convent life suddenly emerge. 'I tell one of the Sisters, when we have leave to talk, about some light that has been given to me in prayer; and she, quite soon afterwards, mentions it to a third party in conversation as if it were an idea of her own; isn't that pilfering? Or again, in recreation, I whisper some remark to the person next to me, a good remark, absolutely to the point; and she repeats it aloud without mentioning where it came from; isn't that a theft of my property?' We hear the voice of a new Thérèse, the hint of the maturity of which tuberculosis robbed the Church. 'I can't say so at the time, but I'd like to; and if opportunity arises, I determine to let it be known, with all the delicacy in the world, that somebody's been misappropriating my thoughts.'[59]

A new, tougher Thérèse, with a clear mind of her own, peeps

out of this utterance, not so much little flower, as a powerful young tree. Yet she still has doubts – why should not her thoughts belong to others, is it pride that fuels her? And envy? She knows she has sometimes feared that Jesus loves others more than he loves her. She struggles on.

She remembers how, little prig that she was, in her early days at Carmel she had longed to set others right and tell them about faults in their behaviour. Nowadays she found herself thinking 'Thank goodness it isn't my job to put her right!' She ponders upon how it is the touchiest, silliest, most ignorant and irritating of the Sisters who need to be spoiled and loved by others, whereas it is always tempting to stick with the nicest and most balanced people. The only way to bear with the difficult ones is to see it as an act of love offered to Jesus.

As death comes nearer Thérèse ponders upon the lines in the Song of Songs 'Draw me after thee; we hasten' believing as she does that death is to be her union with her lover, Jesus. Only the suffering of getting to heaven is very great, is often unendurable to her.

The last six weeks of life were a series of crises. On 30 July they gave her the last rites and the whole community assembled in her room. She recovered but was in acute discomfort in any position she attempted to lie in as well as racked by pain in her intestines. She cried out 'Oh my God, oh my God, I can do no more, have mercy on me, have mercy on me.' The pain continued and Mother Marie continued opposed to the use of the hypodermic needle. 'What is the good of writing beautiful things about suffering?' Thérèse asked in bitterness. 'It means nothing, nothing! When you are going through it, then you know the worthlessness of all this eloquence.'

Receiving Communion had always been amongst the most precious experiences for Thérèse, but after the middle of August when she was continually vomiting blood she felt unable to take the sacrament. Her darkness was now almost total. She indicated to Pauline a well of shadow under the chestnut trees, and said that in such shadow she herself lay, body and soul. Her prayers to the saints fell, it seemed to her, upon deaf ears.

In extremis she took some comfort from lying with her arms extended as if on a crucifix.

On 29 September when the Prioress came to see her Thérèse asked her in a childlike way if this were the final agony and if so, what to do next. 'How does one die?' After another terrible night she rallied briefly and tried to face that she might go on living for months, in acute suffering. She held her crucifix and looked at it continually, often reiterating that she would suffer for as long as God wanted her to.

In the afternoon the end seemed near and the nuns assembled, but after two hours were sent away again. 'Am I not to die yet?' Thérèse asked. 'Very well, let it be so. I do not wish to suffer less.'

At seven in the evening the nuns were again summoned. Gazing at her crucifix Thérèse said, 'Oh, I love him. My God, I love you.' And died. The photograph of her taken after death shows a face beautiful, young, and peaceful.

Chapter Nine

THE SHOWER
OF ROSES

'I will spend my Heaven in doing good upon earth,' Thérèse had
said and when she was buried in the cemetery at Lisieux at a
funeral attended only by Léonie and the Guérins, her sisters
persuaded the Prioress to have these words inscribed on the
cross on Thérèse's grave, in marked contrast to the plain graves
of other nuns. In the weeks and months during which Thérèse
had endured the long agony of her dying her three sisters had
spoken in front of her and behind her back of the possibility that
she was a saint. Now that she was dead there was work to be
done in letting the world know of her spiritual achievement.

Her life, though exemplary and remarkable in many ways
lacked one essential ingredient for official sanctity – miracles.
Since these had not come in her lifetime then, if she was to pass,
as it were, the canonisation examination, there must be miracles
after death. There was certainly an atmosphere of the supernatural at Carmel in the days succeeding her death – rumours of
unexplained perfume in the air, and a nun who had placed her
head upon Thérèse's feet after death being cured of chronic
headache, but this, although reassuring to the three Martin
sisters and their cousin, was scarcely enough to startle the world.
Thérèse had said that after her death she would let fall showers
of rose petals. Whether she meant this as a reassuring sign to her
sisters that she really had gone to heaven, whether she meant it
in some metaphorical sense (i.e. the 'doing good on earth'), or
whether it was even a sort of joke referring to her pleasure in
flinging rose petals as a child in the Corpus Christi procession, is
not at all clear. No rose petals appeared.

It was the custom, when a Carmelite died, to send round an obituary notice to other religious houses giving an account of the nun's life and maybe including a bit of her writing, if she was gifted in that way. The autobiographical writing of Thérèse seemed not only ideal for this purpose, but *so* good that it seemed a pity not to share it with a much wider audience. While Thérèse was still alive her sisters seem to have discussed this idea with her, and so keen was she, not exactly for the personal glory for which she had once longed, but for the chance that other 'little souls' might share her experience, that she had revelled in the idea. She knew that the writing, begun for her sisters, needed polishing if it was to be read by a wider audience. The first section, written out of her love for Pauline, was delightfully unselfconscious in its memories, a piece of work done for domestic pleasure and not for public consumption. The second section, addressed to Marie, and the third section, addressed to Mother Marie de Gonzague, are much more self-conscious and didactic, as if she has become aware of an audience there to be improved. The final pages must also have been affected by her acute physical weakness, her neat schoolgirl writing moving from ink to pencil, and finally into an unreadable scrawl. She entrusted Pauline with the task of doing whatever was necessary to make her little book, or rather series of notebooks, fit for others to read.

What happened next suggested that not only the Martin sisters but also the Prioress and her spiritual advisers had begun to see, as it were, the untapped publicity potential of Thérèse. Pauline added some pious thoughts, cut some of the childhood reminiscences, and altered some details to make the portrait of the would-be saint more complete. Ida Görres suggests that, as Thérèse's first schoolmistress, Pauline quite naturally made corrections and 'improvements'. They somewhat lessened the vitality of Thérèse's style – Pauline, we may guess, would have written a much duller and more sentimental book. Maybe it was Pauline who suggested that the book should have the title *A Canticle of Love, or the Passing of an Angel*, a fancy which an interested cleric fortunately toned down to *The Story of a Soul*.

Work done on the text of *The Story of a Soul* in recent years suggests that some of the more florid literary forms apparently employed by Thérèse – the rhetorical questions, the philosophical ponderings – were Pauline's attempts to make her little sister's homely writing more 'literary'.

An imprimatur was needed from Thérèse's old adversary and friend, Monsignor Hugonin, the Bishop of Bayeux. He could not make up his mind to give this at first, claiming insultingly to be fearful of 'the imagination of women', but eventually did so (within a few weeks of his own death as it turned out), and just over a year after Thérèse's death the convent had two thousand copies printed, an extraordinary number, almost as if the nuns were publishing a novel. And just as if Thérèse was a novelist the book sold amazingly well – five thousand copies within the first two years; not the book alone, but also photographs of Thérèse, often with tiny pieces of her clothing or bed-linen, or wood from the furniture of her cell attached. Carmel had acquired a sort of ghoulish cottage industry for itself.

Not all the nuns liked or approved of this. Some of them did not think Thérèse deserved it, and some thought it was a scheme thought up for the glorification of the Martin sisters. Even the Martin sisters were not happy. Mother Marie de Gonzague had undertaken some final editing of her own when the manuscript left Pauline's hands, altering it so that it seemed as if all three of the texts had been addressed to her instead of only the last of them. She claimed that she had done it to make the book into a literary unity, but Pauline and Marie were very naturally furious. There was nothing they could do about it.

Possibly Thérèse's death and the stream of events which followed it had one other effect on the Martin relatives. Léonie, who must have been deeply ambivalent about religious life, since she had made three abortive attempts at it (once in the Poor Clares and twice in the Order of the Visitation), finally returned in 1899 to the convent of the Visitation and this time stayed there. The sister of a saint could not be found wanting in persistence.

The book had one immediate and striking effect which was

the stream of postulants wanting to enter the Lisieux Carmel. It is interesting to compare this with the flood of novice monks who wanted to enter the monastery of Gethsemani in Kentucky when Thomas Merton wrote a moving book about his experiences there in the 1940s. (It is also interesting to note similarities between Merton's autobiographical style and Thérèse's; he admitted to having a 'devotion' to her, and certain phrases he uses, and even more a sort of wry joking about the hardships of the life are extraordinarily reminiscent.)

Within a couple of years of Thérèse's death her fame was already growing fast. The first edition of *The Story of a Soul* having sold out by 1899, a second edition of four thousand copies was prepared and this too began to sell very quickly. The book was read first by religious and would-be religious, and gradually reached the Catholic public. They liked the sweetness and perhaps the sentimentality, they enjoyed Thérèse's capacity to tell a good story, they were moved, as we may still be moved today, by the sadness of her death at such an early age. Mortal illness, particularly from tuberculosis, was part of people's lives then in a way it is not part of ours, and everyone must have reflected and fantasised about such a death.

In the same way as the book had brought new postulants to Carmel it brought a flood of pilgrims to the cemetery in Lisieux, with renewed requests for pieces of clothing and other relics of Thérèse.

In 1902, too late to correct the final editing of *The Story of a Soul* Pauline was re-elected Prioress, a job which she held with only a brief respite until her death in 1923. During the months of Thérèse's dying she had filled a notebook with her sister's sayings. Over the years she worked at these, finally publishing them as a book – *Novissima Verba* – in 1927. Mother Marie de Gonzague died in 1904, her long struggle with the Martin sisters over at last. Tragically, cousin Marie Guérin, Sister Marie of the Eucharist, died in 1905 in the same painful way as Thérèse.

By 1906 the cult of Thérèse was far advanced. Many thousands of people had read her book, hundreds had prayed at her tomb and treasured pictures of her. Carmel, it was rumoured, was putting forward her case in Rome as a possible candidate for canonisation.

French missionaries had a particular liking for her – 'la petite soeur de France' as they called her. According to Ida Görres they mentioned her so frequently in Africa that the king of one tribe appointed her as 'Regent'. Our Lady herself took second place to her. In Portugal bishops granted indulgences to readers of *The Story of a Soul*, a practice which increased the book's popularity. In England there were requests to the Archbishop of Westminster to grant similar indulgences, but the Archbishop refused with a reply which cast some slight doubt on the integrity of Thérèse's relatives.

One of the fascinations of the story of Thérèse is that it reveals something of the social and psychological process by which a person is transformed into a saint. There is something essentially mysterious about the way in which any life – that of an actor, a writer, a pop star, a 'sex goddess' – breaks out of obscurity and becomes known to thousands, while others who lead similar lives remain largely unknown. Other women led good, pious lives, much like Thérèse's, in and out of convents, others died tragically in youth of the same dreadful disease. Others scribbled their thoughts in exercise books.

To touch public imagination in the way Thérèse did suggests a hunger, a longing, in the unconscious of hundreds of people. When they see pictures or hear a story of this particular young woman then immediately the experience locks into fantasies they scarcely knew they had, fantasies which carry great hope and longing. Thérèse, in her youth and sheltered existence, has the charm of innocence, of goodness, and perhaps of a sort of mediocrity. She is a sort of eternal schoolgirl. Her niceness and relative simplicity – the unspectacular simplicity of a young girl at home for the most part – is pleasant to read about. It is understandable that during the First World War many French soldiers went into battle carrying pictures and medals of her, and French airmen named an aeroplane after her. Not only might they have hoped for her supernatural intervention in the likely event of their deaths, but in the misery and squalor of the trenches she offered a sort of promise that life might hold more than the hell on earth of the fields of Flanders. If, on brief spells from duty, they went in search of a different kind of woman who held out a different kind of promise, this does not make the Thérèse image any less bright – if anything it sharpens and defines it.

Thérèse's death, though by no means an uncommon one in her period, was dramatic, and nineteenth-century readers dearly loved a good death-bed. In fact death-beds evoke fantasies in most of us, fantasies of pathos, heroism, and of having our lightest word raptly listened to. Sanctity and death carry a tremendous imaginative appeal, the appeal of what it might be like to become the idealised self within us, nobly shedding our greedier and more egocentric traits in exchange for a life of austerity or devotion to the poor.

Convents and monasteries, with their ordered lives, their simplicity, poverty and chastity, their prayers and penances, similarly encourage fantasies, as well as fascination at what life in them must be like. Ignorance of it encourages all sorts of projections upon the inhabitants, including the projection that they must be infinitely better than the rest of us. If we cannot be saints ourselves then we are interested in those who live that unlived part of our lives for us. Thérèse, who retired from the world so early, who lived out incredible austerities, who suffered a long and painful death with heroism, and who had her dying speeches carefully recorded by her sisters, was in all these ways a good candidate for spiritual popularity.

Like the saints of the early Church her fame spread through rumour until she was so popular that the Church had to take official notice of her. A fillip was given to the movement which wanted to declare Thérèse a saint by an impressive miracle. In 1906 a young seminarian called Abbé Anne was in the final stages of pulmonary tuberculosis. A novena was said to Thérèse, but without success, and the Abbé's relatives awaited his immediate death. The young man pressed a relic of Thérèse to his heart and begged her to cure him. Instantly he was well. 'The destroyed and ravaged lungs had been replaced by new lungs, carrying out their normal functions and about to revive the entire organism. A slight emaciation persists, which will disappear within a few days under a regularly assimilated diet,' wrote a contemporary doctor.

Here was one major and well-attested miracle to be ascribed to Thérèse. There were to be many more. Not surprisingly recoveries from tuberculosis were high on the list of miracles ascribed to Thérèse, but her name was evoked for every sort of ailment, not least for driving out devils in exorcism ceremonies. Blindness, deformity, human distress of every kind, was healed by the 'little saint', a stream of cures which represented the 'shower of roses' she had once promised.

Meanwhile the 'machinery' of the Church had gone into gear. In 1907 the Bishop of Bayeux had ordered the Lisieux Carmel to hand over its souvenirs of Thérèse, presumably on the grounds that they might be potential relics. In 1909 a Pleader and Vice-Pleader were appointed by Rome (in Rome and France respectively) to prepare the 'Cause' of Thérèse. In August 1910 a 'Process' began to examine her writings, and in September her body was exhumed from the Lisieux cemetery. Aware that Thérèse was, in a sense, 'on trial', the faithful began writing in their hundreds to attest to her holiness – in a year Carmel had received nearly ten thousand letters of this kind. The rain of letters was to grow until in one day in 1918 five hundred and twelve letters would be received. The dossier on her in Rome ran to thousands of words, and necessitated many hours of committees.

In 1914 Rome officially approved of the writings of Thérèse and Pius X signed the document which served as the introduction of the 'Cause'. Privately he had declared that he believed Thérèse to be the greatest saint of modern times.

In spite of this, the Church was slower and more reluctant than public opinion. Supremely in France, but throughout Europe, in South America, French Canada, the United States, Africa and China, Thérèse was invoked. Even Protestants took to her.

In 1921 a decree was promulgated by Pope Benedict XV by

which Thérèse became 'Venerable', as odd an adjective for the
24-year-old nun as it had seemed for Joan of Arc. 'This maiden,
so modest, so humble, this child' as the Pope described her. In
1923 Pope Pius XI promulgated the decree which beatified
Thérèse, describing her as 'the star of his pontifical reign'.
Determined that Thérèse should attain the final accolade of
canonisation, eight hundred to a thousand correspondents a day
wrote to Carmel.

Finally, on 17 May 1925, Thérèse Martin, Soeur Thérèse de
l'Enfant Jésus et de la Sainte Face was canonised at St Peter's in
the presence of thirty-four cardinals, more than two hundred
archbishops and bishops, and innumerable priests, religious and
others. The basilica was decorated with garlands of roses. It was
packed – it was thought there were about sixty thousand people
in the congregation, and the square outside was jammed with
pilgrims. Mass was said and the banner of the new saint was
carried down the aisle. A few rose petals fell mysteriously from
the ceiling during the course of the ceremonies. It was 'gloire'
beyond anything the child Thérèse could have imagined.

CONCLUSION

For years after her death Thérèse played an important part in the Catholic imagination, particularly in France and more particularly in Normandy. Many churches and cathedrals erected statues to her, wearing her Carmelite habit and clutching the white roses which were her hallmark. Village churches in France still display the touching little plaques with which the sick thanked her for prayers answered and for recovery from illness. An opulent basilica was built in Lisieux in honour of Thérèse, inaugurated in 1937 by Cardinal Pacelli, later Pope Pius XII, a huge building for a small town which already has a large cathedral and many churches. Here pilgrims come in coachloads to see the relics of Thérèse, and the graves of Louis and Zélie, who were reburied on the site. There are films about Thérèse on display, souvenirs and books to be bought. On the other side of the town Les Buissonets has its trail of visitors, as does the little house in Alençon where Thérèse was born.

There have been innumerable books about Thérèse, the majority of them written by priests, for whom she seems to have a particular appeal. Certainly the most fulsome biographies of her have been written by men, many of whom emphasise her painful obedience, her penitential life, her submissiveness, her dutifulness – erstwhile womanly qualities that do not make an immediate appeal to twentieth-century taste.

Thérèse was, of course, brought up to know woman's place, which was either in the home, often in childbed, or in the convent. As a good nun she naturally practised obedience (excessively, the modern reader may feel, since she wrecked her health in the process). Yet in spite of this she feels a quirkier and more subversive character than many of her priest-admirers manage to suggest, whether arguing with the Pope at a papal audience when she was only fourteen (something few other papal callers of any age have had the nerve to attempt), or making astringent comments on her death-bed when those who ministered to her – her sisters, the doctor, the chaplain – seemed not fully to understand her point of view. So firmly is this side of her character ignored that it is possible to feel that what appeals to many in Thérèse, is that she can be moulded in fantasy to an image many priests have preferred for women – sexless, obedient, gentle and good – the model of 'safety'.

She can, of course, easily be presented in this light, and her depression and invalidism seem the lot of those who are 'too good'. Yet alongside the rigidities of her class, time and calling, there is something strong, original and irrepressible in Thérèse which I wonder if some of her male adulators recognise and appreciate as eagerly as they appreciate her dutiful qualities – a toughness, a sharpness, a splendidly incurable independence of mind which transcended her meagre education, and which even in sickness and mortal agony did not desert her.

She might be seen, paradoxically, as a model for the power, endurance, and resourcefulness of women, a power which, even when intolerably constricted, crushed and punished by circumstances, reasserts itself with the tenacity of a weed (or little flower) growing on a wall. She is naive, impoverished both by her lack of learning and by her inadequate experience of life outside the convent walls, but neither she nor her superiors succeeded in concealing her untutored intelligence and her native shrewdness. She had one other worldly asset; spoiled child as she was, she had a natural taste for getting her own way without even noticing that this was what she was doing.

What are *we*, a hundred years on, with a different reading of human psychology from the nineteenth century, to make of the life of Thérèse? Even if we share the same religious faith as the saint we have some unease about the traditional interpretations of her life, as, it must be said, did many irreproachable Catholics who were her contemporaries. They were mainly troubled by the sentimentality, and a few of them attributed that to Thérèse's infantility, symbolised by her oft-repeated use of the word 'little', mainly for herself who was not little in any sense of the word. They sensed a spurious humility in it.

Our criticism might have more to do with a sense of being taken in, of a feeling that her sanctity is somehow a trick that has been brought off by the Martin sisters with some collusion from Thérèse. This is not necessarily to accuse the sisters of malice – they had been brought up in an atmosphere in which sanctity was the only imaginable good – yet any careful examination of the facts makes it clear that for what seemed to them an excellent end they were prepared to behave in manipulative ways, towards the convent, the Church, and not least their dying sister.

We may feel that the entire Martin family were the victims of a rigid bourgeois society, complacent in its provincialism, narrow in its culture, restricted in its religious understanding. Louis and Zélie, themselves disappointed in religious vocations, pushed their daughters as inevitably towards the convent as Mrs Worthington pushed her daughter towards the stage. The suffering of Léonie, joining and leaving convents three times before her final submission, would seem to indicate something of the pressure involved. Marie had felt no burning sense of vocation either, yet inevitably she too was confined in the silence and austerity of Carmel. If in doubt, seemed to be the Martin family motto, then you cannot do better than take the veil.

Zélie, a woman of iron will and strict discipline, undoubtedly set the religious tone of the family, a tone that was maintained, despite her early death, by Pauline, in many ways a kind of double for her mother. Marie, a more balanced personality, and Céline, a fairly phlegmatic and unimaginative one, struck a more moderate note. Léonie, always 'different' and unable to conform to her mother's ideas, alone put up a sort of fight, an unequal struggle which condemned her to bitter suffering. Thérèse, as the last and most delicate child, and the one with most imagination and intelligence, also suffered – it was not possible for her to live out the smallest rebellion from a way of life that had been chosen for her in the cradle.

The shock of renewed separations from the first weeks of her life, and the rigidity of Zélie's discipline, gave her a lasting terror of abandonment and of not measuring up to the standards expected of her. Even before Zélie's death, and Pauline's rigorous application of her mother's ideas, Thérèse was a profoundly insecure child tormented with the fear of 'not being good', or of 'not pleasing God', racked with scruples, unable to relate successfully with her peers, somehow stuck in the 'little queen' role assigned to her by her father, one not calculated to appeal to other children. Louis's obvious passion for her in which her lightest word could please or distress him robbed her of the strong, balanced support which might have gone some little way to dissolving her fears. Uncle Isidore came near to filling the role of a father and brings an air of commonsense into the story whenever he is mentioned.

In addition to the particular problem of being Thérèse Martin of Alençon and Lisieux was the more general problem of being a woman in the nineteenth century. Zélie had illustrated the physical strain of perpetual childbearing, the sadness of losing three children to 'heaven' and of an illness, possibily accentuated by childbearing, which killed her at forty-five. Perhaps because of the underlying incestuousness of the relationship with Louis Thérèse does not seem to have been drawn to men except as father figures – any suggestion of sexuality is ruthlessly repressed. So marriage, for these various reasons, could not have appealed to her.

The religious life, the frustrated ambition of her parents, very clearly did. That she found it congenial to her temperament is not in question. But much that emerges in her writings and sayings makes it clear that its relative passivity disappointed a whole side of her character which would love to have been a travelling missionary, a hero, a soldier, above all a priest. To be a woman was to be condemned to confinement, the rule of others, the lack of a voice with which to make oneself heard, and the absence of an attentive audience to listen.

Thérèse was self-confessedly ambitious and she suffered,

therefore, from obscurity, the lack of opportunity to go out and make an active impact on the world, even though her upbringing had made the world seem a dangerous and wicked place from which it was safer and wiser to retreat.

Energies denied their natural expression turn inward. Like many women before her Thérèse made a virtue of the suffering she endured, telling herself that this was what Jesus had chosen for her, though it might seem to others that it was not Jesus but a particular social and religious framework that condemned her to it. In a life that was a sort of death-in-life she was unashamedly enthusiastic for death (as she had been since the age of three), in itself the sign, we may think, of a deep despair. We cannot know how much a longing for death influences the processes of the body, making it vulnerable to disease, but Thérèse, at least, was not in the least surprised or outraged to realise, at the age of twenty-three, that death was already very near. Neither the living conditions of Carmel, nor its attitude to death, made it possible or desirable to put up a fight for life. On the contrary, with its curious mixture of denial of facts, stubbornness and masochism, it pushed Thérèse towards her fate.

Though it aspired to great religious heights, the human reality of the Lisieux Carmel was, by all accounts, a depressing one. The brides of Christ, as depicted not least in Thérèse's own writing, were petty, envious, jealous and downright unkind. Mother Marie de Gonzague may have been seriously unbalanced – indeed that is the kindest diagnosis one can make of a 'Mother' who appears to have 'played off' her daughters' affections one against another, who allowed one of them to struggle on with duties far beyond her strength to the point of irredeemable physical breakdown, and who refused the relief of morphia to a dying patient in intolerable agony. It is a form of Christianity so perverse as to be quite intolerable.

The truly remarkable thing about Thérèse, however, is that she took her own very human failings – her longing for love and attention and acclaim, her overweening spiritual ambition – exactly as they were in all their silliness and childishness, and began to work with them. Almost as if she were considering another person, not herself, she detached herself from the particular shame of such feelings by the process of owning them. Cruelly debarred by the accidents of her upbringing and the blindness of Church and society from leading the rich life her body and brains might have enjoyed, she took the scrap of life allowed to her and transformed it.

It is easy to underestimate how considerable her achievement was, simply because we may resent her collusion with a Church which oppressed women. In a period in which women have begun to claim their birthrights we may resent the acquiescence of Christian women in forms of life which suppressed, silenced and destroyed them. Yet pity and understanding of their plight helps us to interpret the kind of battle they were surreptitiously waging. Thérèse chose to acquiesce because she could not have imagined any other choice, but then she did something daring and interesting with her acquiescence. She was, she knew indistinctly, one of a great army of human beings (the 'little') whom life had robbed of much that might have been theirs. Very well then, she would celebrate the feast of those who have nothing, who have not lived. The Little Way, far from being the tool of subservience (especially for women) that it has often been made into, has an almost ironic quality to it. 'If I may have nothing,' it says gaily, 'then I will turn reason inside out and make having nothing the most enjoyable of possibilities.' Like a St Francis, like a hero of a Solzhenitsyn novel who discovers that when everything has been taken from a man and he no longer has anything to lose then he is free, so Thérèse, on behalf of womankind, charts a way to live out an impossible situation. She also reveals the price that is paid in the attempt to make a true rather than a false response to life.

In a bizarre way, a way that echoes the subversion of the gospels themselves, she triumphs. Paradoxically the voiceless nun finds a voice that is heard more resoundingly than that of any priest or even Pope of her generation. Humble, insignificant, 'little', she intends to find an audience and she does.

What is it she has to say, though? She speaks for those driven, forced, by the cruel necessity of social constraint, religious taboo, accident, physical or mental handicap and disability, into a life they would never have chosen if they had been more fortunate. Cripplingly shy, hysterical, totally ensnared by her family in the net of 'love', debarred by social convention from pouring out her formidable energies in the world, Thérèse turns inward, becomes an invalid (like so many women of her generation) and begins to till the dreary acres of 'submission'. If there is no choice in life, no way out of the trap, then only one response is left; the religious trick is to turn it from masochism into love. Anger gives way not merely to acceptance but to a strange sort of play-acting that gradually turns into the truth – a play-acting that says this is the best of all possible happenings, that this bout of pain is the purest piece of luck. In other words that it is the will of God. By such an act of surrender the unbearable pain of crucifixion is transmuted into the joy of resurrection. The far side of the coin, the opposite side from the face of pain, is the face of joy. 'Love', as e.e. cummings says, 'makes the little thickness of the coin.'

Thérèse, handicapped in Church and society for being a woman, illustrates a favourite paradox of Jesus, that the stone that the builders rejected becomes the carved cornice, a matter of pride. Was she a saint? At the time of her canonisation Cardinal Vico pointed out how in the early days of the Church people became saints by popular acclaim. Nobody collected careful bits of evidence about them. They were those who, for largely inexplicable reasons, became popular among the faithful as somehow illustrating what the faith meant to them. Some performed miracles, some preached marvellously, some lived lives of loneliness in the desert, some were wonderful at hearing confessions and giving advice, some did nothing much except give others a feeling of joy and hope, in bad times as in good. A saint was not somebody who had been put through the Vatican mangle, but was simply a focus of love.

Not for several centuries had there been a popular saint in the sense Thérèse became one, one from whom ordinary people drew encouragement and whom they received as their own.

BIBLIOGRAPHY

Autobiography

Sainte Thérèse de l'Enfant Jésus et de la Sainte Face, *Histoire d'une Ame*, Les Editions du Cerf, Paris, 1985

Thérèse of Lisieux, *Autobiography of a Saint: The Story of a Soul*, trans. by Ronald Knox, Fontana, London, 1960

Books about Thérèse of Lisieux

V. Sackville-West, *The Eagle and the Dove*, Michael Joseph, London, 1943

Hans Urs von Balthasar, *Thérèse of Lisieux*, Sheed and Ward, London, 1953

Etienne Robo, *Two Portraits of St Teresa of Lisieux*, Sands & Co., London, 1955; Newman Press, Westminster, M.D., 1957

Ida Friederike Görres, *The Hidden Face; A Study of St Thérèse of Lisieux*, Burns & Oates, Tunbridge Wells, 1959; Pantheon Books, New York, 1959

Jean-François Six, *La Véritable Enfance de Thérèse de Lisieux*, Editions du Seuil, Paris, 1971

Michael Hollings, *Thérèse of Lisieux*, William Collins Sons & Co., 1981, Fount Paperbacks, London, 1982

Eric Doyle, 'The Ordination of Women in the Roman Catholic Church' (essay), *Feminine in the Church*, ed. Monica Furlong, SPCK, London, 1984

Background material

Teresa of Avila, *The Life of Saint Teresa* (of Avila), Penguin Classics, London, 1957

Rodolphe Hoornaert, *Saint Teresa* (of Avila) *in Her Writings*, Sheed and Ward, London, 1931

Thomas Merton, *The Seven Storey Mountain*, Harcourt, Brace & Company, New York, 1948

Anne Hardman, *English Carmelites in Penal Times*, Burns Oates & Washbourne, London, 1936

Rudolph M. Bell and David Weinstein, *Saints and Society*, University of Chicago Press, Chicago, 1982

Rudolph M. Bell, *Holy Anorexia*, University of Chicago Press, Chicago, 1985

The Oxford Dictionary of the Christian Church, Oxford University Press, Oxford and New York, 1977

The Oxford Dictionary of Saints, Oxford University Press, Oxford and New York, 1978

Dictionary of Saints, Penguin, London, 1965

NOTES

CHAPTER 1: For Ever and Ever

1. Henri Pranzini was tried in July 1887 for murdering a woman, her maid and her eleven-year-old daughter in Paris by cutting their throats – his case aroused enormous interest in France. Although found guilty he refused to admit the crime or show remorse. Thérèse prayed earnestly for him after he was condemned to death, and believed that when he kissed the crucifix before being executed it was because of repentance due to her prayers.
2. Père Pichon: A Jesuit and gifted confessor who had helped Marie Martin with her guilty 'scruples'. He was much influenced by the French spiritual writers François de Sales (1567–1622) and Jean Pierre de Caussade (1675–1751) and preached a more loving and forgiving God than Zélie and Aunt Dosithée had taught the Martin children to expect.
3. Sainte Thérèse, *Histoire d'une Ame*, p. 174, Les Editions du Cerf, Paris, 1985.

CHAPTER 2: The Little Queen

4. Letter from Zélie to Céline Guérin, 2 January 1873.
5. Letter from Zélie to Pauline, 25 June 1874.
6. Letter from Zélie to Pauline, 21 May 1876.
7. Letter from Zélie to Pauline, 22 March 1877.
8. Letter from Zélie to Pauline, 4 March 1877.
9. Letter from Zélie to Céline Guérin, 17 December 1876.
10. Letter from Zélie to Pauline, 13 February 1877.
11. Letter from Zélie to Pauline, 21 May 1876.

12. Etienne Robo, *Two Portraits of St Teresa of Lisieux*, p. 178, Sands, London, 1955.
13. *Histoire d'une Ame*, Manuscript A, p. 31.
14. *Summarium* quoted by Ida Friederike Görres in *The Hidden Face*, p. 52, Burns & Oates, Tunbridge Wells, 1959.
15. *Histoire d'une Ame*, p. 54.
16. *Histoire d'une Ame*, p. 39.
17. Letter from Zélie to Pauline, spring 1877.

CHAPTER 3: Born for Greatness

18. *Histoire d'une Ame*, p. 43.
19. ibid., p. 51.
20. ibid., p. 53.
21. ibid., p. 53.
22. Ida Friederike Görres, p.59.
23. The Abbey school was a sixteenth-century Benedictine foundation, run by the Benedictine Abbey de Notre Dame du Pré in Lisieux. It was destroyed during the Second World War.
24. *Histoire d'une Ame*, p. 63.
25. ibid., p. 65.
26. ibid., p. 70.
27. ibid., p. 70.
28. ibid., p. 71.
29. ibid., p. 72.
30. ibid., p. 75.
31. ibid., p. 77.
32. ibid., pp. 78–79.

CHAPTER 4: A Drop Lost in the Ocean.

33. ibid., p. 91.
34. Thomas à Kempis (c. 1380–1471), *The Imitation of Christ*: An ascetical writer who greatly influenced Thérèse.
35. *Histoire d'une Ame*, p. 97.
36. ibid., p. 103.
37. ibid., p. 104.
38. ibid., pp. 109, 110, 126.

CHAPTER 5: A Toy of No Value

41. ibid., p. 157.
42. ibid., p. 157.
43. ibid., p. 159.
44. ibid., p. 168.

CHAPTER 6: The Little Bride

45. ibid., pp. 179, 180.
46. ibid., p. 183.
47. ibid., p. 181.
48. Billet de Profession, ibid., p. 315.
49. ibid., p. 191.

CHAPTER 7: The Little Way

50. ibid., p. 200.
51. ibid., Manuscript B, p. 220.
52. ibid., p. 221.
53. ibid., Manuscript C, p. 273.
54. Etienne Robo, pp. 152 ff.
55. Quoted by Etienne Robo, source not given.
56. *Histoire d'une Ame*, p. 234.
57. ibid., pp. 245, 246.
58. ibid., p. 285.
59. ibid., p. 262.

INDEX

Adam and Eve, 2
Africa, 125, 127
Agnes, Sister *see* Martin, Pauline
Alençon, 6, 24, 25, 27, 38, 52–3,
   59–60, 99, 129
Anne, Abbé, 126–7
Anne of Jesus, Mother, 102
Aquinas, St Thomas, 3
Assisi, 71
Association of the Holy Angels, 58
Augustine, Saint, 3
Autobiography of a Saint, 1, 44–5,
   78, 84, 99–100, 108–11, 117–
   19, 122–4, 125
Avila, 75

Bayeux, 66
Benedict, St, 74
Benedict XV, Pope, 127–8
Benedictine Order, 74
Berthold, St, 74
Bologna, 69
Bonaventure, 4
Brontë family, 103
Les Buissonets, Lisieux, 11–13, 15,
   38–9, 46, 93, 108, 129
Bunyan, John, 113

Caen, 64, 87
Calvinism, 6, 8
Canada, 127
Carmel, Pauline enters, 47–9;
   Thérèse determines to become a
   nun at, 47–8, 62–3, 64–8,

70–3; and Thérèse's vision of the
Virgin, 51; Marie joins, 59, 60;
Thérèse enters, 8, 11–23;
Thérèse's life as a nun at, 78–88,
92–3; and Thérèse's
autobiography, 123–4; and the
canonisation of Thérèse, 127
Carmelite Order, 74–7
Cecilia, St, 70
celibacy, 3–4
Chalet des Lilas, Trouville, 58
The Children of Mary, 58
China, 127
Christianity, attitudes to women,
2–5
Church Fathers, 3
Church of Our Lady of Victories,
Paris, 50
Convent of the Visitation, Caen, 64
Convent of the Visitation, Le Mans,
13, 24, 33–4
convents, 4–6
Cornières, Dr de, 114
Counter Reformation, 75

Delatroette, Canon, 14–15
Discalced Carmelites, 76
Domin, Abbé, 54
Dosithée, Sister *see* Guérin, Elise
dualism, 2–3
Ducellier, M., 41

England, 125
Enlightenment, 6

First World War, 125–6
Florence, 71–2
Francis of Assisi, St, 4, 134

Geneviève, Mother, 83, 85, 88, 89–90, 91
Genoa, 71
Gethsemani, monastery of, 124
Gonzague, Mother Marie de, 77, 98; and Thérèse's determination to become a nun, 47–8, 14–15, 72; relations with Thérèse, 18, 22, 80–5, 101–2, 105, 109–11; loses position of Reverend Mother, 93–4; becomes Mistress of Novices, 97; and Thérèse's memoirs, 100, 108–11, 123; and Thérèse's illness, 101–2, 103–5, 106–7, 113–14, 117, 119; mental instability, 133; death, 124
Görres, Ida, 40, 43, 122, 125
Great St Bernard monastery, 25
Greece, 2
Guérin, Céline, 12, 38–9, 49, 58, 65, 121
Guérin, Elise (Sister Dosithée), 24, 33–4
Guérin, Isidore (Thérèse's uncle), 6, 14, 24, 42, 58, 121; disapproves of Thérèse's decision to become a nun, 12, 23, 64–5; and Zélie's death, 36–7; Martin family stays with, 38–9; friendship with Thérèse, 49, 50, 132
Guérin, Jeanne, 12, 38–9, 91, 113
Guérin, Marie (Sister Marie of the Eucharist), 12, 38–9, 46, 48, 59, 107, 124

Hugonin, Monsignor, Bishop of Bayeux, 65–8, 72, 87, 91, 123, 127

Italy, 69

Jansen, Cornelius, 6
Jansenism, 6–7
Jesus Christ, 2, 21, 22, 57, 65, 71, 72, 82, 87, 89–90, 94–6, 107, 111, 119, 133, 135
Joan of Arc, 39, 95, 98, 116, 128
John of the Cross, St, 15
Joseph, St, 26, 52
Judaism, 2

Kempis, Thomas à, *Imitation of Christ*, 56, 61–2, 63
Knox, Ronald, 1

Le Mans, 24, 33
Leo XIII, Pope, 70–1
Le Lexovien, 6
Lisieux, 6, 7, 38–9, 99, 129
'Little Way', 7, 96–7, 102, 117, 134
Louise (maid), 34, 36, 38
Lourdes, 36

Madeleine, Sister, 92
Manes, 2–3
Manicheism, 2–3
Marie of the Angels, Sister (Novice Mistress), 14–15, 16, 19–21, 80
Marie of the Eucharist, Sister *see* Guérin, Marie
Marie of the Sacred Heart, Sister *see* Martin, Marie
Marie of the Trinity, Sister, 105
Martin, Céline (Thérèse's sister), 8, 17, 20, 61, 64, 72; childhood, 11, 26, 28, 33, 34–6; and Thérèse's determination to become a nun, 12–13, 19, 62, friendship with Thérèse, 31, 46–7, 62; and her mother's death, 38; education, 39, 45, 54; first communion, 47; and Thérèse's illness, 49; leaves school, 57; grand tour of Europe, 68–72; decides to become a nun, 87, 94; life as a nun, 98; nurses Thérèse, 106, 108, 114; and Thérèse's sanctity, 121, 131; death, 1

Martin, Léonie (Thérèse's sister), 11, 17, 20, 87, 121; childhood, 26, 28–9, 30, 34–5, 44; and her mother's death, 38; education, 39, 45; attempts to become a nun, 12–13, 60, 64, 123, 131; and Thérèse's illness, 49, 50; godmother to Thérèse, 57

Martin, Louis (Thérèse's father), 17, 91, 107; childhood, 25; marriage, 25–6; retirement, 26–7; relationship with Thérèse, 29, 31, 40–2, 57, 61, 132; spirituality, 32–3; and Zélie's death, 37, 38; and Thérèse's education, 45–6; and Thérèse's determination to become a nun, 62–3, 64–8; suffers a stroke, 62–3; grand tour of Europe, 68–72; and Thérèse's entry into Carmel, 11–14, 20–1, 86–7; mental illness, 86–8, 89; death, 87, 94; grave, 129

Martin, Marie (Sister Marie of the Sacred Heart, Thérèse's sister), 16, 49; birth, 26; and Thérèse's childhood, 27, 28, 32, 33; in the Convent of the Visitation, 33–4; runs Martin household, 36; and her mother's death, 38; and Thérèse's illness, 50, 106; and Thérèse's vision of the Virgin, 51; and Thérèse's First Communion, 53–4; becomes a nun, 13–14, 21, 59, 60, 86, 87, 131; and Thérèse's determination to become a nun, 17, 19, 62, 81–2; and Thérèse's memoirs, 99, 123; and Thérèse's sanctity, 114–17, 121, 131

Martin, Marie-Hélène, 26, 30–1

Martin, Marie-Joseph-Jean Baptiste, 26

Martin, Marie-Joseph-Louis, 26

Martin, Marie-Melanie-Thérèse, 26

Martin, Pauline (Sister Agnes, Thérèse's sister), 11, 16, 17, 70, 91; birth, 26; and Thérèse's childhood, 28, 32, 33; in the Convent of the Visitation, 33, 34; runs Martin household, 36; and her mother's death, 38; takes over role of Thérèse's mother, 39–44, 59; becomes a nun, 13, 47–8, 52, 56, 77; and Thérèse's First Communion, 53; and Thérèse's determination to become a nun, 14, 19, 22, 62, 72; relations with Thérèse as a nun, 80, 81–2; becomes Reverend Mother, 93–4, 97; and Thérèse's memoirs, 99, 100, 108, 122–3; and Thérèse's illness, 105, 106, 112; and Thérèse's sanctity, 114–17, 121, 131; re-elected Prioress, 124; publishes *Novissima Verba*, 124

Martin, Thérèse *see* Thérèse of Lisieux, St

Martin, Zélie (Thérèse's mother), 59, 65; letters, 7, 28, 29, 32; childhood, 24; lace-making business, 6, 24, 26–7; marriage, 25–6; children, 6, 26–7, 132; breast cancer, 6, 26, 34, 36–7; and Thérèse's childhood, 27–33; spirituality, 32–3, 131; death, 37, 38, 51, 93; grave, 129

Mary, Virgin, 4, 26; Thérèse sees vision of, 11, 50, 51–2

Mary Magdalen, St, 54

Maudelonde family, 46

Merton, Thomas, 124

Middle East, 2

Milan, 69

Naples, 71

Néele, Dr, 113–14

Le Normand, 6

Normandy, 6, 129

Novissima Verba, 124

Order of the Visitation, 123

Orwell, George, 105

Our Lady of Victories, Paris, 68

Oxford Dictionary of Saints, 9

Padua, 69
Palestine, 74
Papinau, Madame, 57
Paris, 25, 49, 68
Paul, St, 2, 8, 96
Peter, Mother, 86
Pichon, Père, 21, 91, 94
Pisa, 71
Pius X, Pope, 127
Pius XI, Pope, 128
Pius XII, Pope, 129
Pompeii, 71
Poor Clares, 13, 24, 60, 123
Port-Royal, 6
Portugal, 125
Pranzini, 15, 61, 77

Reformed Carmelites, 76
Reverony, M., 67, 68, 70–1
Robo, Etienne, 104
Rome, 68, 69–71, 127–8

Sackville-West, Vita, 1
Saint-Cyran, 6
St Peter's, Rome, 128
saints, 8–10
Semallé, 27
sexuality, Church's attitude to, 2–5
Sisters of St Vincent de Paul, 24
Solzhenitsyn, Alexander, 134
South America, 127
Spain, 75
The Story of a Soul, 1, 44–5, 78, 84, 99–100, 108–11, 117–19, 122–4, 125
Strasbourg, 25
Switzerland, 68

Taillé, Rose, 27, 31
Teresa of Avila, St, 42, 75–7
Tertullian, 8
Thérèse of Lisieux, St, birth and separation from her mother, 27–8; childhood, 6, 27–37; early spirituality, 5, 21, 32, 35; relationship with her father, 29, 31, 41–2, 57, 61, 132; character, 30–2, 44–5; friendship with

Céline, 31, 46–7, 62; and her mother's death, 37, 51; Pauline brings up, 39–44, 59; education, 39–40, 45–6, 54, 57–8; first confession, 41; visits Trouville, 44, 58; and Pauline's decision to become a nun, 47–9, 52, 59; determination to become a nun, 47–8, 52, 62–3, 64–8, 70–3; illnesses, 48–50, 57–8, 82; vision of the Virgin Mary, 50, 51–2; visits Alençon, 52–3; First Communion, 53–4, 55–7; fascination with suffering, 56–7, 95–6, 97; prays for Pranzini, 61, 77; grand tour of Europe, 68–72; enters Carmel, 11–23; life as a nun, 78–88, 92–3, 97–8; relations with Reverend Mother, 80–5, 101–2, 105, 109–11; received into Carmelite Order, 86; profession, 88–91; vision of the devil, 89–90; poetry, 93; paintings, 93; fantasy life, 95–6; 'Little Way', 7, 96–7, 102, 117, 134; writes play about Joan of Arc, 98; tuberculosis, 101–5, 106–8, 111–20; attitude to death, 107–8, 133; autobiography, 1, 78, 84, 99–100, 108–11, 117–19, 122–4, 125; sanctity, 114–17, 121, 124–7, 131; relics, 115, 123, 124, 127, 129; death, 120, 121, 126; miracles, 126–7; biographies, 129; canonisation, 9, 127–8, 135; achievements, 133–5

Trouville, 44, 58

United States of America, 127

Venice, 69
Vico, Cardinal, 135
Victoire (maid), 12, 18, 41, 49, 99
Voltaire, 6

Westminster, Archbishop of, 125
women, Christian attitudes to, 2–5

RYAN QUINN

AND THE REBEL'S ESCAPE

RON McGEE

HARPER
An Imprint of HarperCollinsPublishers

Library of Congress Control Number: 2016936058
ISBN 978-0-06-242164-7

Book design by Victor Joseph Ochoa
16 17 18 19 20   CG/RRDH   10 9 8 7 6 5 4 3 2 1
❖
First Edition

Life is full of daring adventures.
But they're a lot more fun if you have
amazing people to share them with.
So thanks to Mom, Dad, and Brian for
all the great adventures growing up.
And thanks to Eufe, Alex, and Claudia
for all the journeys we still have in
front of us.

—RM

PROLOGUE

**NANSANG PROVINCE,
ANDAKAR**

Lan was only sixteen and about to die.

The Army Services Intelligence agents were narrowing the distance, getting closer every second. Struggling up the steep hill, Lan glanced back, fighting exhaustion and fear. The jungle was dense here, and moonlight broke through only sporadically. The flashlight beams of the ASI agents in pursuit bounced wildly back and forth.

Slipping on wet leaves, Lan stumbled, dangerously close to tumbling back down the steep incline. At the last possible moment, a powerful hand reached out and grabbed hold.

"We just have to make it to the temple. You can do it," the American said. In the gloom, his face was all hard lines and shadows, but there was determination in his eyes. Lan didn't want to disappoint him after he'd risked so much in getting them both to safety. Supporting each other, they made it over the last rise of the hill and onto the open plateau up top.

The grounds of the Mae Wong Temples appeared ghostly in the moonlight. Abandoned for two thousand years, these ancient ruins remained strictly off-limits to tourists. Forty years ago, when this country's military regime seized power, Mae Wong was the site of a bloody massacre of Buddhist priests. It remained a potent symbol of rebellion that Lan had often dreamed of visiting. But not like this. Not just to become yet another victim of the brutal government's soldiers.

"There," the American said, pointing to a small structure about thirty yards to their left. "The hiding place is inside that stupa, the one with the golden dome."

Lan looked back at the flashlights bouncing their way up the hill. "They're right behind us."

"We'll be safe inside the temple. Come on—we're almost there."

Lan wanted to believe it was true. After all the months of secrecy and risk, the constant fear of being discovered, would it finally be over? Could this stranger actually save them? Suddenly, an explosive blast shattered the night and the American jerked forward as a bullet ripped into him. Blood splattered Lan's cheek.

Watching the American fall to the ground, Lan knew that now all hope was lost.

PART *ONE*

WHAT YOU DON'T KNOW CAN HURT YOU

CHAPTER

01

**NEW YORK,
USA**

No more fights.

The promise he'd made to his mother ran through Ryan Quinn's mind as he stood in the school hallway. Drew Stieglitz, a junior and the starting center on the basketball team, shoved Ryan's friend Danny into the metal lockers. Stieglitz was a full head taller than Danny, with a square jaw, giant hands, and the swagger of a guy used to getting his way.

"I told you to leave her alone." Stieglitz slammed Danny into the locker once again for emphasis.

"I thought that was more of a suggestion," Danny said. Short and slim, with spiky black hair and a cocky grin, Danny had a never-ending supply of manic energy. He showed no fear, but Ryan knew his friend was sweating.

Stieglitz leaned in close. "Keep it up, you little dwarf, you're gonna get your butt kicked."

"For talking to a gorgeous girl?" Danny glanced at Kasey, Stieglitz's beautiful and popular little sister, who watched with an alarmed expression. "Gotta tell you, Steeg, even a butt-kicking from you sounds worth it."

A few of the students who had gathered around laughed at Danny's confident attitude.

"Drew, chill," Kasey said, putting a hand on her brother's arm to calm him. She was in two of Ryan's classes, but they'd talked only once. Well, actually *she'd* talked and Ryan had just sort of nodded and stared. And then felt so embarrassed that he couldn't even look at her again.

"Stay out of it." Stieglitz shrugged her off, focused on Danny. "You've a real smart mouth. Think you're funny."

"I'm guessing you're not a fan." Danny tried to sound tough, but his nerves were starting to get the better of him. He looked at Ryan, hoping for some backup.

"You're about to find out," Stieglitz said.

No more fights.

Ryan had been at his new school here in New York for more than two months without any problems. Almost a record for him lately. He'd been in trouble for fighting several times over the last year. The worst was when his family was living in Ghana for a few months. A couple of English teens, tourists visiting Africa with a school group, were throwing rocks at kids from a local village and calling them names. Ryan just wanted them to stop, but things got out of hand. One of the boys ended up with a broken nose, the other with his arm in a sling, and Ryan got hauled off by the police. Luckily, his dad was able to talk the cops into letting him go with a warning.

There were other fights, too. Ryan had a bad habit of getting pulled into other people's problems. It was like he couldn't help himself. Here in New York, though, things were finally going well—really well, actually. And the last thing he wanted was for anything to screw that up.

Like getting dragged into this. But what was he supposed to do, stand by and watch Danny get beaten to a pulp?

Ryan stepped forward. "Let him go."

Stieglitz gave Ryan a dismissive glance, then looked back to his two buddies behind him.

"Did somebody dose all the eighth graders with stupid pills this year?"

"He was just talking to her. Kasey's in a couple of classes with us." Ryan moved in closer, his tone relaxed but making it clear that he wasn't backing away. "No big deal."

Stieglitz turned to face him. Ryan could tell that the jock was keenly aware that people were watching.

"She's my sister. I'll decide what's a big deal," Stieglitz said. Stieglitz shifted position, zeroing in on his new target. Ryan kept his expression neutral, but watched Stieglitz closely, searching for a sign of his intentions.

Stieglitz's first swing was a respectably fast sucker punch, coming in high and from the right. Ryan instinctively dodged, keeping his body weight balanced on the toes of his left foot as he pivoted out of the way. The momentum of the swing threw Stieglitz off-balance and he barely stopped himself from falling. Ryan had a clear shot, but he held back. He didn't want to hit the other boy unless he absolutely had to.

Stieglitz glanced back at his friends. "Kick his butt, Steeg," one of them said, inching forward.

"I don't want to do this," Ryan said. "I kinda

promised my mom I wouldn't get into any fights."

"Should've thought about your mommy before you opened your mouth." Stieglitz shot forward, trying to grab Ryan's well-worn Psychedelic Furs T-shirt with hands that could easily palm a basketball. Ryan stepped back, once more shifting away from the bigger kid so that he missed and stumbled.

"Whoosh—all air! And the crowd goes wild!" Danny said, beaming as Kasey's friends laughed.

Ryan glared at Danny.

"What?" Danny was all innocence.

Students drifted closer, smelling blood in the air and wanting a ringside seat. Stieglitz spun around, angry at being made to look stupid.

"Drew, come on—lay off," Kasey said. She glanced at her brother and then looked anxiously at Ryan. Was she actually worried for him—or did she just think he was nuts for taking on her brother? Ryan couldn't quite tell.

"Big mistake," Stieglitz growled.

Ryan managed to pull his eyes away from Kasey's just in time. Stieglitz charged, determined to ram him into the lockers. Ryan sidestepped with the smooth moves of a dancer. The bigger boy's lack of control would be his downfall. Stieglitz whizzed past and Ryan tapped his shoulder just enough to throw his balance off. Stieglitz crashed into the metal lockers with the force of a bull.

A collective groan went up from the watching students as they heard skull hit metal. Stieglitz dropped to the ground, dazed, as the fourth-period bell rang. Everyone scattered, excited to spread word of how Stieglitz was beaten by a kid half his size.

"That was awesome," Danny whispered to Ryan. "Stupid and probably suicidal—but definitely awesome."

"Mr. Quinn."

Ryan and Danny whirled around to find Principal Milankovic staring at them. The hall cleared quickly as students made themselves scarce. Ryan noticed Kasey's friends grab her by the arm and pull her away. Stieglitz took one look at the principal, then lurched to his feet and stumbled off as well.

"My office, Mr. Quinn," the principal said.

Ryan's shoulders slumped. "I barely even *touched* him."

"Now."

CHAPTER

02

**NEW YORK,
USA**

The International Community School of New York was only six blocks from the United Nations Headquarters and had a student body that included kindergartners all the way up to high school seniors. Many of the kids who attended were the sons and daughters of UN employees. Ryan's algebra class alone had a Saudi Arabian prince, the Minister of Thailand's daughter, and a Somali refugee whose mother was on the Human Rights committee.

It was a perfect fit for Ryan, whose father, John, worked as a director for the United Nations Development Programme. Until recently, Ryan had spent most of his life as a nomad, traveling from place to place. His dad was stationed for a year or two at a time in different countries, and the family had lived all over the world.

When he was younger, Ryan enjoyed living in unusual places. He made friends with local kids pretty easily and each place offered some cool new experience—hide-and-seek in a forest in Belarus, paddleboarding off the coast of Nicaragua, ice fishing in Norway. He never had time to get bored anywhere because they'd soon be off to someplace different.

Out of necessity, Ryan learned to adapt. He studied local kids closely for clues on how to act and then imitated them, becoming good at blending in. He'd change the clothes he wore, the expressions he used, the foods he ate. Whatever made him fit in. Language wasn't much of a barrier when he was young, especially among boys who could occupy themselves for hours playing sports and games.

But as he got older, fitting in was harder. Kids already had their group of friends and weren't as quick to talk to the new guy. Ryan had become something of a chameleon, able to change with each new environment, but he didn't feel like he belonged anywhere. He was always on the outside looking in.

More and more, he just hung out alone. He'd get home from whatever school he was attending and go to his room. Some days, he'd practice the magic tricks his dad taught him when he was growing up, or maybe play guitar. He'd read until his eyes glazed over, then put headphones on and listen to music.

His room became his refuge. Though the location changed every time they moved, one thing was the same: his awesome collection of baseball caps always hung proudly on the wall. Ryan had caps from every Major League team in America. He'd started collecting them when he was eleven and his parents took him to a Washington Nationals game. It was on one of their trips "home," as they called it. Which was totally weird to Ryan since he'd never lived in the States for more than a month or two at a time.

After that trip, though, he started thinking about living in the United States a lot. What would it be like to go to a backyard barbecue and wolf down hot dogs and hamburgers? Or to watch a Friday night football game with cheerleaders and a marching band? Or grow up with the same set of friends who'd known you for more than a few months? Every baseball cap

Ryan added to his collection made him feel a little more connected to an America he knew mostly through books and movies.

That's when the fights started. Ryan insisted to his mom and dad that there was always a good reason: A younger kid was being teased or some bully was picking on Ryan. Kids could be jerks in every country around the world. But secretly, Ryan knew it was more than that. Sometimes, he just felt like he was crawling out of his skin, like he was keeping all this stuff inside that needed some way to get out. The fights didn't really make him feel better, but they kept happening.

One night, he overheard his parents arguing. Ryan's dad thought the moodiness and acting out was normal, just a teenage boy growing up. But his mom understood how unhappy Ryan really was. Their work was starting to hurt Ryan, she told his dad. He needed to plant roots, to make friends. He needed a home. As Ryan sat behind the wall listening, he realized she was right. What he wanted more than anything was to just be a normal American kid with a normal, boring life.

It took a while to work everything out, but now he finally had what he'd been dreaming of:

a home in New York City (which had *two* base-ball teams, the Mets and the Yankees!), a school where he felt like he could finally just be himself, and a best friend he could really talk to.

Everything he'd wanted—and he was about to lose it all.

Principal Milankovic glared at Ryan from under bushy eyebrows. "You understand that fighting is grounds for immediate dismissal?" For a school principal, he was surprisingly big, with massive arms and a barrel chest that made him look more like an aging boxer than a high school principal.

"Yes, sir."

"That's all? You're not going to tell me he started it? That it was self-defense or something?" The principal's Slavic accent was noticeable.

"Would it matter if I did?"

Principal Milankovic smiled. "No, it would not."

Milankovic came around his massive desk, overflowing with stacks of paper piled haphazardly. "Our actions have consequences. The reasons for those actions may be sound; you may be justified in what you choose to do. But you will still have to deal with the consequences of those choices."

Ryan didn't meet Milankovic's eyes, his gut twisted in knots. If he made it through this without getting kicked out of school, he promised himself he'd stay out of the fight next time—no more risking his own neck, even for a friend like Danny.

Sitting next to him, Milankovic shifted his tone and said, "Your grandfather understood about consequences."

Ryan's head jerked up, meeting the principal's steady gaze. "You knew my grandfather?"

"A little. He was an extraordinary man. I was sorry to hear of his passing."

"How did you know him?"

"He did me a great favor once, many years ago."

"What kind of favor?"

For a moment, Milankovic looked thoughtful, his mind far away. Then his eyes snapped back to Ryan's as he dismissed whatever memories had flooded in, stern once more. "You do not fight in my school. Understood?"

Ryan nodded. "I won't—I promise."

"And I know the Quinns always keep their

promises." He stood up. "Get to class. And don't let me see you in here again."

Ryan jumped up and hurried out before the principal could change his mind.

CHAPTER
03

**NEW YORK,
USA**

Ryan saw Danny bouncing down the front stairs toward him as school let out. "Where'd you learn to do that? You were like a ghost—one second you were there and the next you were gone."

"It's just something my dad taught me," Ryan said, acting like it wasn't a big deal. "We lived in some pretty dangerous places. He wanted me to be able to defend myself."

"Can you, like, kill people and stuff?"

"Yeah, but I've only had to do that a couple of times."

Danny stopped on the bottom step, looking back, eyes wide. "Seriously?"

Ryan grinned. "Dude—really?"

"Jerk." Danny was grinning, too.

Actually, Ryan did know how to knock some-body out or break some bones, if he had to. But the last thing he needed was getting a rep as a good fighter. He knew from experience that was a sure way to invite more trouble.

The front of the school was crowded with limos and bodyguards waiting to pick up the kids of dignitaries. Ryan and Danny navigated the black-suited security guards who refused to move out of the way, their cold stares slightly vacant as students flowed around them on all sides.

"Can you teach me how to do some of that ninja stuff?" Danny said.

"Sure—you'd be good at it."

"Course I would—I'm small and fast. Makes me harder to hit."

Danny made Ryan laugh a lot. They had met during Ryan's first week at ICS. Sitting next to each other in physical science class, Danny noticed Ryan's shirt, a vintage concert tee from The Smiths's *Meat Is Murder* tour, and they started talking '80s alt-rock bands. Danny was a die-hard fan of The Cure, and they got absorbed in a debate on which was the better band—a debate that nearly got them both a detention.

Picking up the conversation after school, they didn't stop talking for hours. They'd ended up hanging out at Danny's apartment for so long that Danny's mom invited Ryan for dinner. The family was originally from the Philippine Islands, and they were all shocked when Ryan said how much he loved *kare-kare* stew and rice with *bagoong*. After Ryan said "thank you" in Tagalog—the Filipino language—they practically made him an honorary member of the family.

Since then, Ryan and Danny had hung out often. Both were outsiders in their own way: Danny was a techno-geek who often tried too hard to make people like him, and Ryan felt like his new American school was as unfamiliar as any of the foreign countries where he'd lived. But with Danny, Ryan didn't feel like he had to try and blend in. He could just be himself. Who-ever that was. Ryan was still figuring it out.

"Ryan, Danny—wait up!" a girl's voice called. The guys turned, surprised to see Kasey Stieg-litz pushing through the crowd, joining them at the bottom of the steps.

"Hey, Kasey, what's going on?" Danny greeted Kasey as if it was totally normal for the prettiest girl in the eighth grade to be heading over. Ryan didn't know what it was about Kasey that turned him into a mumbling idiot. It's not like he couldn't talk to girls. He wasn't nearly as smooth as Danny, but he wasn't terrible (at least, he didn't *think* so). But something about Kasey, with her wild, unruly hair and her casual confidence, threw him completely off his game.

"Sorry about Drew," Kasey said. "I told him to stop acting like a jerk."

Danny shrugged. "He doesn't bother us. I just hope we don't have to teach him a lesson again."

Kasey smiled, glancing at Ryan. He just grinned back. And kicked himself inwardly. Talk, he begged himself.

"Which way you going?" Kasey asked.

"Up to the Rose," Danny said. "You?"

"Downtown—got this meeting. Guess I'll see you in class."

As she turned to leave, Ryan blurted out, "Actually, I'm going downtown."

"Yeah?" Kasey said, turning back.

"I help out at my mom's store."

"Mind if I walk with you?"

"I—no—that's . . ."

Danny rolled his eyes. "He'd love it."

Kasey lit up. "Great—let me just tell Lisa so she doesn't wait. Be right back."

As she darted away, Danny whacked Ryan playfully in the chest. "She's totally into you."

"What? No . . ."

"Trust me. I know about these things."

Ryan watched Kasey as she told her friends the new plans and then bounded back toward them. The girls glanced at Ryan, whispering and grinning, the gossip machine shifting into overdrive.

"Dude, kill the smile—you're so obvious," Danny said.

"Shut up." Ryan did, however, do his best to seem cool as Kasey returned.

"Ready?" she said.

Danny backed away. "You two have fun."

Ryan glared at him, but Danny only winked, then disappeared into the crowd.

"He's funny," Kasey said, watching Danny. "Like he stepped out of an anime comic or something."

"He'd consider that high praise."

As they started walking, Ryan was a little nervous that Stieglitz might be watching them together and come after him to start another fight. He scanned the area for trouble and suddenly stopped. Behind an SUV across the street, a man in a dark suit was looking in their direction. Though he was pretty far away, it seemed to Ryan as if the man was staring right at him.

"Coming?" Kasey asked, now a few steps ahead.

"Yeah." When he looked back across the street, the man had disappeared.

CHAPTER
04

**NEW YORK,
USA**

Ryan and Kasey walked along 37th Street, the crisp November air chilly against their light jackets. Determined not to let his nerves get the better of him, Ryan reached inside his jacket pocket for his secret weapon—chocolate.

No matter how different and unusual Ryan found the cultures of the places he'd lived around the world, one thing had always been constant. People loved chocolate. Kids loved it. Adults loved it. And Ryan kind of obsessed over it. He'd had rich, dark chocolate in Belgium; milk chocolate with curry powder in India; even *xocolatl*, the thick chocolate drink made with hot chilies and adored by the Aztecs a thousand years ago. Chocolate was the ultimate icebreaker.

Stopping at the light, he held out several small, brightly wrapped bars to Kasey. "Want one?"

"Thanks. Are they all different?"

Ryan pointed to one in a green wrapper that was long and thin. "This one's from Switzerland—it's just a plain ganache with a cocoa-nib crust. Simple, but delicious. The blue one's from Ecuador. They grow all their cacao beans in the same place they make the bars. Which is very unusual. And the one in gold is chocolate mixed with bacon. Sounds gross, but it's incredible. The chocolatier trained at Le Cordon Bleu in Paris. Only uses the highest-quality ingredients."

Kasey laughed. "You're kind of a chocolate snob, aren't you?"

Ryan could tell her teasing was playful. "I try it everywhere I go. And I've been a lot of places."

"So which should I choose?"

Ryan handed her the one in green. "This one. They make the bars in Zurich, but all the cacao beans are grown on this farm in Cameroon close to where I lived for a while."

The light changed and they started walking as Kasey unwrapped her small chocolate bar. "You lived in Cameroon?" she asked. "Were you there during the education protests last year?"

Ryan looked at her in surprise. "You know about that?"

"I watched videos that were posted online. All those students coming together, standing up for themselves. I wish I could have seen it." She bit into her chocolate bar. "Oh my god—*so* good."

"Right?"

"Did you see any of the protests?"

Most of the kids Ryan met here in the States didn't know a lot about what was going on around the world, much less in a small country in Africa. But Kasey actually seemed interested.

"I was in one."

Kasey stopped short. "No way. Like, really *in* it?"

"A group of students passed right by our school," he told her. "It was mostly young people, and so some of us just joined in. The leaders wanted to block this bridge. We piled up all these tires and things so no one could cross."

"Sounds like the French Revolution when they built those barricades."

"That's what it felt like. Traffic piled up in every direction. The whole city came to a standstill. Eventually, these cops came in with tear gas and machine guns. Everybody just ran. It was chaos."

"You got gassed?" She sounded half-horrified, half-thrilled at the thought.

"A little—my throat felt like it was on fire for hours."

"That's incredible."

"It was. Scary, too." The truth was, Ryan got in over his head before he realized just how crazy the situation would get. Looting and vandalism. Smoke everywhere. Ryan was swept along, enjoying the feeling that he was part of something bigger, that his actions had some purpose and might make a difference. But the protests became more violent as the police cracked down. One of his classmates, a German girl he studied with sometimes, was hit by a cop's baton and dropped to the ground. She was bleeding as Ryan fought through the crowd and pulled her back to safety.

"In the end," Ryan said, "we didn't do much good. Nothing really changed."

"At least you tried."

"People got hurt. I still don't know if it was worth it."

Ryan had never talked to anyone about that day, not even his parents. He was afraid they'd be angry with him for putting himself in danger. Talking to Kasey, though, came easily. "How did you hear about it?"

Kasey gave him a half smile. "I do have some idea of what's going on in the world."

"Sorry, I didn't mean—"

"I'm kidding. I got interested when I was in this bizarre little theater piece last semester."

"You act?" Ryan asked.

Kasey nodded. "Yeah, and the school brought in this Romanian director who was brilliant but totally crazy. The play was all about revolution with real-life characters from all these different time periods—Roman slaves, French peasants, George Washington. It was so insane."

Ryan loved Kasey's laugh. "I wish I could've seen it."

"It was pretty terrible. But it got me interested in things in a way I'd never really been before. I've been reading a lot more history since then, watching more news. Some of it's just so sad, though," she said. "It's like you said. It feels like all this bad stuff is going on and there's not much we can do to help."

As they turned the corner onto Lexington, Kasey stopped in the doorway of an older office building. "Well, this is where my meeting is."

"What kind of meeting?"

"Don't laugh." Kasey took a piece of paper from a folder she carried, handing it to Ryan. It was a flyer that read: "Books Not Bombs!" She continued, "We're trying to get the government to spend more money on schools and education instead of on making weapons. You can come, if you want."

"I promised my mom I'd help her out. Maybe next time?"

"Sure." Kasey pushed the glass door to go inside, but Ryan stepped forward, holding it open for her. "Thanks." She suddenly seemed nervous as she blurted out, "I don't suppose you have any interest in going to the Autumn Carnival Dance on Saturday?"

"Um, I've never really done much dancing."

"Don't worry, I'm a klutz. We can trip over each other's feet."

Ryan forced himself not to smile like a dork. "Sure," he said, "It'll be my first official dance."

"Great!" Kasey started inside. "Oh, you might want to avoid my brother. He's not as horrible as he seems, but he can be protective."

"I got that."

Grinning, Ryan watched her walk away. When she disappeared into the stairwell, he finally stepped back, letting go of the door. As it slowly closed, Ryan froze.

Through the reflection in the glass, Ryan could see across the street directly behind him. The man in the dark suit from the school was there again, staring right at him.

CHAPTER

05

**NEW YORK,
USA**

Ryan fought his initial instinct to turn and stare. Instead, he started down the street at a brisk pace, believing that the stranger was probably watching his movements closely. His parents had warned him about being careful in the places they lived, but he'd thought New York would be safe by comparison.

Ryan took out his cell phone and held it up, thumbs moving over the keys as though he was texting somebody. He held the phone awkwardly, raising it slightly over his shoulder so the camera had a good vantage point behind him.

Click—click—click.

Ryan spun the phone around and pulled up the photos he'd just taken. The man kept several people between them at all times. His gaze, however, never wavered, focused like a laser on Ryan's back. He was of Asian descent, medium height with military-short black hair and a mouth that turned down at the corners in a perpetual frown. Ryan guessed he was probably from Southeast Asia somewhere, maybe Indonesia or Thailand.

Moving quickly, Ryan tried to put some distance between them. He turned at Park Avenue, using the busier street to shake his stalker. Darting in and out of the crowd, he hunched down so the man couldn't see him as easily.

Just before the light changed, Ryan dashed across the street toward the median, which was landscaped with trees and long rows of bushes. Ryan slipped behind the greenery. At the corner, the man was forced to stop as traffic whizzed past. He pulled out a phone and dialed, then began talking via a Bluetooth earpiece, continuing to search for some sign of Ryan.

Watching, Ryan was reminded of the times he and his father had played "Follow-the-Monkey," their own version of "Follow-the-Leader." The follower was supposed to stay hidden and the monkey could go anywhere he wanted. Once, when they were in a crowded market in Rio de

Janeiro, Ryan had done so well staying hidden that his dad had panicked, thinking he'd actually lost his son.

The light changed and the stranger darted across the street, passing the bushes where Ryan was hidden. Halfway across, he stopped and whirled around, his eyes locked on the median, scanning with a professionalism that revealed he was used to tracking. Ryan's impulse was to jump and run again. Instead, he remained still. He recognized that quick turn as a classic misdirection technique. The man was becoming desperate, trying to spook his prey into moving too soon.

A yellow cab honked, zooming toward the man as the light changed once more. He jumped out of the way, hurrying to the other side. At the far corner, he looked in all directions, frustrated at having lost his target, and finally started moving down Park Avenue.

Ryan decided to turn the tables and play a little "Follow-the-Monkey" himself. As the light changed once again, Ryan joined the crowd, pulling off his green jacket and turning it inside out so the black lining showed. He opened his backpack and pulled out one of the baseball caps from his collection: a 1996 World Series

Champions commemorative hat he always kept handy. He assumed the man had tracked him by the green of his jacket and that in the black jacket and cap, he looked different enough to go unnoticed. Blending in came easily to Ryan.

The man was at the far end of the block and Ryan hurried to catch up, keeping his head low and his body hidden as much as possible. When the man stopped and turned around once more, Ryan ducked into the doorway of a bagel shop just in time, flattening his body against the wall.

He forced himself to count to five slowly, his body poised to fight if the man came after him. Reaching five, he peered out. The man was just turning onto 40th Street. Ryan darted out of his hiding place in pursuit, but as he rounded the corner, he stopped short—his follower had doubled back and was about to collide with him.

Ryan veered at the last moment, their shoulders barely missing one another. Luckily, the man was too focused on his phone conversation to notice. He had a deep, guttural voice, and he was angry. Ryan had been right. The man was speaking a Southeast Asian language, though Ryan didn't recognize this one.

As he passed, Ryan distinctly heard the man say "John Quinn." Ryan couldn't help himself.

All his self-control went out the window as he turned to stare from under his Yankees cap, shocked to hear his father's name. Just then, a black Lincoln Town Car screeched to a halt at the curb. The man yanked open the back door and climbed inside.

Ryan wanted to shout, to stop the guy and find out how he knew his dad. On the car's bumper, he recognized the red, white, and blue of a diplomatic license plate. The man tailing him was probably connected to one of the embassies in New York. Ryan snapped a picture of the plate with his phone as the Town Car sped away.

CHAPTER

06

**NEW YORK,
USA**

Jacqueline Quinn held the violin delicately, as if it were made of glass. Her customer marveled at the rare instrument as she explained its provenance. "This one was designed by Giovanni Francesco Pressenda around 1841. The back is made of spruce."

"It's stunning," the man said.

Across the shop, Ryan watched his mother, always impressed by her deep knowledge of the instruments she sold. Jacqueline had a reverence for these musical gems that she conveyed to her customers. It's why they sought her out, no matter where she happened to be living. After all their travels, Ryan figured his mom probably knew just about every person who bought or sold musical instruments around the world. She'd been a consultant for serious collectors and auction houses, but this was the first time she'd been able to open her own shop.

Jacqueline had designed the store with counters made of rich mahogany and beveled glass. It was like a time machine back to the 1800s. She'd even somehow imported the musty aroma of old wood and pipe tobacco.

"Don't be fooled by its appearance," Jacqueline said, her slight French accent adding an essence of sophistication. "What makes this violin so exceptional is what it can *do*. Deep, resonant tones. A purity that blends the best of the Italian and French styles. It may be beautiful on the outside, but the music it produces is what makes it extraordinary."

Ryan spent a lot of afternoons here since they'd moved to New York, helping his mom unpack all the instruments and get the shop organized. Ryan found it kind of boring, but he got paid. Soon, he'd earn enough for the autographed Yogi Berra Mets hat he wanted.

Jacqueline noticed Ryan in the doorway to the back room and instantly recognized that he was upset about something. He didn't want to worry her, so he ducked back into the office and storeroom behind the store. As he left, he heard the customer ask his mother, "And how much is it?"

"One hundred and fifty thousand dollars," she answered, her calm tone making the huge number sound completely reasonable.

Ryan sat at his mom's desk, automatically reaching for the box of chocolate truffles she always kept handy. Chocolate helped him think, and right now that's exactly what he needed to do. He'd clearly heard the man say his father's name—was his dad in some kind of trouble? John Quinn had left on one of his trips two weeks earlier. He was in Thailand for a plastics trade conference. They'd talked on the phone four days ago. John told Ryan he'd be home in time to go ice-skating in Central Park this weekend. That was the last they'd heard from him. Which was strange, Ryan realized, because his dad usually checked in pretty regularly.

Out front, Ryan heard the entry-door chimes ring as the customer left. He expected his mother to check on him, but then heard more voices— somebody else must have come in. Something in Jacqueline's tone caught his attention. Though he couldn't make out the words, he could tell her voice was strained. Something was wrong.

Ryan moved to the doorway that joined the two spaces. The door was cracked open, but as he approached he kept himself partially hidden. He didn't know exactly why he did this; his mom never cared if he listened when she spoke with customers. But some instinct had kicked in, making him cautious. Nearing the door, he heard a man's voice, gruff and abrupt.

". . . You realize that lying to us could have serious consequences," he said.

"Why would I lie to you?" Jacqueline said, sounding bolder—and louder—than normal.

"Mrs. Quinn, we're only trying to help." Ryan craned his neck, peering into the shop. His mother stood in front of a man and woman, both in business suits. The man had gray hair and hard eyes; the woman was African American and tall. "When was the last time you heard from your husband?"

"A few days ago. He called from Bangkok."

"From the International Plastics Exhibition?" the woman said, consulting her notes.

"That's right. Has something happened? Why is the Central Intelligence Agency interested in John?"

The *CIA*? Ryan thought about the Asian man following him. He could have been CIA, too; but then, why the diplomatic plates on his car? And why was he coming after Ryan?

"Agent Calloway, show her the photos," the man said

The woman pulled out a packet of eight-by-ten photographs. Ryan couldn't see the pictures from where he stood, but Jacqueline glanced down and he could tell that she recognized his father. Even from a distance, Ryan could see the tension in her expression.

"These pictures were taken five days ago in Muang Tak, Thailand," the man continued. "Nowhere near Bangkok. The man there with your husband, he's a known smuggler. Muang Tak is his base of operation."

Jacqueline met the agent's stony gaze, and Ryan knew she was over her initial surprise. Her tone was calmer and more under control. "Are you accusing him of something? John meets with hundreds, maybe thousands, of people every year."

"We want to know why he's meeting with a known felon over two hundred miles from where he was supposed to be." He snatched one of the photos from Agent Calloway's hand, pushing it at Jacqueline. "It'll be a lot better for you if you tell us everything you know, Mrs. Quinn."

"I don't know anything about it at all." Ryan could tell his mother was lying—and so could the CIA agents.

"You sure this is how you want to play it?" Agent Calloway said.

"I don't know what to tell you. I'm sure John will straighten it all out."

The two agents shared a look, then turned away. The entrance chimes tinkled as the gray-haired agent opened the door and walked out.

Agent Calloway followed, but suddenly spun around. Across the room, her eyes locked on Ryan. She coolly scrutinized him and nodded her head slightly. Calloway had been aware of his presence all along, and she wanted Ryan to know it.

Drifting back to the desk, Ryan's head was spinning as he sank down into the chair. His father, a criminal? It wasn't possible—but then, why was he meeting with smugglers? And why was his mother lying about what she knew?

Jacqueline came into the back room, all the fight gone out of her. Ryan could see how worried she really was.

"Mom, what's going on?"

"Nothing. Just a mix-up, that's all." She gently brushed her son's hair off his forehead, something she'd done since he was a child.

"Where is Dad? Why hasn't he called?"

"I don't know. I'm sure he's fine," she said. Ryan stared at her, his mind reeling, because one thing had just become clear to him as he heard that louder, bolder tone creep into her voice: *His mother was lying to him, too.*

CHAPTER

07

**NEW YORK,
USA**

The scariest moment in Ryan's life had been three years ago. They were living in a town in Paraguay where Ryan's dad was working to help farmers develop more sustainable crops. He and his mom were alone when a terrible storm hit. The thunder was so loud the house shook. Radio announcers warned of flash floods and reported that roads and bridges were being washed out. Jacqueline and Ryan had hunkered down together, her arms wrapped around him comfortingly as she told him stories of growing up on her family's farm in the south of France.

A loud crack, worse than the thunder, startled them both, and then a giant tree limb crashed through the roof of their small house. Rain poured in as the rest of the roof was torn apart by howling winds. In moments, Ryan and his mom were drenched. Ryan was scared to death, but Jacqueline remained calm and focused. She told him they had to get across town to one of the bigger buildings and find shelter. Ryan refused—they'd get carried away in the rushing water and drown!

But his mom looked him in the eye and asked if Ryan trusted her. Of course, he told her. Then he needed to do exactly what she told him to do. She promised that she'd get them both to safety. Ryan trusted his mom more than anyone—even his dad—and she had always protected him. He finally nodded and followed her out into the violent storm. Hand in hand, they fought their way across the battered town, eventually finding refuge in a stone church.

All his life, through all the places they'd lived, the one constant Ryan could count on was his mom and dad. They had always been a team, and Ryan believed he could trust them with anything.

Now, he didn't know *what* to believe.

As he hurried down 5th Avenue, pushing his way through the throngs of people, Ryan felt confused and alone. He definitely didn't think what the agents said about his father was true. But his mom wasn't being honest with him, so he was going to have to figure out what was going on himself.

To do that, he'd need help—and he knew exactly where to find it.

Ryan arrived at the New York Public Library, passing the famous stone lions without a glance. He took the stairs two at a time to the third floor and burst into the Rose Main Reading Room. Over fifty feet high, the Rose, as it was known among students, had grand chandeliers hanging from a ceiling painted with murals of clouds. Thousands of books lined the walls, long wooden tables with brass reading lamps were filled with students. Normally, Ryan loved hanging out here—it was his favorite spot in the city for people watching—but right now, he was all business. He searched for Danny, which was no easy task considering that this one room went on for two full city blocks.

Danny told his parents that he came here to study, but what he was really interested in was the untraceable WiFi connection. Danny was a hacker, and the library was the ideal place to hone his cyber talent. With hundreds of laptops running in the Rose Room at any given time, he was virtually invisible online.

Of course, for Danny, it wasn't just the WiFi. The library also had girls. Lots of them. From all over the city. They came to study at the Rose after school.

Ryan spotted Danny across the room, whispering with two girls in private-school uniforms. They were probably fifteen, a couple of years older than Danny, but they hung on his every word. Danny just had a way.

"You'll never get those concert tickets trying to buy them through the website," Danny was telling them. "They'll sell out in seconds. But I can build a bot that'll get the best seats in the house for you."

"A bot?" one of them asked. "That's some kind of computer program, right?"

"Mine are more like works of art. I could get three tickets, we'll all go!" The girls shared a skeptical look, unsure if Danny was for real or just blowing smoke.

"Hey, you got a sec?" Ryan interrupted.

Danny was surprised to see Ryan here. "Don't tell me you blew it with Kasey already."

"I need to talk to you. Now."

Danny could tell something was up. "Think

about it," he told the girls. "You know where to find me."

As Ryan moved away, Danny caught up with him. "What's up?"

"You have your laptop, right?"

"I'm breathing, aren't I?" Danny slid into a seat at another table. He flipped open his tricked-out laptop and the screen came to life, displaying the words: THIS COMPUTER WILL SELF-DESTRUCT IN 15 SECONDS.

As the timer started counting down, Danny quickly tapped in the seventeen-digit password, his fingers moving across the keys like he was playing a piano.

"Will it really self-destruct?" Ryan asked.

Danny smiled. "Hope you never have to find out. All right, *mi amigo*, what can I do for you?"

Ryan pulled out his cell phone and opened it, showing Danny the picture he took of the man who'd followed him. "This guy was following me today. At first, I thought maybe he was CIA."

Danny rolled his eyes. "Riiight. I may be gullible, but I'm not an idiot."

"This isn't a joke—I swear."

Danny's grin faded as he realized Ryan was serious. "You're not screwing with me?"

"Not even a little bit." Danny looked back at the picture as Ryan continued. "The car he got into had diplomatic plates. So maybe not CIA, but he definitely gave off that Secret Service, spy kind of vibe. I need to find out who he is. I overheard him say my dad's name. I think my dad may be in trouble."

"What kind of trouble?"

"I don't know. Here, I snapped a picture of the plates on his car." Ryan showed him the picture of the license plate.

"You want me to hack into the Department of Motor Vehicles?"

"Can you?" Ryan knew it was a long shot, but Danny was his only chance. His mother was a member of UNESCO, the United Nations agency that dealt with cultural and educational affairs, and Danny had used her access to get into all sorts of databases and software servers around the globe.

Danny stared at his computer, brows furrowed, thinking hard. Suddenly, his face lit up with an idea. "I don't know if I can hack into the DMV, but I could probably get access to the UN's diplomatic vehicle registry. I know my mom has to fill out a form every year for her car."

"You think it'll work?"

"It's worth a try," Danny said, "but it's gonna take a while."

"Like what, a couple of days?"

Danny looked at Ryan like he'd lost his mind. "Like, a couple of *hours*. Email me all the pix."

Ryan sent the photos, then stood. "You're the best."

"Oh, I think that's already been firmly established, brother." As Ryan left, he glanced back. Danny was already deeply immersed in his search. The one thing that could distract his friend from girls was a serious hack.

CHAPTER
08

**NEW YORK,
USA**

Ryan emerged from the subway station at Lexington and 63rd cautiously, searching the face of every passerby for signs of danger. The streets were now dark and quiet. Ryan worried that he was being paranoid but then remembered something his father told him before his first ice-hockey game the winter they lived in Croatia: Never second-guess your instincts. Good instincts make the difference between winning and losing. Ryan had tried to take his dad's advice but ended up getting creamed on the ice. Turns out, Croatians kick butt at hockey.

The Quinns' brownstone on 62nd Street was a prewar four-story walk-up that had been in their family for almost a hundred years. Both his grandfather and father had grown up there. Some of Ryan's favorite memories were the times spent with Granddad on his family's visits to New York. Declan Quinn told the best stories. He'd sit with Ryan in the big chairs in his study, the fire blazing and crackling, and spin tales of knights and dragons, leprechauns and windigos, the Russian witch Baba Yaga and the Japanese samurai Masashige. Stories from cultures all over the world that spoke of bravery, loyalty, and sacrifice. Ryan never forgot any of them. When Granddad died last year, it took Ryan a long time to accept that he was really gone. Living in the brownstone these past months, he thought of Granddad often.

Ryan approached the home from across the street, pausing behind a parked truck and searching the shadows. Did the man who followed him know where he lived? Not spotting anything suspicious, he headed inside. Just in case, he had his key out and ready as he ran up the steps to the front door.

Entering, he shut the door and locked the deadbolt, then started flipping on lights. Mom wasn't home yet. Perfect. Ryan wanted answers, and he knew the best chance of finding any was in the study on the bottom floor. Dumping his backpack, he hurried down the long central hallway and took the stairs down.

The entire lower floor of the brownstone had been carved out decades ago by Granddad as a large study and library. Shelves lined one entire wall, filled with an array of books on geography and history. The bottom shelf was crammed full of old maps and atlases. Ryan passed the fireplace and the two wingback chairs where he'd spent so many hours listening to his grandfather and headed to the massive desk that sat in the middle of the study.

He started opening and closing drawers, not even sure exactly what he was looking for. Paid bills, old financial statements, files on the various UN projects his father coordinated. None of it helped. As far as he could tell, everything looked totally normal.

"It's never enough. It's never enough. . . ."

Ryan jumped out of his skin at the loud noise. It took a moment for him to realize the music was the ringtone assigned to Danny on his cell phone, The Cure crooning their displeasure. Ryan snatched the phone from his pocket and answered, "Hey."

"Dude, what have you gotten yourself into?"

Danny was clearly worried.

"You found something?"

"We need to talk."

"What about the plates—"

"Not on the cell," Danny snapped. "Just stay inside and lock the doors. I'm already on the way." The connection was cut.

Ryan had never heard Danny sound so intense, and he wondered what could have him so worked up. He sat heavily in the desk chair, frustrated and anxious to have some answers.

Looking around the room, a memory drifted in at the edge of his subconscious. He was around six years old and his family had been visiting. Upstairs, Ryan had heard arguing coming from the study. Curious, he had wandered down, listening from the stairwell.

". . . It's too dangerous," his father had said.

"It's always dangerous, John. Always has been." Granddad's tone was deadly serious.

Ryan remembered a strange sound, like something metal rolling, then silence. He'd crept down the stairs and peered around the doorway.

No one had been there. His father and his grandfather: gone.

Just then, his mother had arrived upstairs, yelling out that she'd brought home his favorite ice cream. Chocolate won out over a mystery any day. He raced upstairs, forgetting all about the strange occurrence.

Sitting at the old desk now, Ryan spun around, looking at the room. Where had they gone that day? There were no doors other than the entrance from the stairs, and the only windows were up high at street level and didn't open. Ryan stood, looking at the room more closely now, analyzing everything about it. Something was bothering him, but he wasn't sure exactly what it was.

His gaze drifted up to the ceiling. The floor above this one held the living room, a dining room, and the kitchen at the far back of the brownstone. As he pictured it in his mind's eye, Ryan realized this floor and the one above weren't quite the same size. They should have been, as the brownstone was built straight up from the bottom.

Ryan moved to the exposed-brick wall at the end of the room and inspected it more closely. There were no lines in the mortar, though. Nothing to indicate that it was anything other than a normal wall. He felt stupid. What was he thinking, that there was some kind of secret entrance here? His dad was a diplomat, not Batman!

He looked down, annoyed with himself, and turned back toward the desk.

Then, he stopped.

Ryan spun back toward the wall. The mortar lines on the wall were all in perfect shape. Three bricks from the bottom, however, the mortar was cracked in strange places, almost as if it had been cut. Kneeling, he looked more closely at the bricks. Using the tips of his fingers, he grabbed the loose mortar. It pulled out with little effort and he began working more quickly. Several more pieces came out until Ryan had outlined four of the bricks, one each on top and bottom and two in the middle, making a lowercase *t* shape.

Grabbing the top brick, Ryan pulled. It came out and he looked at it in surprise; it wasn't even a full brick, only the front half of one. He set it aside, his heart beating faster, wondering what exactly he'd stumbled onto here. The other three half bricks came out just as easily, and Ryan peered into the opening he'd created.

A metal handle was nestled inside the cavity. Ryan took a step back and finally got it: The brick wall was fake. He pulled the handle. It was heavy, but the wall pivoted straight up like a garage door. Behind it was a hidden room.

CHAPTER
09

**NEW YORK,
USA**

Against the back wall, a chest-height worktable had been carved from cedar, the smell of the old wood permeating the enclosed space. Ryan approached, passing a rack filled with equipment. He wasn't a techie, but this looked pretty sophisticated: a high-quality laser printer and scanner, a laminating machine, and a couple of other devices that he didn't recognize at all.

The worktable was covered with maps, photos, and piles of computer printouts. Ryan picked up the photos, which were grainy and taken from a long distance, like surveillance pictures. He didn't recognize anyone in them. A map of Southeast Asia was open and had been heavily marked up. The map included south-west China, Laos, and Thailand. But the focus seemed to be on the country of Andakar.

Above the table hung a giant corkboard covered with tacked-up information. Train and airline schedules were pinned beside photos of parks and what looked like old Asian temples. Ryan noticed that the train schedules were all from Andakar and looked closely at the printed captions under the temple photos. Same thing—everything here was pointing toward Andakar.

Ryan had never been there, but he knew a hard-core military government ruled Andakar with an iron fist, imprisoning, torturing, and even executing citizens who spoke out against it. Ryan had read that they recently opened their borders to tourists and were trying to promote travel in order to make money. Which seemed like a terrible idea. Who'd want to vacation in a place that treats its own people like that?

On a shelf next to the table, Ryan noticed a stack of passports from various countries—Germany, England, South Africa, Canada. Ryan flipped open the top one, his stomach sinking as he recognized his father's picture above the name Benjamin O'Hara. The others were all the same: Each one showed Dad with a different name.

Ryan glanced at the equipment on the rack, understanding its purpose now. His father had been making forged passports. Good ones, from what Ryan could tell. The next one showed a picture of his mother and another fake name. So Mom was involved, too. And there were others— a redheaded young woman and two different men Ryan didn't recognize—all with passports made out to multiple identities. Ryan's head was spinning, scrambling to process all this information.

When he opened the last one, an Irish passport, his heart nearly stopped. Looking back at him was his *own* photo and the name Thomas Dylan O'Hara. It said he lived in Dublin and that he was sixteen years old!

Ryan threw the passport down on the table and took several steps back. This couldn't be possible. The people he loved most in the world—the people he *trusted* most—what kind of secrets were they keeping from him? The CIA agents had said his father was dealing with smugglers and known criminals. Seeing the fake passports, Ryan couldn't help but wonder if it was true.

He had to find his mother. He'd make her tell him the truth, no matter how bad it was. No more lies. That was the one thing he knew: No more lies.

As he turned to leave the secret room, a scream from upstairs pierced the silence. It startled Ryan, but then instinct kicked in and he started running.

"Mom?" he yelled.

Ryan took the stairs two at a time as something crashed in the upstairs hall. His mother was in serious danger, and no matter what else was going on, Ryan would do everything possible to protect her.

Leaping up the last couple of stairs, Ryan burst around the corner to find grocery bags scattered on the ground in disarray and his mom struggling in the arms of an Asian giant, a dark-suited powerhouse of a man. In front of them stood a second man—the same Asian guy who had followed Ryan earlier!

The man held her chin with an iron grip, forcing her to look at him. "Where is Myat Kaw?"

"You'll never find out if you hurt me!" Jacqueline was scared but defiant.

Just then, the giant holding her saw Ryan at the end of the hallway. "Aung Win—the boy!"

Aung Win turned. His eyes were so dark they were almost black.

"Let her go," Ryan said, shifting instinctively into a fighting stance.

"No, Ryan—run!" The defiance was gone from Jacqueline's voice. She was kicking, thrashing, fighting like a wildcat, but the man who held her was too strong for her to break free.

Ryan charged forward, trying hard not to be completely freaked out. His father always warned that if you lose your head, you lose the fight. Dad had mostly trained in a fighting style called Krav Maga, the same street-fighting technique used by Israeli Defense Forces. It's brutal and effective—all about finding weakness and adapting to the situation, no matter how perilous or impossible it seems. And this seemed pretty impossible. Ryan had to take out at least one of the men quickly if he was going to stand a chance. He came in hard and fast with a throat strike.

But Aung Win sidestepped the blow; Ryan barely glanced his shoulder. Aung Win's retaliation was swift and fierce, a hammer blow that caught Ryan right in his solar plexus. The hit knocked the air out of Ryan. He stumbled back, gasping for air. He grabbed a side table, trying to keep his balance.

"Leave him alone. I'll tell you!" Jacqueline was desperate.

Pulling out a gun, Aung Win turned from Ryan as if he was insignificant. "I had planned to take your son. It's convenient that he has come to me." He pointed the weapon at Ryan, but his eyes never left Jacqueline's. "You will tell me where John Quinn is. You will tell me where I can find Myat Kaw. If I think you are holding anything back, I will shoot your son."

Ryan fought the panic rising in his chest. Aung Win's moves were those of a practiced killer. Ryan struggled to think of something he could do to even the odds. He glanced at the side table and saw two carved jade candlesticks his parents had bought in China.

Jacqueline looked defeated as she said, "The last time I spoke to John, he was in Thailand. He was going to cross into Andakar." Before she could continue—*Bam! Bam! Bam!*

"Dude, open up, it's me!" came from outside the front door.

The adults all turned, but Ryan took the opportunity to grab one of the candlesticks. He slammed it down on Aung Win's forearm, hearing bones crack. The gun clattered to the floor as the man gasped in pain.

"Danny," Ryan yelled, "Call the cops!"

Aung Win reacted quickly, furiously striking out at Ryan with his left hand. The blow caught Ryan on the shoulder, hitting the nerves so that his arm fell to his side like a dead weight. He staggered back, spying the gun under one of the ornate legs of their kitchen table.

In their native tongue, Aung Win barked an order to the big man, who had moved to protect Aung Win like a bodyguard. The bodyguard shoved Jacqueline forward, turned, and opened the front door.

Ryan saw Danny on the front stoop, frozen at the sight of the Goliath who towered over him. "Look out!" Ryan screamed, snapping Danny back to his senses. Danny ducked just in time, using his smaller size to evade the bodyguard's grasp, and jumped down the stairs.

In the hallway, Ryan saw Aung Win had Jacqueline by the throat. He winced, forced to use the arm Ryan had just injured to pull a plastic bag out of his pocket. Ryan dove for the gun as Aung Win ripped the bag open with his teeth and noxious fumes from the chlorophyll-soaked rag inside seeped into the air. Jacqueline jerked backward, but Aung Win held her tight with his good arm, forcing the rag over her nose and mouth.

"Let her go!" Ryan shouted, pointing the gun unsteadily at Aung Win as his mom lost consciousness. The man hefted Jacqueline in front of him as he backed toward the door.

"Go ahead and shoot," he taunted.

Ryan tried to look confident, but he'd never shot a gun before in his life. Even worse, the blow from Aung Win had left his right arm limp, and he was stuck using his bad hand. There was no way he could risk taking a shot.

"Leave us alone!" Ryan said. "Just let her go and we'll pretend this never happened." He was trying to buy time. Maybe someone heard. Maybe Danny got to make the call. Maybe someone would come to help if he could just stall them long enough. Ryan took another step forward.

"Your family should not get involved where you don't belong."

"What are you talking about? We just moved here," Ryan said. Aung Win ignored him, pulling Jacqueline out the front door and slamming it behind him. Ryan ran after them, but stumbled over the groceries that had scattered everywhere. He fell hard.

Hearing the screech of tires outside, Ryan jumped to his feet, dropping the gun so he could use his good hand to open the door. He threw it wide and saw his mother tossed into the back-seat of a dark sedan. Aung Win followed right behind.

"No!" Ryan screamed, coming down the stairs. The car raced away down the street. "Stop!" But it was no use. In seconds, the car sped around the corner. Ryan watched help-lessly as his mother disappeared.

CHAPTER

10

**NEW YORK,
USA**

For a few moments, Ryan stood in the empty street, frozen in shock. Only when Danny appeared at his elbow, urging him back to the sidewalk, did he notice that he was holding up traffic. Cabbies honked and swore and revved their engines, impatient to get by.

"Was that him?" Danny asked. "The guy that followed you?"

Ryan nodded, numb with fear. "They've got my mother."

"Sorry I ran—I thought that guy was gonna squash me."

"I heard them talking. They're trying to find

my dad. They think she knows where he is. She said something about him crossing over into Andakar."

"That's where it was from," Danny said. "That license plate—it's a diplomatic plate registered with Andakar's embassy."

"We need to call the police," Ryan said, turning back to the house.

"I wouldn't do that, if I were you."

Ryan and Danny both stopped short, surprised to see a young woman now standing between them and the stairs to the brownstone. With her short, severe hairstyle and alabaster skin, knee-high boots, tight pants, and leather jacket, Ryan thought she looked at least twenty. Maybe older. She seemed to have appeared out of nowhere, but then Ryan recognized her—this was the woman whose picture was on one of the forged passports in the secret room!

"If you go to the police now, both your parents are as good as dead." The woman spoke with calm assurance, but she radiated an aura of danger. Ryan wasn't sure what to make of her.

"Who are you?"

"Tasha Levi," she said, with a slight accent,

scanning the street as she spoke. "I can help your parents, but I need some information. Information that's inside your house."

"What kind of information?" Danny asked.

Tasha glanced at him, as if noticing him for the first time. "We should really have this little chat inside."

"No one is going inside or anywhere until I get some answers." Ryan was getting over his initial panic, and his tone was firm. "Who were those men?"

"I don't know."

"How do you know my parents?"

"I can't tell you that."

"Well, what are you looking for that you think you're going to find in my house?" he asked, exasperated.

"The trip your father is on, I need to know exactly where he went. I need to find out everything I can about the route he was taking."

"Why do you need to know that?" Ryan asked.

"How else am I going to find him and bring him back?" Her steady gaze was confident, and Ryan knew she was deadly serious.

"Come on," he said, pushing past her up the stairs.

Danny leaped after him, grabbing his shoulder. "What are you doing? You trust her?"

"My parents did. And right now, I've got to trust *someone*."

CHAPTER 11

**NEW YORK,
USA**

oly crap." Danny's eyes were huge as he
looked at the secret room in the study.
"What are your parents into?"

"I don't know. But I think she does." Ryan
showed Tasha the passport he'd found with
her photo inside. "This has your picture, but it
doesn't say Tasha. It says Kathleen Connors."

Glancing at it, Tasha frowned. "I hate that
name. But I do look good with red hair." She
turned her attention back to the marked-up map
of Andakar and all the notes, photos, and computer printouts on the worktable. She searched
through everything, setting certain items aside.

"Are my parents criminals?" Ryan asked,
afraid of the answer.

"Yes," she said. "In at least eight countries around the world, both John and Jacqueline Quinn would probably be put to death if they were ever caught."

Ryan felt as if he couldn't breathe, but then Tasha's expression softened, "But a criminal in one person's eyes is a hero in someone else's."

"A hero?"

"You come from a long line of them, actually. Going back over seventy years."

Ryan felt like he was on a roller coaster. "Can you please just give me a straight answer? What's going on?"

"Have you ever heard of Varian Fry?" Tasha continued her search as she spoke.

Ryan exchanged a glance with Danny, both of them shaking their heads. "Who was he?" Ryan asked.

"In the beginning, nobody. An American journalist who was a foreign correspondent in Europe during the 1930s. But as the Nazis came to power in Germany, Varian Fry saw firsthand how the Jewish people were being treated. It sickened him, and it made him want to do something. To help in whatever way he could."

"What does that have to do with Ryan's parents?" Danny asked. "They weren't born yet."

"Shut up and you'll find out." Tasha gave him a withering look.

"Wow," Danny said. "Harsh."

"Over the next several years," Tasha continued, "things in Europe went from bad to worse as World War II erupted and Adolf Hitler's power grew. By 1940, the Germans had occupied France and anyone of Jewish descent was in danger of being sent to a concentration camp."

As she told the tale, Tasha's impatience faded. This was not merely history she was repeating, Ryan understood, but something deeply personal to her.

"As a foreign correspondent, Varian Fry was allowed to visit France after the occupation. On the surface, he appeared to be just another American reporter writing about the war. Secretly, though, he was working with a group of people who felt the same way he did. A group of regular people like himself who refused to sit back and do nothing while atrocities occurred all around them. They called themselves the Emergency Rescue Committee."

Ryan looked back to the hidden room, to the map and all the information, starting to figure out where this might be heading. He looked back to Tasha. "My great-grandfather, I think he was in France during World War II."

Tasha nodded. "He was. In fact, he was one of the first members of the Emergency Rescue Committee. It was formed here in New York, with the mission to save as many of the refugees as possible. Everyone knew that Hitler was intent on killing every anti-Nazi intellectual, artist, and writer he could get his hands on. People like Marc Chagall, Marcel Duchamp, Max Ernst. All trapped in France, knowing they could be dragged off at any moment, never to be seen again. The committee's goal was to help them escape."

"Like an underground railroad," Ryan said.

"Exactly. Over the next year and a half, Varian Fry, your great-grandfather, and a network of allies managed to smuggle over two thousand people out of France to freedom in the United States. It was the most successful operation of its kind during the war."

Ryan wanted to believe what she was telling him, but certain things still didn't make sense. "But why wouldn't they tell me that my great-grandfather was some kind of hero? I never heard anything about that."

"Yeah," Danny said, "and what does any of

that have to do with *Andakar*?"

Tasha rummaged through the drawers of the worktable as she continued. "Eventually, politics and infighting brought about the end of the group. The last thing the American government wanted was a bunch of rebels off fighting their own secret war. Fry was forced to return to the United States and, publicly at least, the Emergency Rescue Committee was disbanded."

Tasha leaned down and pulled open a drawer beneath the table, revealing rows of files, some of them quite old. She pulled a handful of files out as she spoke. "But your great-grandfather and a few others refused to let it go. If they couldn't rescue people with the support of the American government, then they'd do it on their own. The Emergency Rescue Committee lived on—even if it had to exist in secret."

She shoved the files into Ryan's arms. "For over seventy years, your family has been part of a network that helps people escape from some of the most dangerous places in the world."

She went back to the worktable as Ryan looked at the names on the files he held. *Tibet—Cuba—North Korea—Sri Lanka*. Each one held information and photos on another person rescued from imprisonment or death. Putting the pieces together now, Ryan realized that his father's job as a diplomat had been the perfect cover, allowing him to go from country to country without being suspected. Until now. Now, something had gone wrong. He looked up, remembering what Aung Win had asked his mother.

"Who is Myat Kaw?" he asked.

"With any luck," Tasha said, picking up the fake Kathleen Connors passport, "Myat Kaw is the person that's going to lead me to your father."

CHAPTER

12

**NEW YORK,
USA**

ait!" Ryan had to hurry along the sidewalk to keep up with Tasha's quick pace. "What about my mom? We have to find her."

"Where would you even start looking?" Tasha carried the map and printouts in a file under her arm. She had spent fewer than ten minutes booking flights and making calls before leaving the study, with Ryan right on her heels. "Your mother could be anywhere. The best chance we have of getting her back is finding your father."

"Then I'll go with you."

"No way. I can't help them if I have to babysit you." Tasha lifted her leg over the seat of a slick, black Kawasaki motorcycle parked at the curb.

Grabbing her helmet from behind, she gave Ryan a sympathetic look. "Go stay with your friend there for a few days. And don't come back to the house—it's not safe anymore. I'll be in touch."

Before he could argue, she hit the ignition switch with her right thumb and the motorcycle roared to life.

"But how do I get in touch with you?" Ryan asked over the noise.

"You don't. Just keep out of sight until this is over."

"Tasha—" Ryan started, but she was already racing down the street and into the night.

Ryan was sick of people disappearing on him, and Tasha was nuts if she thought he was just gonna sit tight and do nothing. He sprinted back to the brownstone, fueled by anger and frustration. He had to find some way to help his parents.

By the time he got back downstairs to the study, Danny was already typing at a furious pace on Ryan's father's computer. "Andakar's main embassy is in Washington, DC, but I'm accessing New York property records. If the embassy owns a place in the city, that might be where they took your mom."

"Good," Ryan said, moving past him to the secret room.

"So your parents are, like, insanely awesome."

"My parents are liars." Ryan jerked open drawers, searching through the remaining files.

Danny spun around in the desk chair. "They would have told you, eventually."

"They should have told me a long time ago."

"Look at all that's happened. It's dangerous. They were just trying to protect you."

"Well, that didn't work out so well, did it?" Ryan couldn't help the anger he felt and, in a way, he actually needed it. Fear would stop him cold, but anger kept him moving.

Ryan found a folder filled with credit cards, all made out to the identities on the various passports. He flipped through them, finding that one of the credit cards was made out to Thomas O'Hara, the name on his own fake passport.

Ryan's cell phone vibrated in his pocket and he snatched it out, praying it was his mother. But when he read "Blocked" on the Caller ID screen, an ominous feeling gripped him.

"Hello?"

"Ryan! Don't listen—"

"Mom?!" Her cries tore right to his heart. He wanted to leap through the phone somehow and save her. But all he could do was helplessly hold the phone in his clenched hands. "Mom, I'll find you!"

"I want to speak to John Quinn. Now—or you will never see your mother again." Ryan recognized Aung Win's voice and tried to calm down.

"He's not here. I don't know where he is."

"Then your mother dies. I want Myat Kaw!"

"Don't hurt her. I swear I don't know this Myat Kaw or where my dad is or *anything*."

There was a moment of silence, and Ryan feared Aung Win had hung up. "Fine. Tell John Quinn I will trade your mother for Myat Kaw."

"Aren't you listening—I don't know where he is!"

"I'm sure you have some way to contact him. Tell John Quinn he has five days. If I do not have Myat Kaw by Saturday, your mother dies. And if I even suspect you've spoken to the police or anyone else about this, I will kill her immediately. Five days."

"How am I supposed to find—"

But the call was already disconnected.

"Oh my god," Danny muttered. "We have to tell the cops."

"He said he'll kill her. And he's a total psycho—he'll do it."

"What choice do we have? Your dad's missing, that motorcycle girl took off—we have to do *something*."

Ryan didn't know what to do. Maybe Danny was right. Calling the police made the most sense. But what if his mom died because he did what Aung Win told him not to, and it was all his fault?

"Tasha said the best way to help Mom was to find Dad . . ." Abruptly, he stopped, a thought popping into his head. In three long strides he was at the worktable, picking up the fake passport with his picture.

"O'Hara . . ." he mumbled, wheels spinning. Ryan had an idea—a crazy idea, but it might be his only chance to save his mom.

CHAPTER 13

**NEW YORK,
USA**

"Flight two-eight-one, China Star service to Taiwan, is now boarding. All passengers please report to gate five."

Ryan dodged in and out of the crowd at JFK Airport. He was cutting it close after getting caught in the long security line. If he missed this flight, he knew he might never make it to Andakar. He gripped the plane ticket and the fake passport tightly, his backpack bumping as he ran.

Without Danny's help, he never would have made it this far. Danny had been able to track back through the history on his father's computer and find information on the plane ticket that Tasha had purchased. Using the credit card with the Thomas O'Hara name, Ryan had booked a seat for himself on the same flight out.

Ryan finally made it to the boarding area for gate five, scanning the line of impatient passengers. There! Near the front, he saw a woman with brilliant red hair. Ryan pushed his way through the passengers, hurrying to reach her before she handed over her ticket and disappeared into the plane.

"Hey, cuz, wait up!" Ryan called.

The redhead swiveled around and Tasha stared at him in disbelief. To her credit, she never broke character, but Ryan could see the daggers in her eyes.

"Hey . . . *cuz*," Tasha said, as the agent taking tickets glanced between them.

Ryan handed his ticket to the agent. "I thought you were gonna wait to get in line until I got back from the bathroom?"

Tasha looked ready to throttle him but played along. "No. I think you completely *misunderstood* what I told you."

"Oh, I understood," Ryan said. "But when a guy's gotta go, he's gotta go."

The gate agent handed Ryan's ticket back. "You're not seated together. Maybe you can ask one of the other passengers to change with you."

"We'll do that. Thanks." Ryan and Tasha moved into the gangway leading to the plane.

The moment they were out of earshot, Tasha whispered fiercely, "You can't come with me."

"They're my family."

"You'll only slow me down," she hissed.

"I can help."

"How? You're just a kid!" They were nearing the plane, and Tasha knew she was running out of options.

"I don't know how—yet," Ryan admitted. "But you're crazy if you think I'm sitting around here and doing nothing." Ryan stepped across the threshold and onto the plane. "I'm going to Andakar."

PART TWO
INTO THE LION'S DEN

CHAPTER
14

**OPEN SKIES,
ANDAKAR**

Ryan executed a Hindu Shuffle and a One-Handed Triple Cut, then worked on his Double Lifts for a while. He always kept a deck of cards with him to practice these sleight-of-hand skills, the most important element in most magic tricks. Though he'd been practicing for years, his growing hands were finally big enough for him to manipulate the cards more easily. He didn't even have to concentrate on the movements anymore, making it almost like a form of meditation. The cards helped him think, which was about all he'd been doing for the last twenty hours as he and Tasha flew halfway around the world.

How could he not have known his mom and

dad were living this secret life? It didn't seem possible. Through all the different towns and countries, the one constant he could always rely on was his parents. They were his rock.

But now he was questioning everything.

Was this stupid Emergency Rescue Committee the reason he had been forced to move all the time? Was it why he never had a regular life or got to stay in one place long enough to make real friends? Why were all those people whose names he saw in the ERC files more important to his parents than their own family? Because obviously, being part of this underground group was dangerous. Ryan's dad was missing and his mom had been kidnapped—it didn't get more dangerous than that!

All Ryan wanted was a normal teenager's life. To hang with friends, hear all the ridiculous drama and gossip, maybe play baseball on a real American team. He was finally living the life he'd dreamed of. For the first time, Ryan was starting to feel like a regular kid. He should be doing homework or grabbing a slice of pizza with Danny.

Instead, he was on a plane flying around the globe again.

"Your father furrows his brow just like you do

when he's angry." Tasha studied Ryan from the seat next to him.

"I'm not angry," he said, packing his playing cards back into their case.

Tasha looked away again. "Whatever."

Ryan still didn't know what to make of this mysterious young woman. For the entire first flight, from New York to Taiwan, she had mostly slept, barely acknowledging his presence. He had a million questions, but she pretty much blew him off, still mad that he had come along. Now, their second flight was about to end and they'd be in Andakar. Ryan wanted some answers.

"How come I've never met you?" he asked. "I know most of my parents' friends."

"Members of the committee have as little outside contact with each other as possible."

Ryan was surprised to finally get an actual response. "Did you do these rescues with my parents?"

"Occasionally. That's how the ERC works, a network of people around the globe, each just a stop along the way. Only a few people know who all the members are. It's safer that way."

"Then how do you contact each other? Because maybe we could get other people to help us. Maybe someone knows where we can find my dad."

"That's not how it works, kid."

"We need all the help we can get. How are we supposed to find one man in a whole country of people?"

"I'll find him. It's what I do." Tasha leaned her head back, closing her eyes as if the conversation was over.

Before Ryan could protest, the flight attendant broke in with an announcement, which she repeated in several languages: "Ladies and gentlemen, we will be landing shortly at Panai International Airport. As we start our descent, please make sure your seat backs and tray tables are in their full upright positions. Welcome to Andakar."

Ryan turned to the window, taking in the harsh and unforgiving landscape passing beneath them. Dense forests of towering trees covered rocky hillsides. This close to the city, there was still no sign of civilization. As the plane cleared the hills, Ryan spotted a lone pagoda perched precariously halfway down a steep slope, the sun glinting off its dome. It was massive, but looked impossible to reach, isolated by the wilderness around it.

"Wow," Ryan said, craning his neck to get a better glimpse.

Tasha glanced past him through the window. "Andakar is a land of contrasts. Ancient, yet wracked with modern problems. Primitive, but starkly beautiful. It's also one of the most perilous countries in the world. There are eyes and ears everywhere, and the secret police won't hesitate to lock you up."

"I thought they were trying to attract tourists. Throwing people in jail doesn't sound like the kind of thing you put in a travel brochure."

"The military regime only opened up the borders because they want Western countries to invest in their economy. Tourists see only what the government wants them to see: remarkable temples, colorful parades, exotic jungles. The ruling class in Andakar gets richer every day while the people starve."

"And this Myat Kaw, what did he do to make them so mad?"

"Exposed them for the liars they are. Myat Kaw's been blogging about Andakar for over a year now, revealing secrets about the military regime. No one knows Myat Kaw's identity, but judging from the information he's released, it seems likely that he's high up in the military. He has access to details that only someone on the inside would know."

"And my dad went there to rescue him?"

Tasha looked unsure. "From what I read in his files, I think Quinn was planning to sneak Myat Kaw out of the country and across the border to safety."

"Then he must have known who Myat Kaw was. How else could he help him escape?"

"If he did, he didn't leave any record of it at your house. Which isn't a surprise. Quinn has always been insistent on keeping information secret. He believes it's safer for everyone that way." Tasha's frustration was clear. "Your father can be quite irritating."

"How do you know Dad didn't get Myat Kaw out already? Maybe they're just hiding somewhere until things blow over."

"I don't think so," she said. "Quinn's never off the grid for this long. Something went wrong."

Ryan was quiet a moment, then asked what had been in his mind the whole time. "Do you think he's already dead?"

"I certainly hope not." Tasha didn't even try to be comforting.

Ryan looked out the window once more. Up ahead, the outskirts of the city appeared. The rugged terrain of the hills gave way to urban sprawl. Factories belching smoke were surrounded by older apartment buildings that spread out in all directions. Even from up here, the disorder and poverty were evident.

As the plane landed, Ryan couldn't shake the question that kept plaguing him: Why was his father willing to risk his life to save some guy he didn't even know?

CHAPTER
15

**PANAI,
ANDAKAR**

*T*he moment he got off the plane and took his first steps into Andakar, Ryan could sense how different things were there. It was weirdly quiet, a kind of hush in the terminal where all the passengers disembarked. The airport itself had an aura of faded glamour, as if it had once been impressive but had been neglected for far too long. The smell of mold, like in the boy's locker room at school, hung in the air.

There were only a handful of tourists and they were generally older. Ryan and Tasha were by far the youngest people arriving.

"Remember, we're cousins, Thomas O'Hara and Kathleen Connors, traveling from Ireland—"

"I *got* it," Ryan shot back, annoyed. They'd been over the cover story multiple times. But being a chameleon is what Ryan had done most of his life, and he was good at it. Faking an accent, changing his body language to fit the situation—that was easy for him. Of course, he'd never traveled under an assumed identity. He took a deep breath, calming his nerves.

Ryan followed the line of passengers toward passport control. As they entered the security area, soldiers in pale gray uniforms stood on each side of the passage, watching everyone with undisguised suspicion. The soldiers wore black tactical vests over their uniforms and carried submachine guns. But Ryan was used to tight security at a lot of the places they had traveled, so he wasn't intimidated.

One of the soldiers shifted his gaze to Ryan, who was caught by surprise. Ryan looked away a moment too late. The soldier's full attention was now on him, eyeing the backpack Ryan wore slung over his shoulder. As he followed Tasha through the doorway, Ryan's path was suddenly blocked by the soldier's submachine gun.

The man barked at him in his native language, which Ryan now recognized as Andalese, the same language he had heard on the plane and from Aung Win back in New York. Ryan adopted what he hoped was a confused, naive expression. Reminding himself he was supposed to be Irish, he said, "Sure lookit, I'm just visiting. What's the problem then?" A few steps ahead, Tasha stopped and turned back.

The soldier spoke again in his language, and Ryan smiled sheepishly. "Sorry—you speak English?"

"Parent?" the soldier asked. "Where is parent?"

Tasha responded before Ryan could. "I'm his cousin. We're traveling together." Tasha's own voice lilted with a perfect Irish accent.

The soldier looked between them, then motioned Ryan away from the others. "This way," he said. Tasha took a step to follow, but another soldier stopped her.

"Not you," the second soldier ordered. "You, there." Ryan could see Tasha struggling with what to do, not wanting to lose Ryan, but not having any good options.

"It's okay, cuz," he told her with more confidence than he felt. "I'll see you in a few minutes." Ryan walked in front of the soldier who guided him away. As they arrived at the security checkpoint, the soldier began speaking to a uniformed immigration official and pointing at Ryan.

Ryan had been going through security checkpoints all his life. There were usually long lines and waiting always felt like forever. His parents would play games with him to help pass the time. One of his favorites was "I've Got a Secret." His dad would whisper outrageous "secrets" to him, usually something that made him laugh, like the man checking passports was nicknamed Mr. Fart-a-Lot. They'd joke about it while they waited, but once it was their turn to hand over their passports, the goal of the game was to keep a straight face and never let on.

Ryan wasn't too good at it in the beginning, and there were plenty of officials around the world who probably thought he was a little nuts as he laughed hysterically for no apparent reason. But over the years, he got better, until he could keep a straight face no matter how hysterical the secret was.

"You are visiting Andakar on your own?" The immigration official spoke perfect English with a slight British accent, holding out his hand for Ryan's passport.

Ryan handed it over with a smile. "I'm with my cousin. She's my legal guardian. This guy wouldn't let her come with me."

"Someone else will speak with your cousin. Thomas O'Hara," he read, examining the passport carefully.

"Tommy," Ryan said. "That's what my friends call me."

The official looked up at him with a cold, fake smile. "And what is the reason for your visit?"

"To see this incredible country—they say it's bang on! We're gonna go down to the beaches, and then, hopefully, get to do one of those zipline tours through the jungle. You ever done that? The lads say it's deadly cool." Ryan told himself to tone it down a bit, he was sounding a little *too* Irish.

The official appraised him, then reached out a hand for his backpack. "You have no drugs?"

Drugs? Is that what this was about? "Absolutely not," Ryan said. "I'd never do drugs." That was one thing Ryan *didn't* have to lie about.

The official looked through the bag, which contained mostly clothes, toiletries, a stash of chocolate, and a couple of baseball caps. "We have difficulties with young people believing they can come here and . . . party? That is the word, yes?"

"I'm just here to see your beautiful country,"

Ryan said with complete conviction. The immigration official nodded, handing Ryan his backpack. With one efficient movement, he stamped the passport, then held it out.

"Enjoy your stay."

"Thanks. I plan to." Ryan took his passport and hurried away, trying to keep the grin off his face. Across the hall, he saw with relief that Tasha's passport was also getting stamped. They'd done it.

But even more important, Ryan had made a discovery that he was just beginning to understand. The games he'd grown up playing with his parents, like "Follow-the-Monkey" and "I've Got a Secret," weren't just for fun. They were training exercises. Ryan's parents had been secretly preparing him for this kind of assignment his entire life.

CHAPTER
16

**PANAI,
ANDAKAR**

Ryan had been right about the city—the streets of Panai were chaotic. The sidewalks were crammed with people pushing past one another, knocking into Ryan without a second thought as he tried to keep up with Tasha. A decrepit old bus spewed a cloud of exhaust right into his face as it pulled away from the curb. Ryan hacked and coughed, wishing he could stop at one of the countless vendors that lined the sidewalk and grab a drink. But Tasha never looked back, and he wasn't about to risk losing her.

Ryan had traveled throughout Asia and his family had even lived in Bangkok for six months, but he had never seen such a vibrant display of color as here in Panai. Though the roads were dirty and most of the buildings in disrepair, everywhere Ryan looked there was purple, pink, orange, or yellow. It was as if the locals refused to allow the reality of their daily lives to define their world. The only thing detracting from the festive atmosphere was the presence of gray-uniformed soldiers with machine guns on every corner.

"We have to hurry," Tasha said.

Ryan ran to catch up as she navigated through the crowd. "Where are we going?"

"Across town. We'll stay with a friend tonight, then start out first thing in the morning."

"Who's this friend? Do they know where my dad is?"

Tasha never stopped scanning the faces around them as she answered. "Friends are people who help out the ERC. They provide places to stay, transportation, sometimes just information or access. They put themselves at risk every time they open their doors to us."

Ryan and Tasha arrived at a large, open plaza teeming with people. An ornately carved pagoda occupied the center of the busy square. The pagoda's roof, a carved dome that tapered to a long, thin spire, was almost four stories high and covered in gold leaf.

"Take my picture," Tasha said. Ryan was confused by her goofy grin as she took a few steps backward so he could get a better shot. They didn't have time for sightseeing! But Tasha was insistent, "Take my picture, *Tommy*."

Ryan pulled out his phone, switching it to camera. As he raised it to snap a few pix, Tasha's bizarre actions became clear. While he shot pictures, she was looking *behind* him, searching the crowd. Ryan realized he still had a lot to learn.

Tasha came close and whispered, "Cross the plaza to the opposite side, then keep going straight down the street on the other side. Be natural, not obvious. Take your time. You're a *tourist*." She started to walk away.

"Where are you going?"

"I want to make sure we're clear before we travel to the safe house." Before Ryan could protest, Tasha was gone, disappearing like a ghost into the crowd. His instinct was to look for anyone following them, but he stopped, reminding himself to be natural. He was a tourist.

Ryan made his way across the plaza, focusing on the pagoda. It was pretty awesome, covered in intricate carvings and surrounded on all sides by hundreds of small sculptures of the

Buddha. He stopped in front of a sign, reading that the Ashoka Temple was over two thousand years old.

As he passed the entrance, Ryan noticed an old monk, bald and wrapped in a blood-red robe, watching him. The monk smiled and bowed slightly. With a nod of his head, Ryan returned the bow and was surprised when the monk stepped forward. The man took Ryan's hand and gently slipped a string bracelet around his wrist. It was simple but beautiful, with inter-woven strands of red and yellow.

"Tasmati ca niva," the monk said, bowing once more. Ryan had no idea what he was saying.

"It is a blessing," said a passing woman, noticing Ryan's uncertainty. "Very good luck. You say, '*Tin ba dai*.'"

Ryan turned back to the monk, making another small bow, the bracelet firmly in place. *"Tin ba dai,"* he repeated, then faced the helpful woman. "Thank you."

But she was looking beyond him now, her expression darkening. She nodded curtly and abruptly walked away. Ryan turned to see what had spooked her: One of the soldiers was staring right at him with suspicion. Ryan gave what he hoped was an innocent smile, and then started across the plaza once more.

Making it to the other side, he crossed the street, as Tasha had instructed. He kept walking, unsure how far he should go. What if they really were being followed? If something had happened to Tasha, he had no idea where he was supposed to go or what he should do. Only now, standing by himself in the middle of this busy foreign city did Ryan realize how alone he'd be if he lost Tasha. He didn't know anybody here, didn't know the language, and had no idea how he'd ever find Dad on his own. And if he didn't find his dad, how could he hope to help his mom? He felt his stomach twisting, panic threatening as the minutes dragged by.

Where *was* she?

The screech of tires startled Ryan and he whirled around. An old Peugeot hatchback that had seen better days stopped at the curb, the passenger door swinging open and nearly hitting him.

"Get in," Tasha commanded from the driver's side.

Ryan didn't hesitate, jumping in and slamming

the door closed. The car's engine made a grinding noise as Tasha shifted into gear and sped off.

"Where'd you get this?" Ryan asked.

"Stole it," Tasha said matter-of-factly. Ryan stared at her—was she being serious? Seeing his expression, she rolled her eyes. "Don't worry, we'll give it back. Eventually."

Ryan leaned back against the seat. "So we're thieves now."

Tasha grinned. "You're just like your father." The way she said it, Ryan knew it wasn't meant as a compliment.

CHAPTER
17

**PANAI,
ANDAKAR**

Darkness had fallen by the time the Peugeot rattled to a stop on one of Panai's countless winding roads. This neighborhood was more residential, the streets lined with apartment buildings, most of which were falling apart. Telephone cables and power lines snaked through the air, and the sounds of families eating and laughing wafted from open windows.

"We have to hurry," Tasha said, getting out of the car. "The show starts in less than five minutes."

"What show?" Ryan grabbed his backpack, following as she moved quickly down the street.

"You'll see." Ryan was almost getting used

to the way Tasha seldom answered a question directly. He didn't even bother asking anything further because he had the feeling she kind of enjoyed tormenting him.

They made it to the end of the block. Tasha paused, confirming once more that they were in the clear, before she turned the corner onto a busier street. A few storefronts away, a small crowd of adults and children were gathered on the sidewalk. As Tasha and Ryan approached, the group began filing inside what Ryan could now see was a theater. The marquee was in a language Ryan couldn't read, but it was translated into English at the bottom: "Mama Nan's Marionette Theater!"

"Puppets?"

Tasha didn't even bother to respond, mixing in with the patrons as they drifted inside. Ryan followed, falling into step beside two chattering younger kids.

The theater wasn't very big, but was surprisingly nice, with red velvet seats for the audience and heavy curtains on all sides. Down front, the proscenium surrounding the stage was decorated to look like an imperial palace. Almost as soon as Ryan and Tasha took their seats, the lights dimmed and the curtain rose.

A gong struck three times, then a burst of music erupted, a strange melody of ill-timed drumbeats and tinkling bells. Against a mountain landscape backdrop, two marionettes appeared, their strings rising above their heads to where the unseen puppet masters controlled them. The puppets were tall and elaborately decorated. One appeared to be a demon of some kind, with emerald-green skin, red-jeweled eyes, and fangs like a vampire; the other was a young princess with silk robes that twirled when she spun around.

Ryan was so transfixed by the show that he jerked in shock when a hand grabbed his shoulder. He spun around to find a young man right behind their seats. The man put a finger to his lips and motioned for them to follow. Tasha got up immediately and slipped out. Ryan cast one sidelong glance back at the show, then joined them.

Moving through the shadows, they followed the young man behind the stage. All around, lifeless marionettes hung from the ceiling, seeming to stare at Ryan as he passed. Backstage, the magic was gone. These puppets gave Ryan the creeps.

They arrived at a rickety wooden stairway

and the young man motioned for them to go up alone. He disappeared into the shadows and Ryan followed Tasha up the steep stairway. At the top was a single door that she entered without hesitating. As Ryan came in, Tasha closed the door behind him.

"What do we do now?" The distraction of the theater already fading, Ryan was anxious to get started. The flight to Andakar had taken almost a full day, and he couldn't stop worrying about his parents.

"Now," Tasha said, "we sleep."

"What? I don't want to sleep—I want to find my dad."

Tasha tossed down her bag. "My contact in Panai says it's not safe for him to meet until ten tomorrow morning. And you barely slept on the plane. In the ERC, one of the first things you learn is to sleep when you can. You may not get another chance for a long time." Tasha looked over the room, which had a small sink in the corner and a large worktable filled with string, wood, and paint for making marionettes. "Not bad for a crash pad."

Ryan watched in disbelief as Tasha bunched up some fabric to create a makeshift pillow, then settled down to sleep. She glanced up at him. "Seriously. There's nothing we can do right now." She turned over to face the wall, ending the conversation.

Ryan crossed the room and sat, discouraged and angry. He'd brought a stash of chocolate and grabbed a small square from his backpack. Unfortunately, it did nothing to help his anxiety. He pulled a photograph from his pocket, unfolding it to see his mom and dad smiling back at him. It was a family picture taken on one of their countless camping expeditions. Though he was still upset by the secrets they'd been keeping, all he cared about was getting his parents back home. The fear that he might never see either of them again was overwhelming.

After a few minutes, Ryan was surprised to hear steady breathing coming from Tasha. She really did know how to grab sleep when she could!

But Ryan couldn't just do nothing. Time was of the essence. Folding the picture and returning it to his pocket, he looked back to the window. Outside, a fire escape led to the roof. He quietly pulled out his cell phone and powered it on. Because of all his traveling, Ryan had a phone that could work pretty much anywhere in the world as long as it had a signal.

Ryan crept over and raised the window carefully. With one last glance at Tasha, he stepped out onto the fire escape.

CHAPTER
18

**PANAI,
ANDAKAR**

From the roof, Ryan could see Panai extending in all directions. For a city this large, there was surprisingly little light, not at all like the near-constant brightness of New York. The phone beeped as it finished powering up and connected to the local service carrier. Ryan was excited to discover he had two voice mails. He hit the play button, praying one of them was from his dad.

But the first was Danny, telling Ryan he had some new information and to call no matter what time it was. He hit play on the second message.

"Ryan, it's Mom. I'm okay . . ."

Hearing his mother's voice, Ryan was flooded

with relief. She was still alive! He hadn't even realized how scared he was that it might already be too late to save her. At least now he knew he had a chance. But his hope was dashed as the message continued.

"I've told these men we don't know about any of this—"

Aung Win's gruff voice barked through the speaker. "Four days. You will produce Myat Kaw or you will never hear Jacqueline Quinn's voice again."

"Let go!" Jacqueline's tone was indignant, but then the message abruptly cut off.

Ryan stared at the phone a moment. He felt so powerless. But he knew sitting up here agonizing about his mom's situation wouldn't help her—he needed to *do* something. He dialed Danny's number. Whatever information he'd found might be useful. The time difference between here and New York was twelve hours, so Danny would be in school now. The phone rang three times, and Ryan worried that Danny wouldn't answer.

"Ohmygod, dude, you're still alive!" Danny's hushed voice over the line made Ryan instantly feel a little better.

"Yeah, we made it to Andakar. But we still

don't know where my dad is."

"Hold on," Danny whispered. Ryan could hear shuffling and realized Danny was hiding his phone. "Miss Ellison, so sorry—kind of a crisis—can I run to the bathroom?" Ryan couldn't hear Miss Ellison's response, but he assumed it wasn't positive because Danny suddenly wailed, "Ooooo! Total emergency! Maybe both ends!" That must've done the trick because he could hear Danny moving now. "Thanks, Miss Ellison!"

Moments later, Danny had made it out of the classroom. "You owe me," he told Ryan. "I'm gonna be living that down for years."

"Did you find anything?"

"Maybe. I took your dad's computer with me and spent last night digging through it. He had some pretty impressive encryption."

"But you got in?"

"It took a while, but yeah. I got a little obsessed. Deep down in one of the root directories, I found a whole group of deleted emails from right before your dad left."

"How'd you find them if they were deleted?" Ryan asked.

"Delete doesn't really get rid of anything from your computer. It just hides it. If you know where to look, you can find it again. The thing is, it's gonna take me a while to put the emails into a shape where we can read them. Right now, it's like they went through a paper shredder—all little bits of data that have to be put back together."

Ryan was disappointed. "So they're no real help?"

"Slow down, Dr. Downer, I'm not done yet. I was able to find an IP address in the email headers. The IP address tells you where the emails were sent from."

"This is the good news part, right?"

Danny didn't hide his excitement. "All the emails came from Panai!"

"Myat Kaw," Ryan said, getting a first tingling of hope. "It had to be Myat Kaw and my dad arranging the rescue."

"That's what I figured, too. The problem is, I can't get a physical address from an IP number. I've got my desktop at home running a program to patch the emails back together, but so far the only helpful thing I dug up was the name Kali Thawar. It came up a few times in the last couple of emails."

Ryan started back toward the fire escape. "I'll ask Tasha. Maybe she knows what it is."

"*Hello?* Did I *say* I was finished?" Danny

chided. "I did some research and found out that the Kali Thawar is this hotel that was built there by the British back in the early 1900s. Google says it closed down years ago but doesn't say what it is today. It's about a mile from where you are right now."

"You know where I am?"

"I'm looking at your location on that cell tracker app I created. It uses your phone's GPS—but I can only see you if your cell's on. I'm texting you the address now."

Ryan finally had something he could use. "Okay, I'm gonna check it out. Thanks. I'll have to turn off the phone to save the battery, but I'll call you if anything comes up." Ryan ended the call and stepped back onto the fire escape stairs.

For a moment, he considered waking up Tasha and telling her about the old hotel. But she'd just want to wait until morning. This was Ryan's first real lead to find his dad, and he wasn't willing to waste another second.

Ryan hurried down the fire escape, dropping the last few feet to the ground. He raced off through the murky alleys of Panai.

CHAPTER
19

**PANAI,
ANDAKAR**

The Kali Thawar had obviously started out as a grand and luxurious hotel. Standing three stories high and occupying an entire block, it was a massive building. Even now, after years of neglect, Ryan could see how impressive it must have been in its day, with a sweeping entrance, huge bay windows, and elegant columns. But it sure wasn't a hotel now.

Instead of bellboys greeting guests, the Kali Thawar had soldiers with machine guns slung over their shoulders keeping everyone out. The gates were closed, and barbed wire adorned the top of the metal fence that surrounded the property.

Staying in the shadows, Ryan circled the

building, trying to figure out its purpose. He spotted a few soldiers roaming the grounds and two more at a smaller back gate, which looked like it was probably used for deliveries. All these soldiers wore the same dark-blue uniforms, different from the drab gray of the men at the airport and in the city. None appeared particularly alert. This seemed to be their regular routine.

The guards and heavy security convinced Ryan his father must be a prisoner here. That would explain why they hadn't heard from him. Dad and Myat Kaw had discussed the Kali Thawar right before he disappeared. Ryan had to get inside and find his dad. But how was he going to get past the security patrols? The metal fencing and barbed wire surrounded the compound on all sides.

Every fifty feet or so, palm trees had been planted that rose higher than the hotel itself. They were thin and regal, creating a stately appearance. Looking at them, Ryan was struck by an inspiration: Those trees could be his way onto the grounds.

When he was nine, Ryan's family had lived for several months in Belize, a country in the Caribbean with gorgeous beaches, incredible snorkeling, and thousands of palm trees. Ryan got to know the local kids and they laughed at him when they learned he couldn't climb a palm tree; they'd all been doing it their whole lives. It took a lot of painful falls and scraped skin on the soles of his feet, but Ryan was soon able to climb the tallest palms with the best of them. He even learned to carry a machete on his back so he could hack off coconuts.

The only way he knew to climb a palm tree was barefoot, so Ryan unlaced his high-tops. Stuffing his socks in his pocket, he tied the laces of the shoes together and wrapped them loosely around his neck. He waited in the shadows until the roaming sentries passed, knowing he had to time this perfectly, then darted across the street.

The secret to climbing a palm is knowing how to apply pressure in the right directions. With his back to the metal fence, Ryan wrapped his arms around the thin trunk. At the same time, he placed his bare feet, one on top of the other, in front of him on the tree. By *pushing* with his feet while *pulling* with his hands, Ryan maintained a constant balance of pressure that kept his body in place. After every step, he raised his arms a little higher. Once you got the motion down, it was easy—the kids of Belize could scale the highest palm trees in seconds.

And that's exactly what Ryan did, the movements coming back to him instinctually even though he hadn't climbed in a few years. He could feel the tough bark scraping the soft skin on the bottom of his feet, but he didn't stop. When he was up far enough, Ryan looked behind him. He was a couple of feet higher than the barbed wire, which meant this was at least a ten-foot jump to the ground. If he missed, he'd be cut to pieces, and would probably get arrested and thrown in jail.

Before he could talk himself out of it, Ryan counted down—three, two, one!—and pushed out with his legs as hard as he could. Ryan soared over the fence and the razor-sharp wire, hanging in the air for what seemed like forever. He landed on the ground with a hard crunch. Ryan rolled with the impact, throwing himself into a somersault that knocked the breath out of him.

Gasping for air, Ryan turned over, shocked and surprised to discover he hadn't twisted an ankle or broken any bones. He knew he couldn't stay out in the open like this. He forced himself to get up and move. Keeping low, he ran to the side of the hotel, gravel stinging the soles of his feet like needle pricks, making it hard to move fast. He hid behind the shrubbery that lined the walls, listening hard for any indication that he had been spotted. After a moment to catch his breath, Ryan put his socks and shoes back on and scanned the area. The coast was clear.

Creeping around to the back, Ryan spotted an entrance that had apparently been used by the hotel's staff. There was no one around, so he cautiously moved to the door and peered through the glass panes. The door opened onto a back hallway that was empty. He tried the handle. It was unlocked.

With a deep breath and a quick, quiet prayer, Ryan slipped inside.

CHAPTER

20

**PANAI,
ANDAKAR**

Whack! A cleaver chopped the head off a long fish as several soldiers chattered among themselves, slicing and dicing large bowls of seafood and vegetables. Their curved knives moved with frightening speed as Ryan watched, hidden behind a counter in this industrial-sized kitchen. These guys must be on food detail. And they were cooking a *lot*, which made Ryan wonder how many soldiers were actually stationed here.

He ducked back down, suddenly hit with the realization of how crazy his plan was. He was locked inside this place with who-knew-how-many guys carrying machine guns and knives that looked like they could cut him right in two!

Get a grip, he told himself. Finding his nerve once more, Ryan scurried quickly across the kitchen, hidden from the soldiers' view by the counters. He darted into a hallway, hoping he wouldn't run into anyone.

Fortunately, the hallway was deserted, but Ryan could hear voices just beyond it. He moved closer to the swinging door at the far end, which had a round window in the middle. Ryan guessed the door led to what was once a restaurant and that this was the hallway the waiters used back when it was a working hotel.

Ryan peered out the round window into a huge room that still had the trappings of British Colonial design: dark wood floors, wicker chairs, and palm-leaf fans hanging from the ceiling. But it wasn't a restaurant anymore. One whole wall was lined with computer stations, each manned by a technician wearing a headset. The other wall was filled with sophisticated flat-screen TVs and a sea of flickering, shifting images. Ryan saw maps, newscasts, and a whole bank of monitors showing surveillance-camera footage of the hotel's grounds.

It didn't take a genius to realize the hotel was some kind of command center.

Before Ryan could see more, a movement in

his peripheral vision caught his attention. One of the soldiers was heading right toward him! Ryan bolted back down the hallway. He passed the kitchen door and spotted a staircase just as the door behind him opened. Ryan dodged behind the staircase. He pressed his back against the wall and held his breath, not making a sound.

Hearing the soldier give orders to the kitchen crew, Ryan exhaled in relief: He hadn't been spotted. But the hallway was getting busy now. He had to get out of there. He darted up the stairway to the second floor.

It was much quieter upstairs. Ryan stayed close to the walls as he snuck down the hall, passing doors that opened into what had once been guest rooms. After checking the doorsills to make sure no lights were on, he tried the handles. A few opened to offices. He searched them briefly but found nothing that helped him figure out what this place was. At the end of the hallway, one of the doors opened into a much bigger room. Ryan stepped silently inside.

It was completely dark. Ryan knew he couldn't turn on a light. He used the glow from his cell phone to look around. The room must have been a suite way back when, but it was being used as a storage area now. The walls were lined with shelves stuffed with thousands of file folders.

Ryan pulled one down, careful to remember where he'd found it. On the front of the folder was a red-and-gold shield with a white triangle floating in the middle. It was some sort of logo. Ryan couldn't read the language of the writing underneath it, so he snapped a photo. Maybe later Danny could figure out what it was. He opened it and found a dossier written in a language he didn't understand. A picture of a middle-aged man was clipped inside, along with what appeared to be all his essential information. Ryan could recognize dates and times strewn throughout, but he couldn't read the entries themselves.

Ryan guessed that these were files on Andakar's citizens. With all the communications technology and surveillance equipment he saw downstairs and the files up here, Ryan was pretty certain the hotel was currently the base for some kind of intelligence agency. All the emails Danny found to Ryan's father had come from Panai, and some mentioned Kali Thawar. That meant Myat Kaw could have had access to lots of top secret information. No wonder they wanted to find him.

After putting the folder back, Ryan left the file room and continued down the hall. From the front of the building, someone was yelling, sounding more scared than angry. Creeping closer, Ryan arrived at the end of the hallway. It opened onto a landing that overlooked the old hotel's lobby.

Crouching low, Ryan sidled up to the balcony rail and peered over. The lobby was connected to this upper floor by a wide, gently curving staircase. Down below, two of the blue-uniformed soldiers held a frightened man between them, his desperate cries turning to pleading sobs. An officer stood imperiously before him, questioning the man in a cold, emotionless tone.

Ryan wanted to get a better look, but he couldn't risk being seen. The officer in charge spat out a command and the soldiers dragged the prisoner away, his pleas echoing uselessly. They took him to a stairway on the opposite side of the lobby that led to whatever was downstairs.

Backing carefully away from the rail, Ryan hurried once more toward the staff stairwell. If the soldiers were taking their prisoner to the basement, then maybe Ryan's dad was down there, too.

CHAPTER

21

**PANAI,
ANDAKAR**

The basement was like something out of a horror movie. Half the lights were out or flickering, and the bare concrete walls and underground dampness gave it a cold and threatening atmosphere. There was a stench down here, too, which Ryan thought was probably a combination of filth, body odor, and fear.

A confusing network of corridors ran underneath the building. Ryan didn't think the soldiers used this part of the old hotel much, as he'd passed a couple of forgotten laundry carts and found a closet still packed with rotted-out supplies. He got completely turned around in the hallways, which all looked alike, until he didn't know where he was.

Finally, he spotted a pair of steel doors at the end of yet another hallway. Cautiously, he opened one of the doors and immediately heard the buzz of machinery from the other side. This seemed to be an entrance to a whole other section of the basement housing the generators and equipment that kept the building functioning. Ryan stepped inside, careful not to let the heavy door slam.

A long chamber stretched out before him, lit only by a couple of bare bulbs. Several giant, rusted-out furnaces lined one side of the room. At the far end, a hallway led off into darkness. Through the hum of the machinery, Ryan now noticed other sounds. People's voices, moaning and crying out in desperation.

He started that way, then froze, hearing something else—footsteps. Coming closer quickly. Ryan moved to the furnaces, slipping silently into the shadows between them as a soldier entered from the hallway at the other end of the room. The man passed within a few feet of Ryan but didn't stop. He exited through the steel door and was gone. The moment the door clicked shut, Ryan hurried toward the voices. If his father was here, he could only imagine what condition he might find him in.

Around the corner, he could hear what sounded like an interrogation. The hallway was empty of guards, so Ryan risked a peek through an open doorway. His heart stopped at what he saw inside.

Rusted pipes spanned the ceiling of a long room that once housed the water tanks for the hotel but was now a makeshift torture chamber. Ryan saw a man and a woman chained to the wall with iron manacles. In the middle of the room, Ryan recognized the guy who had been dragged away upstairs, his shirt now off. He was tied to a chair, whimpering. Behind him, the officer raised a riding crop. Ryan flinched as the officer swung, viciously striking the man's exposed back. The man screamed and Ryan turned away, horrified.

Down the hall, Ryan discovered a series of rooms that had been converted into jail cells. He counted six in all, three on each side. There were still no guards in sight. Ryan took the opportunity to look inside each cell.

But his dad wasn't here. The prisoners in the cells were all locals, and they looked miserable. Ryan wished he could help them escape, but that would alert the guards in the interrogation room.

"Hey." Ryan spun around at the whispered voice behind him. A young woman stared out from behind the bars of a cell, her face streaked with dirt and tears. "You have to get out of here."

Ryan's shock turned to surprise at her perfect English. "I'm looking for someone. A man, an American—"

"There's no American here. Go."

"Are you sure? His name is John Quinn—he's helping Myat Kaw."

The young woman's expression changed at the mention of Myat Kaw's name. "You know Myat Kaw?" she asked.

Ryan moved to her, noticing that other faces were now appearing at the cell doors. "John Quinn is my father. He was trying to get Myat Kaw to safety. I have to find him."

One of the other prisoners, an older man, whispered something in their native language. The young woman listened, then translated for Ryan. "He says he knows your father. That he's very brave."

Ryan turned to the man, trying to keep his voice down despite the excitement he was feeling. "Do you know where he is?" The man shook his head, then spoke once more to the young woman. He went on for some time and Ryan couldn't help feeling impatient, hearing the cries from the interrogation just around the corner. He didn't have much time.

"There is a student at the Panai Teaching College," she said. "His name is Ashin Myek. He says to ask this student. He may know where your father went."

"How does he know?"

"Many of us helped Myat Kaw." They both turned at the sound of a door swinging open around the corner. Her eyes met his in fear, "You must go—hurry!"

Ryan's hand went to the lock on her cell. "I'll let you out—all of you."

"No," she whispered. "This is Andakar—there is nowhere to go, and it is worse for those who run. *Go! Save yourself!*"

Ryan hesitated, but he could hear the soldiers dragging their mumbling prisoner toward the cells. He took off, racing for the steel door, frustrated at not being able to do more for the people who had helped him.

Making it through the steel door, Ryan raced for the stairs, more intent on speed than on stealth at this point. But the corridors were confusing, and Ryan's rush ended with him getting hopelessly lost. He tried to backtrack, but couldn't tell one hallway from the other. Frustrated and annoyed with himself, he turned a corner and came face-to-face with one of the soldiers!

Ryan and the soldier were equally startled, but Ryan was the first to recover. As the soldier went for his pistol, Ryan brought a knee up into the guy's stomach! The soldier doubled over, gasping for breath.

Unlike the fight at school, Ryan didn't have to be careful and pull his punches. He was a couple of inches shorter than the soldier, but he delivered a Palm Heel Strike that sent the man to his knees. The soldier raised his gun, but Ryan grabbed it and dealt one final Hammer Fist Punch that sent him to the ground, unconscious.

Ryan could hardly believe what he'd done. His body had reacted instinctively, all those years of practice paying off in a big way. But after seeing the way these soldiers tortured people, he didn't feel bad at all. He ran up the stairs, the gun still in his hand.

At the top, Ryan paused to make sure no one was around, and then went out the back door. He darted across the expanse of lawn, keeping to the shadows as he raced for the back gate.

There weren't any palm trees on this side to climb, so he had to find another way out.

Ryan crept along the back wall, getting closer to the gate. Two soldiers were stationed at the entrance, one along the road and the other inside the guard shack. Ryan still had the gun, but he didn't even know how to use it. Out of options, he raised the weapon, hoping he could fake enough confidence to force the soldier to open the gate. He took a step forward, but the night suddenly erupted with shouts from the main building.

An alarm was being raised! The soldier he'd hit must have come around. The man in the guard shack came out and joined his comrade on the road. They both looked quizzically toward the hotel. This was the only opportunity Ryan was going to get. Slipping inside the guard shack, he searched for the button to open the gate. Spotting one with an icon of an open door on its face, he pressed it and hurried back out.

Hearing the metal gates creak open, the two soldiers whirled around. Before they could raise their machine guns, Ryan fired two shots into the air, high over their heads, but loud enough to make them both duck for cover. Without a backward glance, he squeezed through the gate.

Ryan sprinted down the street as a siren began to wail from the compound. He was out, but they would soon be hot on his trail.

CHAPTER
22

**PANAI,
ANDAKAR**

Stopping to catch his breath, Ryan looked back over his shoulder. He'd been running for blocks, making sharp turns, going down alleys, anything he could think of to shake the men chasing him. But there were too many. Every time he thought he was in the clear, they'd appear once more, cutting off his escape.

The streets he'd taken had been dark, with virtually no electric lights on anywhere. But a block away, he spotted a busier area with bright lights, noise, and people. Ryan had hoped he could lose the soldiers by hiding in the shadows, but that wasn't working. Needing a new plan, he headed toward the crowd.

Old-fashioned neon signs assaulted Ryan from both sides of the street. The garish colors and blinking lights reminded him of a carnival. Locals were everywhere, eating, drinking, and chatting at a variety of small cafés and food stands. Dressed in jeans and T-shirts, they didn't look that different from people hanging out anywhere else in the world.

Ryan slowed down and tried to blend in, but being the only American around, he stood out in the crowd. Still, he received hesitant smiles from most of the people he passed as he made his way to the far end of the street. He nodded and smiled back. The distraction almost got him caught.

Ryan stopped short. Less than thirty feet ahead, blue-uniformed soldiers shoved people out of the way. A woman was pushed to the ground, but the soldiers just stepped right over her. Ryan lowered his head and turned around. Moving as quickly as he could without rousing suspicion, he headed back the way he'd come. He didn't get far before he saw another group of soldiers fanning out as they roughly pushed their way through the crowd from the opposite end.

Ryan was trapped.

Desperate, he looked frantically for an escape route. He stood in front of a crowded café open to the street, where patrons sat at plastic tables so low to the ground they seemed better suited for little kids than adults. The soldiers closed in from both sides, and Ryan made his move.

Three men looked up in surprise as Ryan plopped himself down in a red plastic chair opposite them. "Hi," he said, keeping his back to the sidewalk.

The men exchanged curious looks. One of them looked toward the door and his expression darkened. Out of the corner of his eye, Ryan could see the blue uniform of a soldier on the sidewalk. The man spoke a few words to his friends, and they saw the soldier as well. Their gazes all turned to Ryan.

Were they going to give him up? Ryan tried not to let the anxiety show on his face, but he knew if they did, he'd be toast. Glancing down, he had a sudden inspiration. He loosened the string bracelet the monk had given him at the Ashoka Temple. Taking it off his wrist, he took the hand of the man across from him.

"Tasmati ca niva," Ryan said, trying to imitate the sounds of the words the monk had spoken to him.

For a breathless moment, Ryan thought the stranger was going to jerk his hand away. Instead, a smile spread across his face.

"Tin ba dai," he replied.

One of the other men suddenly laughed, throwing an arm out and draping it over Ryan's shoulder in a fatherly fashion. The other two joined in, smiling as if nothing was out of the ordinary and talking loudly among themselves once more.

Ryan couldn't understand a word, but he nodded as if he belonged here. He could practically feel the eyes of the soldier on the back of his head.

After a moment, the men's chatter subsided as they looked beyond him. One of them nodded to him, his face serious. Ryan checked, and, sure enough, the soldier had moved on. The man next to him pointed toward the back of the café, making it clear Ryan should leave that way.

Ryan thanked them again and then weaved his way out through the crowded tables. A long hallway led past the kitchen, where the smell of curry and garlic made him realize how hungry he was.

Ryan pushed open the door at the back, disappearing quickly into the night.

CHAPTER
23

**NEW YORK,
USA**

An airborne French fry smacked into Danny's laptop screen. The guys at the table behind him were goofing off, but he didn't have time to get distracted. Cleaning the greasy smear with his T-shirt, he went back to reading.

The school cafeteria wasn't the best place to be researching the most feared military dictatorship in Southeast Asia, but Danny didn't have much choice. History class started in twenty minutes, and he was using every spare second to help Ryan.

So far, he'd managed to locate sixteen blog posts written by Myat Kaw. They were difficult to find because the website where they were originally posted had been shut down. Danny assumed Andakar's government was responsible for that, hoping to limit the damage Myat Kaw was causing. Fortunately, people who cared about Andakar's future had copied the posts before they were removed and put them up on other sites.

Danny was seriously impressed by what he read. He suspected Myat Kaw might be a world-class hacker who had infiltrated Andakar's most secure networks. That would explain how this anonymous blogger had access to information the military dictatorship desperately wanted to remain secret. There were reports of Andakar covertly purchasing missiles from the Chinese that had made headlines around the world, proof that some German tourists had mysteriously gone missing, and an exposé of the lavish lifestyle enjoyed by Andakar's top generals while much of the country went hungry. The revelations in the blog posts were creating huge problems for the government. Myat Kaw was doing what no one had been able to accomplish for over thirty years—making the country's iron-fisted rulers sweat.

"Daniel." Danny looked up to find Principal Milankovic approaching his table. With nimble fingers, he cleared his screen, replacing Myat Kaw's blog posts with a map of the thirteen colonies. "Have you spoken to Ryan in the last couple of days?"

"Um, yeah—he's really sick."

"That's too bad." The principal regarded Danny with skepticism. "The school emailed his parents but didn't get any response. You're sure they're not off somewhere?"

"No, sir." Danny tried his best to sound convincing. "He has the flu—the *Samoan* flu. So does his mom, supercontagious. Ryan's dad is spending all his time taking care of them."

"The Samoan flu?" Principal Milankovic raised his eyebrows.

Danny had a feeling he'd gone too far, but he couldn't back down now. "Fever, hives—not pretty. Trust me, you're glad he's not here."

The principal nodded. "If you speak to him, please have Ryan remind his parents that the school needs to be notified about all absences."

"Will do, sir! I'm sure it's just an oversight." Danny waited until Principal Milankovic was out of the cafeteria, then grabbed his backpack from under the table. He pulled out John Quinn's laptop and flipped the cover open. One email excuse from Ryan's dad, coming up!

As he was typing, Kasey sat in the chair next to him. "Hey, Danny, whatcha doing?" Danny slammed the lid closed. Smooth, he chided himself, very subtle.

"Nothing much. Just hanging."

"Two laptops? Isn't that a lot, even for you?"

"Sometimes I'm just too much for one computer to handle!"

Kasey laughed. "I bet you are."

So often, Danny didn't know where the cocky things he said came from. He certainly wasn't as confident inside as he acted. The truth was, for years he had felt much more comfortable lost inside digital worlds—video games, the web, challenging hacks—and so he didn't even bother much with Real Life. When he was younger, that had worked well for him. At the small elementary school he attended, Danny had only a couple of friends and spent most of his free time alone.

But everything changed in middle school. Suddenly, he had to deal with an eclectic variety of students in a school with well over a thousand kids. Danny had been overwhelmed at first, not fitting into any particular group and not really knowing how to make friends. People seemed to look right past him, hardly noticing he was even there. He'd had a few tough months and then, one night as he was listening to The Cure's "Just Like Heaven," Danny decided he'd had enough of being ignored.

Taking down his concert poster of Robert Smith, the eccentric and brilliant lead singer of The Cure, Danny had gone to his bathroom. He grabbed a tube of hair gel and squirted a glob of it into his hand. Looking between the poster and his own reflected image, Danny spiked his hair up in every direction just like his musician hero. It was wild, but he loved it. Whoever this new kid looking back at him in the mirror was, Danny liked him.

The next morning, he ripped a few strategic holes in his jeans, then put on a T-shirt and a burgundy sport coat his mom had made him buy for the occasional opera they attended. Danny slipped out of the apartment before his mom saw him, and headed to school, excited but scared.

Nobody had ignored him, that's for sure. For the first time, people paid attention. It wasn't always good—Danny got picked on some, the way anybody does who's different. But he also met some interesting kids who'd never really noticed him before. He wasn't entirely comfortable in his new role, but he faked the confidence he didn't feel. Danny started making friends for the first time. It wasn't until he and Ryan connected a couple of months ago, though, that he found someone he could totally relax with and just be himself. He never had to put on an act with Ryan. And now that his best friend was in trouble, Danny was going to do anything he could to help.

"So I texted Ryan a couple of times, but I didn't get any response," Kasey said. "Is everything all right?"

"He's sick."

"Too sick to answer a text?"

"His, um, hands are *swollen*. You should see his thumbs—they're like cucumbers."

Kasey wasn't buying it. "Look, if he doesn't want to go to the dance with me, I'm not gonna be mad or anything."

"He asked you to the dance?" That was news to Danny.

"No, I asked him. He didn't tell you? I thought you were his best friend."

"I am, yeah, but he's been superbusy lately—and sick. Really, really sick."

Kasey seemed genuinely disappointed. "Whatever. He doesn't want to go. It's fine—

but he doesn't have to avoid me." She stood as Danny's phone dinged with a text message. He opened it instantly when he saw it was from Ryan. "That's him, isn't it? Guess his cucumber thumbs suddenly got better."

"Kasey, wait—it's not what you think." Danny glanced at Ryan's text, a photo of a red-and-gold shield with a white pyramid floating over it and the message: *Can you find out what this is?*

"It's okay. Maybe my brother is right about you two. I just thought you guys were different. Tell Ryan not to bother about the dance. I'll ask somebody else."

She turned to go when Danny blurted out, "His dad's missing, his mom's been kidnapped, and Ryan used a fake ID to sneak into one of the most dangerous countries on earth!" Danny was surprised by his own outburst. "So he's been a little busy."

Kasey stared at him a beat. "Wow. When you lie for someone, you really go for it, don't you?"

But Danny's expression was serious. "I know it sounds crazy. I wish I was lying."

CHAPTER

24

**PANAI,
ANDAKAR**

A re you insane?" Tasha got right in Ryan's face. "You could've gotten yourself killed!"

She'd been waiting for him when he snuck back in the window and was reading him the riot act. Ryan knew she had a point, but he didn't like being treated like a child. "I didn't get killed. Or caught. And I got information we can use."

"A name of some random person who *might* know something about your father, given to you by a stranger in a jail cell."

"It's more than you've found."

Tasha looked like she wanted to clobber him, but Ryan stood his ground. They stared each other down a moment, and then she turned away, struggling to get her temper in check. "You said he's a student?"

"At the Panai Teaching College. Ashin Myek."

"And how do we contact him?" Tasha asked.

"I don't know."

"Where does he live? Does he have a phone number we can call? An email address—anything?"

Ryan realized it wasn't much to go on. "We can check at the college. They must have a directory or something."

Tasha looked out the window past the fire escape. "And you're sure you weren't followed?"

"Positive," Ryan said. "I was careful—that's why it took so long."

Unfortunately, he had more bad news for her. While he was hiding out, Danny had sent him the information he'd uncovered on the logo Ryan had found at the hotel. "This hotel where I went, it's run by the Army Services Intelligence division."

"The ASI? You snuck into a command center for the ASI?" To his surprise, Tasha laughed. "You really *are* insane."

"I didn't know what it was when I went in."

"Well, let me educate you. The ASI is one of

the most feared, hated, and ruthless spy agencies in the world."

"I saw what they're capable of," Ryan said, remembering the brutality of the riding crop striking the prisoner's bare back. "They torture people."

"They do worse than that. They learned from the KGB and China's MSS. And now, they've probably captured your handsome face on numerous security cameras. Congratulations—by tomorrow, you'll be the most wanted man in Andakar."

Ryan leaned against the wall and slid to the floor. Tasha was probably right; with all the monitors he'd seen at the compound, at least one of them likely got a good image of him. His fake identity would be blown soon, and he had no other way to travel. The half-finished puppets hanging around the workshop seemed to stare at him, taunting. Who was he kidding? There was no way he could pull this off. He was in way over his head.

"You need to sleep." Tasha's tone had shifted, becoming gentler. "The adrenaline's wearing off. You're exhausted."

"I'm fine," Ryan muttered, knowing it was a lie.

"Will you just shut up and do what I say for

a change?" She came over, grabbing some of the fabric as she approached. As she had done for herself, Tasha bunched it into a ball. Forcing Ryan to lie on the floor, she placed it under his head like a pillow. "You're no use to anyone like this."

"I can't . . ." Ryan protested. But he never finished, falling instantly into a deep slumber.

CHAPTER
25

**PANAI,
ANDAKAR**

Tasha had been busy.

Since Ryan had zonked out a few hours ago, she had gathered materials to create disguises, found some food, and even tracked down an address for Ashin Myek. She had thought hard about taking the opportunity to ditch Ryan. But the kid had actually done pretty well by getting them a name. He might still prove useful.

She shook him awake, and he stirred groggily. "Rise and shine. Unless you want to hang around here and wait for me all day."

Ryan sat up, rubbing his eyes, his mop of brown hair sticking out in all directions. He looked outside. "It's morning."

"Your powers of observation are astonishing. Here, eat this. And drink the tea, whether you like it or not. Your body needs it." She set down a bowl of cold noodles and a wooden cup of steaming, cloudy tea. Ryan gulped a large bite of noodles and made a face.

"Those are awful," he said.

"They flavor them with fish sauce."

"For breakfast?"

"It's an acquired taste. But it's all we've got, so eat up." Tasha held out a long cotton shirt and one of the traditional sarongs Ryan had seen on the streets of Panai. "When you're finished, change into these. You'll have to leave your backpack. Put your clothes and high-tops into one of the cloth bags."

Ryan took the sarong. "But this is a skirt."

"And you're man enough to wear it well," she teased. "They'll be looking for an American teenager, so we'll hide you in plain sight. You'll look like a local." At the workshop table, she held up a jar of black liquid. "I found some acrylic paint. We're dyeing your hair, too."

Tasha observed Ryan's confusion as he wrapped the sarong around his waist, trying to figure out how it worked. "Don't tell me in all your travels, you've never worn a sarong?"

Ryan looked at her with concern. "I get to keep my underwear on, right?"

"That depends on how wild and funky you're feeling. But yeah, keeping it on is probably a good idea."

When he'd finished the noodles, Tasha pulled on a pair of plastic gloves, and they got busy dyeing Ryan's hair at the sink. As she worked the black liquid through his untamed mane, he admitted, "I nearly got caught last night."

Tasha tugged his hair roughly, eliciting a yelp of pain. "Would've served you right for sneaking out."

"The only reason I got away is because these strangers helped me—some prisoners at the ASI headquarters and then three men at one of the cafés. They didn't have to."

"You seem surprised. The citizens here hate the ASI."

"But they could've been killed. Why would they risk getting caught?"

"Life is full of risk. Sometimes doing what's right is the riskiest move of all." Tasha picked up a paintbrush. "Now shut up and let me concentrate."

Thirty minutes later, they left through the back door. Considering their limitations, Tasha thought she'd done a good job disguising Ryan. Wearing the traditional sarong, long shirt, and sandals, he definitely looked less American. The acrylic paint had turned his hair jet-black. Not as natural as she would have liked, but it helped him blend in a little better.

Tasha had ditched the red wig and sewn a simple, floor-length skirt for herself from fabric she'd found in the workshop. It covered her feet, which allowed her to wear pants and boots hidden underneath. She wrapped an embroidered silk scarf around her head, covering her hair.

"Look down as much as possible so people can't see your face," she told Ryan.

"Are we going to the college?"

"Yes, but we have to hurry. We need to catch Ashin Myek before he leaves his apartment."

"How did you find him?" Ryan asked, as they crossed the street.

"I called my contact. He sent me everything he could dig up on short notice."

Ryan grinned. "Thought you said it wasn't safe to get in touch with your contact until ten this morning? Sounds like I'm not the only one who breaks the rules."

Tasha could see that some food, a few hours of sleep, and a real lead to follow had done Ryan a world of good. He was less anxious this morning, more sure of himself.

She was actually starting to like this kid. Which was a shame.

It made her *real* mission that much harder.

CHAPTER
26

**PANAI,
ANDAKAR**

The Panai Teaching College was in the midst of a celebration of some kind. Ryan could see over a hundred students gathered in the sprawling courtyard of the main building. Some were dancing to traditional music, while others waved banners and twirled paper umbrellas. The plaza was boisterous and busy, a riot of color and noise.

"That's where Ashin Myek lives," Tasha said, pointing to a plain, two-story building at the edge of campus. Students were leaving and walking toward the festival. She held up her cell phone and showed him a photo. Ashin was in his mid-20s with a gaunt face, high forehead, and bushy hair.

"We have to be careful," Ryan said. "The prisoners at the Kali Thawar told me the ASI was rounding up anyone they suspected of being connected to Myat Kaw."

They found a bench that afforded a view of the building and sat, watching students make their way to the plaza. Ryan was having trouble getting used to the sarong, which was wrapped around his waist and knotted in front. He shifted his legs, uncomfortable and not knowing how to sit so it didn't fall open. After fifteen minutes, Ryan's patience was wearing thin. "Maybe we should just go inside and see if he's home?"

Tasha suddenly stood. "There."

Ryan joined her, slinging the cloth bag with his clothes, shoes, and phone over his shoulder. Following Tasha, he spotted Ashin walking with a couple of friends toward the festival. They laughed together over some private joke.

As they closed in, Ryan noticed a man in a dark suit strolling several feet behind Ashin. The cut of the suit and the way the man carried himself reminded Ryan of Aung Win back in New York. He grabbed Tasha's elbow, holding her back.

"What? We're gonna lose him."

"He's not alone." Ryan nodded subtly toward

the man in the suit and Tasha followed his gaze. The moment she saw him, she understood.

Her eyes expertly swept the area. "Another over there."

And Ryan had just noticed a third, this one dressed more casually, but as laser focused on Ashin as the guy in the suit. "At least three of them."

"Come on." Tasha started moving again, keeping pace with Ashin and the men trailing him, but holding back so they weren't seen.

Ryan tried to keep the desperation out of his voice but didn't quite succeed. "We have to talk to him. He's the only person who may know where my dad is."

"We will," Tasha said.

Ashin and his friends made it to the festival, standing together. Revelers in traditional costumes of richly embroidered silk danced to the beat of drums. Huge papier-mâché elephants dotted the crowd. Neon green and psychedelic pink, they bounced and boogied beside others outfitted with more ceremonial Asian decorations. It took Ryan a moment to realize that there were people inside the giant elephants. At least two or three students were hidden under each costume.

Tasha positioned them in the middle of a small crowd of onlookers who were cheering on the dancing elephants. "They're not moving in, just keeping him under surveillance." She looked from Ashin to the ASI agents, calculating a strategy. "If they stay in the crowd, maybe I can get close enough to talk to him."

"But if the ASI suspects anything, they'll pull him in. Probably torture him like that guy I saw. You, too."

Tasha's uncertainty was apparent; she knew this wasn't a good plan. "Like you said, we don't have any other leads and we're running out of time."

She began to move closer to Ashin, when Ryan stopped her. "Wait, I've got a better idea." Before Tasha could protest, he grabbed her hand and pulled her in the opposite direction. Annoyed, she had no choice but to follow.

Just behind the crowd, Ryan had spotted another of the beautiful elephant costumes—only this one was sitting on two wood tables, supporting it from head to tail. Ryan scanned the area, but everyone's attention was focused on the parade. Nobody was paying any attention to the elephant costume.

"You're the butt," he whispered. She glared

at him and he realized what he'd said. "I mean, you're *in* the butt—no, that's not—just take the back, okay?" She rolled her eyes, then nodded.

Keeping low so they didn't attract attention, Ryan pulled back the decorative panels that formed the elephant's body. Tasha dipped underneath, disappearing inside the elephant's torso and Ryan followed. Inside the papier-mâché elephant, it was hot and humid. Ryan discovered that sections of the costume, which had appeared solid from the outside, were actually made of a mesh material that he could see through. It was kind of like looking through a window screen.

Two wooden handles came down from the top of the elephant's head. Ryan grabbed them, glancing over his shoulder to see that Tasha had hold of another handle in the back that held up the tail end. He gave her the signal and they carefully lifted the elephant.

"Who's the thief now?" she said.

Ryan guided them around and into the crowd. Seeing through the mesh made walking challenging, and he bumped into a couple of students as he figured it out. One of them spun around in anger at being hit, but broke into a grin as he saw the elephant head looming over him.

"Dance, *rahu*, dance!" he yelled. The student began to bob and weave, leaving Ryan no choice but to dance with him, moving the handles up-and-down, then side-to-side, creating a rhythmic motion.

"Really?" Tasha whispered.

"All the other elephants are *dancing*. You want me to blend in, don't you?" Ryan moved forward once more, feeling uncoordinated as he walked and controlled the elephant at the same time. Up ahead, he caught sight of Ashin and his friends and maneuvered in his direction. Festivalgoers parted for the elephant, giving Ryan a straight shot at their target.

"We won't have much time," Tasha advised. "Get close and I'll grab him. Work your way deeper into the crowd—the busier, the better."

"Got it." Ryan spotted one of the ASI agents several feet behind Ashin. He navigated so that the elephant's body was between the agent and Ashin, blocking his view, then spat out, "Now!"

Holding the tail handle with one hand, Tasha timed her movements perfectly, reaching out and grabbing Ashin as they passed. Ashin stumbled but managed to stay on his feet, shocked to find himself suddenly inside the elephant. Panic filled his eyes until Tasha whispered, "We're friends of Myat Kaw—keep walking!"

Ryan slowed his pace, giving Ashin an opportunity to get in step with them. "You can't be here," Ashin warned. "I'm being followed!"

Tasha tried to sound comforting. "We know. We just need information. We're trying to find John Quinn—do you know where he is?"

Ryan glanced to his left and suddenly saw the looming figure of one of the ASI agents right beside them. He was searching the crowd and talking into a handheld radio. The man seemed to look right at Ryan, who held his breath as he swerved away. Ryan knew the agent couldn't see inside the costume, but he was unsettled anyway.

Ashin spoke urgently. "I don't know where John is now. I left my car for him several days ago and gave him directions to the village of Thanlin. That was the last I heard of him."

"How far is Thanlin?" Ryan asked, making a wide circle through the crowd.

"Four or five hours depending on how many times the bus breaks down. In the mountains." Ashin looked through the mesh as his friends came back into view, Ryan's circle having brought them around once more. "Good luck!"

As they passed close to his friends, Ashin ducked back out, laughing joyously as if it had all been a lark. His friends laughed with him, making a convincing show of it. Ryan saw one of the ASI agents look at the elephant, then glance down toward Ryan's feet. Ryan could only hope that seeing his sandals and sarong would be enough to convince the agent that nothing was wrong.

Ryan steered the elephant back to where they found it. Two students saw them approaching and were furious, gesticulating wildly and cursing at them. For once, Ryan was happy he didn't speak the language as the owners continued to scold them. Ryan and Tasha placed the costume back on the wood tables and hurried off as the students railed at them.

Moving away from the crowd, Ryan couldn't help smiling at Tasha. "We make a pretty good team, huh?"

She didn't even glance his direction. "I don't do teams."

CHAPTER
27

**NANSANG PROVINCE,
ANDAKAR**

Ryan pulled the paper bag to his mouth, puking for the third time as the rickety bus careened around yet another hairpin turn. By this point, though, he didn't have anything left to heave. The combination of noxious fumes and erratic motion had kept him nauseated since they first started their ascent into the mountains.

The bus was in terrible shape, rattling and spewing gray-black exhaust as it struggled up the incline, gears grinding in complaint at every turn. Ryan couldn't stop glancing out the window, his stomach churning every time he saw the steep drop from the road's edge. He could see straight down to the bottom of a watery chasm hundreds of feet below.

"Why do they go so fast?" he asked Tasha. She barely seemed to notice the wild ride, eyes closed as she tried to nap. "If the bus goes over the cliff, they're gonna die, too."

"They're Buddhists. They believe in karma and rebirth. The drivers figure if we go over, they'll just come back in their next life as something better."

"Great."

They had been traveling for hours. The farther they got from the city, the more rural the area became. Factories were replaced by vast fields of sugarcane and rice paddies. Ryan couldn't help but notice the extreme poverty in which most of the citizens of Andakar lived. Their homes were simple, with wood walls and rusted-out, corrugated metal roofs. Oxen mingled freely with villagers, and barefoot children in threadbare clothes ran alongside the bus, waving. Ryan smiled and waved back. No matter how tough things were, kids always found ways to play.

But as the bus lumbered through the mountains, Ryan had little to smile about. Two hours of twisting and turning made him a wreck. He tried distracting himself with the deck of cards, practicing his sleight-of-hand techniques, but even that didn't work.

"Where are we now?" he asked Tasha.

"Nansang Province. It continues over the mountain range and down to Andakar's border with Thailand."

Ryan remembered the CIA agents in New York showing his mom those photos of his dad. They said he met with smugglers in Muang Tak, Thailand. So maybe his father had used the smugglers to sneak him into Andakar from Thailand? It made sense that he'd return by the same route once he had Myat Kaw. But things must have gone wrong somewhere along the way.

A short while later, Tasha sat up, looking out the window. "We're here—this is Thanlin. Ashin gave your dad directions to this village, which means it probably wasn't part of his original plan."

"Are there any friends of ours here?" The bus jerked to a stop, engine clattering as it died. Ryan, Tasha, and a couple of locals stood, making their way to the front.

"None that I know of," Tasha said. "Don't talk to anyone. I'll take a look around, see if there's anyone I trust enough to ask a few discreet questions."

"What am I supposed to do?"

"Nothing. Got it?" There was no room for argument.

"Got it," Ryan agreed.

Getting off the bus, Ryan quickly tossed his puke-filled bag into the trash. He took a gulp from his water bottle, rinsing out his mouth, then finished the rest. Tasha took off down the street, doing her best imitation of a tourist.

Ryan wandered through the center of the village. It was mostly comprised of little houses with walls made from tightly woven strands of bamboo and thatched roofs. The scenery surrounding it was breathtaking, though. Thanlin was perched on a hillside with sweeping views of the jungle in every direction.

He sat on a ledge and opened his knapsack. Digging to the bottom, Ryan found his last thin box of chocolate treats. The chocolate was probably soft and squishy from the heat, but he didn't care. As he brought the box out, his hand grazed the folded photo of his family.

He wasn't sure if looking at it would give him renewed determination or just make him depressed, but he took it out anyway. As he opened it, he realized that he was being watched.

Trying to act casual, Ryan looked up. A few feet away stood a cute little girl in a Hello Kitty T-shirt, with long black hair and smudges across her nose. She was very curious and pointed at the box of candy in his hand. Ryan held it up.

"This? Yeah, they're really good." He opened the box and pulled out a long stick that was actually a cookie, most of it covered with delicious chocolate. "It's called a pocky stick. It's from Japan. The chocolate's yummy."

Ryan took a bite of the pocky, showing her how tasty it was. He knew the girl probably didn't understand a word he said, but he figured chocolate was a universal language. He pulled another stick out of the box and held it out. "You can try one, if you want."

The girl's eyes got big as she took it from him. She crunched into it with gusto, chomping down until it was gone. Before she finished swallowing the last bite, she was ready for another one. Ryan noticed a few more kids watching from a short distance away and handed her the whole box. "Take it all," he said, then gestured to her friends. "But you have to share, okay?"

The girl nodded eagerly, taking the box. She paused, noticing the photo Ryan had set on the ledge next to him. Her expression clouded as she looked at it. Ryan picked it up, so she could see it better.

"Do you recognize him? This man?" He pointed to his dad and she nodded. Ryan pointed between the picture and himself. "He's my father. Have you seen him?"

The girl took the photo, looking between it and Ryan. Abruptly, she turned and walked away. Ryan grabbed his bag and followed. "Wait—I need that."

She kept going, not looking back. One of the other children suddenly called to the little girl, and she spun around. All of them were instantly on alert, their attention focused toward the entrance to the village. Only now did Ryan hear the sound of approaching vehicles as the kids scattered in all directions.

"Hey!" he called, as the little girl took off running.

But she didn't slow down. Ryan was normally pretty fast, but in the sarong and sandals, he felt clumsy and uncoordinated. As he ran, he noticed villagers hurrying to their homes and disappearing inside. The girl turned the corner, and Ryan lost sight of her.

As he came around the bend, he spotted her

on a rocky path along the cliff's edge. "Please!" he called, when she looked back at him. "I need that picture!" But she took off once more along the path toward a group of trees.

Ryan kicked off his sandals and put on a burst of speed as he sprinted away from the village. It was much easier to run like this, and he closed the distance quickly. As the little girl vanished into the undergrowth, Ryan was only a few steps behind. Bursting through the trees, he stopped, looking around to see which direction she had gone.

Which is when a man's hand reached around from behind him, covering Ryan's mouth and jerking him backward!

CHAPTER
28

**THANLIN,
ANDAKAR**

"Quiet!" Ryan strained to break free as the man spun him around. He was surprised to see the Hello Kitty girl right behind him. The man whispered fiercely, "If anyone sees us talking, my daughter and I will be in great danger."

The girl looked up at Ryan with big brown eyes.

"You understand?" the man asked. Ryan nodded, relaxing enough that the man finally let go.

The girl held out the photo to the man, who studied it, and then looked at Ryan warily. "Who are you?" he demanded.

"Ryan Quinn. That's my father. You know him?"

The man was short, but powerfully built with deeply bronzed skin. His daughter cuddled into his side, and he placed a protective arm around her. She clutched the box of pocky sticks tightly to her chest, her eyes never leaving Ryan.

"He came several days ago," the man told Ryan, handing him back the photo. "He needed to get out of the country. I sometimes take English and European tourists on expeditions into the jungles, so he asked for my help."

"Was he okay? Nobody's heard from him in almost a week." Ryan couldn't stop the flood of questions. "Did you take him somewhere? Do you know where he is?"

"He didn't want me to go with him. I gave him directions to the border. He was fine when he left. But others came looking for him. Soldiers from the ASI."

"Did they find him?"

"I don't know." The man's tone was grave. "There were many of them."

Ryan's heart sank, but he refused to believe the worst until he knew for sure. "Where did he go?"

"Up the mountain and through the jungle. At the top of Mount Bana there is a holy place—the Mae Wong Temples. There are places to hide in the temples—secret chambers known only to the villagers of Thanlin. I hoped he might be safe there."

"Can you take me?"

"You're just a boy—you could never make it. And if the ASI find out I helped you—or your father—they will come after my family."

Ryan didn't want to put anyone else at risk, but he had to do something. "If my dad made it there, then I will, too."

They were interrupted by a shout: "Ryan!" It was Tasha, her tone urgent. Ryan hurried out of the trees and saw her searching for him along the rocky path.

"Tasha! I found someone—"

But she didn't let him finish. "They're here. Two trucks of ASI soldiers just pulled in. Come on!"

Suddenly, a shot rang out and Tasha dropped to the ground. Ryan ducked back, terrified she had been hit. He glanced behind him. The villager had taken the girl's hand and was moving deeper into the trees. Ryan looked between the man and where Tasha had fallen, not knowing what to do.

Then, Tasha stood and scrambled behind one of the big rocks. She was okay—she hadn't been shot! But ASI soldiers appeared, cutting her off from Ryan and the trees. Tasha looked at him across the expanse with a fierce expression. Ryan had the weirdest feeling that she actually seemed *angry*.

Another gunshot reverberated through the canyon, and Tasha had no choice—she raced off in the opposite direction, away from Ryan. They were now separated by a squadron of soldiers with rifles. But Ryan couldn't afford to even think about that. If he lost sight of the villager and the girl, he'd also lose any chance of finding his dad.

He cut back through the trees, only to find that the man was already far ahead. "Wait!" Ryan yelled, his bare feet stinging with every step.

The man didn't slow down until his daughter pulled his arm, urging him to stop. It was just enough time for Ryan to catch up. "Please—at least tell me which way to go."

The man's focus was on getting to safety. "There is no time. If they catch us helping you, they will kill us."

"You're the only chance I have of finding my father." Ryan didn't even try to keep the desperation from his tone.

The man wavered, then let out a heavy sigh. "There is a path—easy to follow, but difficult to climb. It will take you down from Thanlin and up Mount Bana on the other side."

"Can you show me?"

The man debated with himself a moment more, then turned to the girl. He spoke to her in their language and she nodded. "This way," he said to Ryan.

Ryan started after him, then turned back briefly. "Thank you," he said to the girl.

She held out the box of candy and repeated, "Thank you."

Ryan hurried to catch up with the villager. Behind him, he heard soldiers shouting and the roar of more vehicles arriving. He had no idea what lay ahead, but he knew there was no turning back.

Ryan was now completely on his own.

CHAPTER
29

**NEW YORK,
USA**

Ever since Kasey learned what was going on with Ryan and his parents, all she'd thought about was how she could help. Before their walk downtown, Kasey had tried to talk to Ryan a few times during their classes, but hadn't had much luck. He was quiet around her, but she could tell there was something special about him. And she'd been right. Their conversation had been so great. True, she really didn't know him that well yet. But she'd sensed a real connection, like they'd been friends for years. When they talked, it didn't feel like he was interested in her because he thought she was popular but because he cared about what she thought.

Kasey and Danny had met up after school yesterday, and he had shown her what he found in New York's property records database. Danny had tracked down three buildings around the city that were owned by companies with ties to Andakar's military regime. One of them was a warehouse pretty close to their school.

She had convinced Danny they should go investigate the buildings themselves, and he had finally agreed. They were standing across the street from the warehouse now, but they didn't have much time before school started. Kasey had lied to her dad, telling him she was heading in early for a rehearsal. She hated lying to him, but she figured it was for a good cause. With three older brothers and a single father who had raised them all, Kasey had been treated like a breakable doll her whole life. She loved her family but felt increasingly suffocated by them. The Stieglitz men still saw her as a little girl they needed to protect. Well, she was done with that.

"I'm going in," she told Danny.

Danny lowered his camera and looked at her like she was nuts. "You can't just walk in there—these guys have guns!"

"What else are we gonna do? Call the police?"

"I told you, we can't," Danny said. "That Aung Win dude said he'd kill Mrs. Quinn if Ryan told the cops."

"But the police know how to handle this kind of thing. We don't."

"It's not up to us—it's Ryan's call. He thinks if he finds his dad, then he'll know what to do."

"Well, we can't see anything from out here," Kasey said.

They looked back at the warehouse across the street. It was a brick fortress, square and flat with no windows, bearing a sign across the top that read: Assured Moving and Storage. The front door was gated, and a large, rolling metal door for trucks had been closed since they arrived.

"How would you get inside?" Danny asked. "It looks pretty sealed up. We can't just go in through the front door."

"Actually," Kasey said, "that's exactly what we're going to do. Switch the camera to video. I'll ring the bell and see if I can angle it to shoot inside."

"That sounds like a *terrible* plan." Danny went ahead and put the tiny camera in video mode.

"You got a better one?"

"Nope. But that doesn't make yours good."

Kasey took the camera, knowing he was right. She crossed the street, thinking of clever things to say that might get her inside. She could pretend she was a Girl Scout selling cookies—or maybe she should tell them she was working on a school report about the Lower East Side? Those both sounded kind of lame, but they might work. People often underestimated Kasey, assuming she wasn't very smart because she was pretty. Truth was that Kasey was curious about almost everything: How things worked, why people acted the way they did, what other people's lives were like.

Just as she was about to ring the front bell, the metal garage door made a grating sound and began to lift. Thinking fast, Kasey walked right past, stopping instead at the next building down, which was under construction and sur-rounded by scaffolding. She hid behind a beam and watched as the garage door slowly opened. A truck rolled out and idled on the edge of the sidewalk.

Across the street, Danny silently motioned her to stay hidden and safe. But Kasey knew this could be the only chance they had to see inside. In a heartbeat, an idea came to her—crazy maybe, but it might work.

Kasey scanned the scaffolding and spotted what she needed: a jagged edge of metal sticking out dangerously. With only the briefest hesitation because she knew her dad was gonna be pretty pissed, she used the sharp metal to slash a tear in the seam of her jacket. Holding the coat to the metal with one hand, she jerked hard, ripping the sleeve wide open. Kasey ran her hands through her hair, messing it up as much as she could. She hit record on the camera and took off running for the garage door.

"Help!" Kasey screamed, waving her arms in panic. The truck had just started rolling again, but jolted to a stop. "Please, somebody, help me!"

She ran past the startled truck driver and into the warehouse. Kasey stopped in the center of the cavernous space. She spun around as if looking for someone to come to her rescue, but she was actually sweeping the camera in every direction to film as much as she could. The driver jumped out of his vehicle and several workers hurried toward her.

Three men surrounded her, all with East Asian features. One of them was older and seemed to be in charge. "You must leave this place," he said. But he seemed to believe her act, not at all worried that a thirteen-year-old girl might pose a threat.

"This weird man," Kasey cried. "He was following me and then he grabbed my arm and I just ran." Kasey glanced all around the warehouse, hoping for some indication that Ryan's mom might be here. Except for a small office, though, it was one huge open space. Lots of boxes and equipment around, but there was no obvious place to hide a hostage.

"You must go!"

"What if he's still out there?" Kasey knew she was almost out of time, keeping the camera hidden in her palm as she tried to film behind her.

The man finally noticed the awkward motions she was making with her hand. He stepped toward her threateningly, reaching for her hand.

"Watch it!" Kasey snapped, stepping back.

But the man had seen the camera and he grabbed for it once more. Kasey dodged, running for the garage door. The truck driver grabbed her as she passed, but he only caught the torn sleeve. It ripped the rest of the way, coming off completely in his hand!

Kasey dashed out the garage door as the men yelled behind her. She never looked back as she raced toward Danny. "Go! *Go!*"

Danny jumped from his hiding place and ran with her around the block. "I told you it was a terrible idea," he said.

Four blocks and several turns later, they finally slowed down, checking behind them. Breathing heavily, Kasey said, "I think we lost them." She leaned against the wall, her hands and legs shaking. That was the scariest, stupidest, best thing she'd ever done in her life!

"Oh my god, you're as crazy as Ryan," Danny wheezed.

Kasey handed him the camera. "I filmed the whole place, I think. But Ryan's mom isn't there. The warehouse doesn't have any rooms to hide her in."

Danny was disappointed. "There're still two other properties to check. Think we should take a look?"

"Definitely," Kasey said. "But it'll have to wait until after school. First bell's in six minutes and I can't afford a tardy. My dad's already gonna be mad enough I ruined my new coat."

Danny smiled. "Really? You bust into a building filled with guys who might shoot you on sight, run for your life through the streets of New York—and you're worried about a *tardy*?"

CHAPTER
30

**NANSANG PROVINCE,
ANDAKAR**

Gunshots echoed through the night as Ryan fought his way up the hillside. After changing back into his high-tops, T-shirt, and jeans, Ryan had started along the perilous path. The jungle's thick undergrowth made the climb difficult, but Ryan forced himself to keep moving forward. He had been on the run for what seemed like hours and had actually come to look forward to the occasional gunshots. Every time he heard another shot it gave him hope. If the ASI soldiers were still firing, they probably hadn't caught Tasha.

Not much moonlight penetrated the canopy of leaves overhead and, twice already, he had nearly twisted his ankle when he failed to see an obstacle hidden in the shadows. But this wasn't Ryan's first time trekking at night. Over the years, his family had been on camping trips to all sorts of crazy spots: on a camel trek in the Sahara desert, at the top of a volcano in Ecuador, and in the shadow of Mount Everest in Nepal.

During every trip, they would take a "Moon Hike," where no flashlights or lanterns were allowed. As a kid, he'd been scared of the dark and always dreaded these excursions. But when he was eight, they took a trip to Iceland and camped by a series of towering waterfalls. His mom took him out on the "Moon Hike" that night, and they trekked up the falls. At the top, Ryan was shocked to discover the sky was lit up with a cascade of violet and green pulsing lights. It was his first glimpse of the northern lights, the most beautiful thing he'd ever seen. It was also the last time Ryan was afraid of the dark.

Scrambling over a fallen tree, Ryan stopped for a moment, looking back. There was no sign of pursuit, so he took a moment to sit and catch his breath. He pulled out his phone and turned it on, but couldn't get a signal.

During the difficult climb, Ryan had dumped

everything from his knapsack other than food. All that was left was one last piece of fruit, a red mangosteen. He tore it open to reveal the white pulp inside and ate every juicy bite. Getting to his feet, Ryan folded the bag and stuck it in his pocket in case he needed it later.

The steep path got increasingly challenging and for the next ten minutes Ryan struggled. It ended at a vertical outcropping of rock, and Ryan had to find a foothold in order to lift himself high enough to grab the upper edge. Physically exhausted and emotionally drained, it took all the strength he had to haul himself up and over the ledge.

But Ryan was surprised and excited to discover that he'd finally made it to the top. Breathing heavily, he looked out across the plateau before him. Misty fog and silvery moonlight gave everything an eerie glow. Ancient stone temples were scattered across the field, their whitewashed domes pale against the night sky. The villager had told him these were the Mae Wong Temples, a Buddhist stronghold abandoned long ago. Ryan wondered if his father had made it this far.

The man had directed John Quinn to a secret chamber located inside a temple with a gold-plated dome. That was the first place Ryan wanted to check, and he headed directly to the closest of the temples. But in the moonlight, it was hard to tell which domes were gold and which were regular stone.

Ryan was so preoccupied with searching for the right temple that he almost missed the ASI soldier patrolling fewer than fifty yards ahead of him. Just as the soldier turned, Ryan saw him. He dropped to the ground, not moving a muscle. Ryan held his breath for what seemed like forever. Finally, the soldier moved on, passing behind one of the pagodas.

Keeping silent, Ryan raced across the open ground and pressed against another of the numerous temples. Peering around the corner, he saw a second soldier pass in the distance. When the sentry wandered out of sight, Ryan darted toward the next pagoda, using it to shield him from view. Through the fog, he caught a glimmer of light shining off one of the domes, taller than the others. Could that be the gold temple the villager described?

Hearing a shout from behind, Ryan whirled around, just in time to see a soldier raise his rifle and fire. Ryan dodged around the side of the temple as the bullet shattered the stone where he'd been standing.

Ryan sprinted away, zigzagging so he didn't make an easy target. Another shot rang out, this one from the second sentry. They were cornering him from two directions. His best chance to stay alive was to take out these two before they could radio for help—and pray there weren't even more of them lurking in the shadows.

Darting around another building so he couldn't be seen, Ryan abruptly stopped, crouching, waiting silently. The two soldiers yelled to one another as they gave chase, attempting to cut Ryan off and trap him between them. But as the first soldier came around the corner, Ryan swung around and smashed his foot, heel first, into the man's right knee! The soldier screamed in pain as he tumbled to the ground, dropping his rifle. Ryan was pretty sure the kick had broken his leg.

Ryan grabbed the weapon, only to see the soldier wasn't giving up. He had pulled a handgun from its holster. Ryan smashed the butt end of the rifle at him, obliterating the man's nose and knocking him out cold.

Hearing boots approach from the other direction, Ryan pressed his advantage. Instead of running, he dropped the rifle and charged forward, meeting the second soldier just as he rounded the corner. Using his smaller size to his advantage, Ryan grabbed the man around the waist and lifted him straight up. The soldier flipped over Ryan's shoulder, landing on his back with a thud. As he struggled to sit, Ryan delivered a perfect Krav Maga chop to his neck, striking the vagus nerve and rendering him instantly unconscious. The guy dropped back to the ground. He'd be out of it for a while, and when he did wake up, he'd have a heck of a headache.

Ryan turned, only to discover he was staring down the barrel of a rifle. Another soldier! Ryan knew there was no getting away this time. It was over. There was no one left to help his parents now.

But as the person holding the rifle stepped out of the shadows and into the moonlight, Ryan saw it wasn't another soldier, after all. It was a girl, probably only a few years older than him.

The rifle never wavered as her finger hovered over the trigger. She said something to him in Andalese, her tone fierce and accusatory.

Ryan raised his hands in surrender. "I'm sorry. I don't understand."

Her expression changed, confusion replacing suspicion. "Who are you?" she asked, in perfect English.

Ryan's instinct told him that the truth was the only thing that might save him. "My name is Ryan. I'm looking for my father, John Quinn. He came to your country to help Myat Kaw."

She slowly lowered her rifle and looked him right in the eye.

"My name is Lan," she said. "I am Myat Kaw."

PART THREE

NO WAY OUT

CHAPTER
31

**MOUNT BANA,
ANDAKAR**

Lan never intended to become a rebel.

Two years ago, she was just a normal schoolgirl. Well, maybe not normal exactly. Lan's life in Andakar was more comfortable than most kids. She knew that now.

Lan's father was a lawyer with the Ministry of Justice, which meant the family was part of the government's inner circle. That came with a lot of perks: a nice house, plenty to eat, and people to help with the cooking and cleaning. She had good friends and went to a school that was only for the children of Andakar's government workers. If it weren't for her father, Lan would never have even questioned how easy they had it.

But Lan's dad didn't allow her to simply

accept the comfortable life they led. He worked inside the system, but insisted it was only so that he could help change it. He represented the citizens of Andakar in the government's courts where they didn't stand a chance of being treated fairly. Lan's father would fight for them even though he knew it was usually point-less. Occasionally, he would win some small victory. On those rare days, he would be filled with passion, insisting that change would come to Andakar, but that it moved as slowly as the sluggish Chin Yon River.

Back then, Lan was impatient with her fa-ther's lectures. She was fourteen—she was in-terested in her friends and music and boys. What happened outside her comfortable world didn't seem to matter that much.

But everything changed after the car crash.

A freak accident, they told her. Both her par-ents killed instantly. She could barely function. Nothing made sense.

And then her uncle showed up. Aung Win was her father's brother, but the two had grown distant. Lan had not even seen him in over a year. She had always been a little afraid of her uncle. He watched everything with suspicion and disapproval. She didn't know much about him, really. Only that he was high up in the government and had no other family. He disagreed strongly with her father's belief that the people of Andakar should be given more freedom and real justice. The brothers argued about it whenever they were together.

When Aung Win told her that she would be coming to live with him in Panai, she didn't understand at first. She wouldn't leave her friends, her school, everything she'd ever known. Her uncle tried to be comforting, but she could tell he was annoyed by her protests. In the end, she had no choice. It had already been decided. There was nothing she could do about it.

Lan soon learned that her uncle was a general with Andakar's feared secret police, the Army Services Intelligence agency. Her new home was a penthouse on the top floor of the Kali Thawar Hotel. The old hotel was now ASI headquarters, its lower floors housing the strategic command center. The suites on the upper floors had been modernized and now provided luxurious apartments for the ASI's top officers.

From the beginning, Lan and Aung Win had problems. No other kids lived at the Kali Thawar. Lan felt isolated and depressed, lost in this new and unfamiliar place. Her uncle was gone most of the time, leaving her with a caretaker and a teacher who would come to their suite. She was virtually a prisoner in the old hotel.

Eventually, bored and restless, she snuck into her uncle's study—which was, of course, strictly off-limits—and began to explore. This was her first hint of the horrors that her uncle oversaw in his role as the head of the Internal Security Division. From what she could tell, Aung Win's job was to spy on the citizens of Andakar and to arrest anyone suspected of working against the military rulers. She discovered photos of torture that made her run to the bathroom and vomit.

Lan realized she was living among monsters. Not just Aung Win, but the entire ASI and the government itself. She finally understood how sheltered her life had been and how tough it was for most people in her country. She thought often of her father's lectures—how she wished she could hear him go on and on about justice and freedom just one more time! She needed a reason to move on, a purpose. And now she had one.

Inside the walls of the ASI, Lan had access to the country's most closely guarded secrets. All of the ASI soldiers were men, and no one thought anything of the quiet teenage girl who was always around. It took months of watching her uncle and winning his trust, but she gradually discovered the password to his computer and learned the inner workings of the command center downstairs. Piece by piece, Lan gathered intelligence. She taught herself how to get past the security firewalls on the internet that kept Andakar's citizens cut off from the rest of the world. She would use the hated spy agency's own resources against it.

As a child, Lan loved a bedtime story her father told of the monkey and the tiger. The two met in the jungle one day. The tiger put its giant paw on the monkey's tail, pinning it down. The tiger roared and prepared to take a deadly bite. The monkey knew it was hopeless—the tiger was so much bigger than she was—but she didn't give up. Instead, she dug down deep and roared right back at the tiger! The tiger had never been roared at before and was quite surprised. For just a moment, he let go of the monkey's tail. In a flash, the monkey ran away and climbed high into the trees. Lan loved to hear her father do the monkey's roar. The little monkey's name was Myat Kaw.

Using the alias Myat Kaw, Lan began to release the secrets she had uncovered. She learned to hide her tracks and watched in disbelief as the information slowly made its way around the world, outraging the public. For months, she had been exposing the corruption at the heart of Andakar's military rulers. She never set out to be a rebel, but that's what they called her.

Lan realized it couldn't last forever. Her uncle was leading the hunt to find Myat Kaw, so she was able to follow the investigation. They were getting close: tracing the blog posts, breaking through her cyber defenses, cracking down on anyone suspected of supporting Myat Kaw. She knew she'd have to leave soon and made plans to escape.

But she'd waited too long.

Five days ago, Lan had entered the large apartment she shared with her uncle to find Aung Win waiting. He was furious, but his anger was cold and quiet.

"You made a mistake," he told her.

Lan's survival instincts had kicked in. She instantly adopted a passive, confused expression. What was he talking about?

Aung Win showed her a report he'd received on a dissident they'd arrested several days ago. The ASI techs had analyzed his computer and found a communication between the man and someone inside the Kali Thawar. Aung Win admitted he had become suspicious of Lan and the way she had watched his movements all the time, thinking he didn't notice. But he couldn't believe his niece was really capable of betraying him like this.

He had used the dissident's computer to set a trap. He sent an email with a tracking program expertly hidden in the data. And a response had just been received from one of the offices on the second floor. Aung Win held up a tablet that showed surveillance footage of the office: Lan was right there, sitting at the desk using the computer in a room she had no reason to be in.

Aung Win's anger erupted violently then. He had taken her in when no one would! He was the only family she had! How could she do this to him?

But over the past year, Lan had become an excellent liar. She pretended she had no idea what he was talking about, insisting she would never do anything to hurt him after all he'd done for her. It killed her to say those words, but she knew she was fighting for her life.

Aung Win wasn't convinced, but her forceful denials surprised him. He got called away, promising they would finish this when he returned. She would tell him the truth, one way or another. He locked her into her room when he left.

Which was just what Lan wanted. She had a rope stashed outside her window and used it to slide all the way down to the ground. Months of sneaking around the Kali Thawar command center had prepared her for an escape. Within minutes, she made it out of the compound and into the streets of Panai.

If not for John Quinn, she was sure the ASI would have found her within hours—they had eyes everywhere. The American had rescued her, but he'd paid a terrible price.

Now, his son stood in front of her, waiting anxiously for the answer to the question he had just asked.

"Yes," she told him. "Your father's alive."

CHAPTER
32

**MOUNT BANA,
ANDAKAR**

Ryan tied the hands of one unconscious soldier as Lan bound the feet of the other. His head was swimming with the quick download of information she had given him.

"Shot?" he repeated. "How bad? Is he okay?"

"He's getting better. It went straight through his leg."

"Where is he? Take me to him."

"He needs water," Lan said. "We both do. Help me get supplies, then we'll go."

Ryan didn't want to wait another second. "I want to see him now."

But Lan was adamant. "He's feverish and fighting infection. We ran out of medicine and water yesterday. We need to grab whatever we can find before more soldiers show up."

Frustrated, Ryan wanted to argue but knew she was right. "Fine—let's just hurry."

"Are you out here by yourself?" she asked, dragging one of the soldiers out of sight.

"Why?" Ryan grabbed the other one by the ankles and pulled.

"You just seem young, that's all."

"You're one to talk. You've been single-handedly taking on the entire government." Ryan was still having trouble believing this teen-age girl was the notorious Myat Kaw. Lan wasn't at all what he expected. She actually looked rather delicate, short and thin with a round face, high cheekbones, and black hair pulled back into a ponytail. But her eyes betrayed the feroc-ity of a survivor. This girl was a fighter.

"We need to find their jeep," Lan said, scan-ning the area. She led the way, cautiously check-ing around the corner of every temple before moving forward.

"How'd you get hooked up with my dad?" Ryan asked. Lan glanced over, and Ryan could tell she was debating how much to tell him. "I think you can trust me—my dad got *shot* for you."

"Sorry. It's been hard to trust anyone the last few months." Lan kept moving as she spoke, trying to locate the jeep. "A few weeks ago, things started getting really bad. The ASI was coming after me with everything they had. I knew, eventually, they'd find out who I was. I needed a way out of Andakar. Some supporters put me in touch with this group that helps people like me out of bad situations."

Ryan nodded. "The ERC."

"John Quinn contacted me and offered to help. But I thought we still had time. A few days ago, everything went wrong and I had to run. I got word to your dad and then hid out until he could get here." Lan suddenly pointed. "There!"

The jeep was parked under the outstretched boughs of a banyan tree. They watched from behind a stone wall for a few moments, making sure no one else was around, then moved forward.

"I'll take the back," Ryan said. As they searched the jeep, opening bags and searching compartments, he asked, "How did my dad get shot?"

"The ASI agents were always close behind. I think someone in Thanlin must be an informer for them because they were on us almost immediately. We had just made it to the temple grounds when the bullet hit your father. I thought we were dead."

Ryan stopped searching, looking at her. "What happened?"

"Your dad's stubborn. He yelled at me, and I finally snapped out of it." Ryan remembered plenty of times his dad had pushed him in the same way. Lan continued, "We barely made it to the temple. John was about to pass out by that point. And then I couldn't find the secret entrance the guide told us about. I could hear more soldiers arriving, shouting. They were so close."

Reliving it, she lapsed into silence. Ryan prodded her, "But you made it."

"Yeah. I dragged him inside and we were finally safe. We had a first-aid kit and medicine in our packs, so I patched him up the best I could. I've given him all the antibiotics. His fever has come down a lot since yesterday." She held up two canteens. "Water."

Ryan realized that she had probably saved his father's life. Of course, his dad would've never been here in the first place if not for her.

He unzipped a canvas bag, dumping out the ammunition inside. "Here—we can carry everything in this."

Lan tossed him the canteens and a flashlight she pulled out of the glove compartment. "I don't think the ASI knows he got shot. The area was crawling with soldiers that night and all the next day. They searched everywhere, but then they all left except for the two we tied up. The rest moved on toward the border. They must think we got away."

The squawk from a radio startled them both. Lan found it wedged between the front seats, the size of a brick with an antenna sticking out the top. She listened to two voices communicating for a moment, then translated for Ryan. "We're okay for now. They're searching on the far side of Mount Bana."

Ryan felt his stomach clench. "Did they say anything about capturing anyone?"

"No."

So there was still hope for Tasha. Ryan found a box filled with rations, cans of meat and individual meal bars, and dumped the whole thing into the bag. Lan clipped the soldiers' radio to her pants as Ryan zipped the canvas bag, slinging it over his shoulder. "Let's go."

Their raid complete, Ryan and Lan made their way to the temple with the golden dome. Its walls were covered with elaborate depictions of scenes from the life of the Buddha. Vines covered much of the surface, wrapping across the stone like serpents consuming the ancient structure. Lan ducked into the pitch-black entrance without hesitation, swallowed by the shadows.

With its ghostly emptiness and the buzz of jungle insects echoing all around, the place gave Ryan the creeps, but he fought his anxiety and followed.

Inside, shafts of moonlight lit the temple with a pale glow. He was in a huge room, the ground littered with debris. Lan stood in front of a massive, solid wall.

"Help me. It's heavy."

Confused, Ryan approached. A sculpture of a man and woman, palms pressed together in prayer, was carved into the stone. They were kneeling on some kind of raised altar engraved with intricate symbols. Lan put both hands on the edge of the altar as if to push it.

"It's a solid wall," Ryan said.

"That's exactly what the king's guard believed when they came to slaughter the monks that lived here five hundred years ago. They were wrong." With a grimace, Lan pushed on the altar and, to Ryan's amazement, it moved. She looked back. "You just gonna stand there?"

Ryan joined her and, together, they pushed. The sculpture was heavy but had been engineered to move smoothly. It pivoted on its axis, revealing a dimly lit tunnel just beyond. When it was wide enough, they slipped through the opening, and then pushed the stone back into place.

The tunnel wasn't long but it led to a hollowed-out chamber. A battery-powered lantern gave enough light for Ryan to see the crumpled form of his father resting against the far wall.

John Quinn raised his head, looking up in utter disbelief. "Ryan . . . ?"

"Hey, Dad. You're not an easy guy to find."

CHAPTER
33

**MOUNT BANA,
ANDAKAR**

Seeing his father again, Ryan remembered a time when he must have been around five years old. His dad was about to leave on another of his many trips and Ryan begged him not to go. It was the third time in a month he'd left. When Ryan was little, he had always missed his dad to the point of tears.

John had pulled his son up into his arms and held him close. He smelled like he'd just shaved. "I know it's hard to be apart," his father told him. "But the work I do, it's important. It makes a difference in people's lives."

"I don't care," Ryan had insisted. "I just want you here."

"You might not care now. But one day, I hope

you will. You know how much I love you, right?"

Begrudgingly, Ryan had nodded.

"And I always come back, don't I? No one in the world is more important to me than you and your mother. So give me a kiss, and we'll be back together before you know it."

Now, Ryan sat next to his dad on the hard, stone floor of the temple. John's leg was bloody and bandaged, his face filthy. Was this what those trips had always been like? How many times had Ryan come this close to losing his father and never even known it?

"The leg's healing. It's just taking time." John was doing his best to convince Ryan he felt better than he looked.

"You need a hospital," Ryan said.

"I'll be okay. Another couple of days of rest and I can travel." John took a long drink from one of the canteens. "You shouldn't be here."

Ryan was confused—it sounded like his dad was mad at him. "You shouldn't be, either." Across the chamber, Lan ate quietly, trying to give them privacy. But in this small room, Ryan knew she could hear every word.

"Where's Mom?" Dad asked.

"I don't know."

"She's not with you?"

Ryan lowered his voice. "She's been kidnapped. Because of *this*. Because of her."

"What?" John's tone was sharp, not caring
that Lan could hear them. "What happened?"

"These guys were following me. Then, they
came to the house. I tried to fight them off,
but . . . I wasn't good enough. They took Mom.
They were from Andakar—the one in charge is
called Aung Win."

"Aung Win is in New York?"

"He was a couple of days ago. You know
him?"

But it was Lan who answered. "Aung Win is
my uncle. He's a general in the ASI."

Ryan's dad was confused. "He targeted my
family, which means he knows who I am. How
could he have identified me? We were careful."

"I did exactly what you told me," Lan said.
"I only used that private chat room you set up,
and I never wrote anything down."

"No one's blaming you." John turned to Ryan.
"Is Mom okay? Have you talked to her?"

"She was when I left. It's why I came." Ryan
glanced at Lan, not sure how to continue with
her standing right there. Lan understood and
moved away, sitting back down against the wall.

"Aung Win wants to trade," Ryan whispered.

"Mom for her. He said we have five days. That's three days from now."

"That's not going to happen," John said. He tried to stand before Ryan could stop him. "We have to get home."

"Dad, stop—"

John faltered, grabbing his leg, grimacing in pain. Ryan helped him back down as Lan came over, opening a bottle of pain pills from the medical kit. "Give him these. They're the last two."

Ryan helped his father take the pills and sip some water. "We'll figure it out, Dad. Mom's gonna be okay." He said the words but didn't really believe them.

For several minutes, John leaned his head back against the wall, eyes closed. When he opened them, he looked at Ryan. "You must have a lot of questions."

"You think?" Ryan was glad to see his dad smile. For a brief moment, it felt almost normal.

"But I have one first," John said. "How did you even get here?"

"It wasn't that hard. I just used my new credit card. The one I found with my fake passport in the secret room behind the wall of your study." Ryan couldn't keep the bitterness out of his voice. "And then I tagged along with this really obnoxious woman who showed up on a motorcycle. Turns out, she knew more about my parents than I did."

John's expression clouded. "Wait—are you talking about Tasha Levi?"

"Yeah. We got separated."

"Why is Tasha here?"

"She's trying to help me find *you*. Which may have gotten her captured or killed!" Ryan knew he must be exhausted because it was hard to keep his emotions in check. Now that he was with his dad, part of him just wanted to let go and be a kid. To throw a tantrum or even cry, which he almost never did. Instead, he asked, "When were you gonna tell me about the ERC?"

"When you were ready."

"You didn't think I could handle the truth?"

"Mom and I wanted you to have a normal life. We've been training you practically since you were born. But you needed to be old enough to make your own decisions before you chose whether to get involved or not."

"I don't want to be involved. And I don't want you to be, either. I just want to go back to our regular lives and forget all this." Ryan could see the disappointment in his father's eyes, but he didn't care. He'd believed if he could just find his dad, then everything would be all right. John Quinn would figure out what to do. He always had.

But looking at him now, Ryan knew his father wasn't in any condition to fix this situation. Not in time to help Mom. Only three days were left before Aung Win carried out his threat to kill her if he didn't get Myat Kaw. And it would take a whole day just to fly back to New York.

Which meant that time was running out fast.

Ryan and Lan locked eyes across the room. He had the feeling she could tell exactly what he was thinking: *He'd make whatever sacrifice was necessary if it meant saving his mom.*

CHAPTER
34

**NEW YORK,
USA**

anny and Kasey met after school, sitting close together on a courtyard bench so they could share Danny's computer. He had uploaded the video recording Kasey shot of the warehouse, making it easier to see on the bigger screen.

"What *is* all that stuff?" Kasey asked, pointing to the boxes stacked all around. "I know they weren't hiding Ryan's mom there, but they sure seemed like they were being secretive about something."

Danny highlighted the area of the screen with the boxes and hit a couple of keys. The image enlarged so they could see the side of one of the boxes, which was labeled: LTV Technologies. Danny Googled the company. "Looks like LTV does a lot of work with the US military. Wow—missile-guidance systems, lasers—this is super-high-tech."

"The United States would never let LTV sell that kind of stuff to a dictatorship like Andakar. It's too dangerous."

"Which means they're probably stealing the technology, then shipping it back to Andakar secretly." Danny fast-forwarded the video to another section showing a small forklift moving a stack of crates. "Yeah, see there? Those crates are marked with a Red Cross logo. I bet that's how they get it all out of the country."

Kasey was excited. "We could use this with the police. I bet this is enough for them to arrest those guys. Maybe they can force them to tell where Ryan's mom is?"

"But what if they don't know? Or what if this Aung Win finds out the police are asking questions and just kills her?"

Kasey wasn't ready to give up on her idea, though. "He could do that anyway. We can tell them they have to be careful."

Danny thought about it and finally nodded. "Maybe you're right. But let me email Ryan first. Make sure he's cool with it."

"Deal."

As Danny typed the email, Kasey stood. "But we're still checking out that other address to-night, right?"

"Will you be able to sneak out?" Danny asked.

"I think so. My dad's got some event, so it's just me and my brothers. I'll tell them I'm crash-ing early and close my door." Kasey seemed un-sure, admitting: "I've never snuck out before."

Danny nodded. "Me, neither. My mom'll ground me for a year if she finds out."

"Then maybe you'd better not do it." Danny and Kasey both jumped at the voice behind them. The African American woman was tall and imposing, dressed in a dark blue suit and wearing sunglasses. "Sneaking out can lead to all kinds of trouble."

Kasey recovered first, facing the woman. "It's really rude to eavesdrop on people."

"But you hear such interesting things." The woman smiled, taking off her sunglasses and staring at Danny. "You're Danny Santiago?"

"Nope. Never heard of him." Danny stuffed his laptop into his bag and stood next to Kasey.

"Danny, my name is Agent Calloway." The woman flashed her credentials, revealing the bald-eagle logo of the Central Intelligence

Agency. "I'm concerned for a friend of yours."

"For Kasey?" Danny widened his eyes in mock surprise. "Kasey's fine—aren't you, Kasey?"

Agent Calloway smiled, but she wasn't at all amused. "You know who I mean. Ryan Quinn. He may be in trouble, and I'd like to help."

Before Danny could deny it, Kasey cut him off. "What do you know about Ryan?"

The agent turned her cool gaze on Kasey. "I know that he hasn't been seen since Monday evening. Neither has his mother. And his father's been associating with some bad men. I'm afraid that somehow Ryan and his mom got caught in the middle."

"Wait," Kasey said. "You think Ryan's dad is some kind of criminal?"

"I'm not sure. That's why we want to talk to him. But maybe you know something about him that I don't?"

"He's a hero, not a criminal—"

Before she could say anything more, Danny jumped in. "That's right—a *hero* to all of us kids who like to hang out at their house—and order pizza and sodas!" Both Kasey and Agent Calloway were perplexed by Danny's outburst. "Because John Quinn orders great pizza! And buys tons of soda. To drink. Which is totally heroic."

Agent Calloway regarded the two of them. "Your friend could be in danger. You sure there's nothing you'd like to tell me?"

"Ryan's just sick," Danny said, with a warning look at Kasey. "But if we hear from him, we'll tell him you're looking."

Agent Calloway pulled business cards from her suit pocket. "You do that. Here's my number." She gave a card to each of them. "I really do just want to help."

She stared at them each a moment more, letting her words sink in, then moved off. When she was out of earshot, Kasey turned to Danny. "Why do they think Ryan's dad is a criminal?"

"Ryan said they had some pictures of Mr. Quinn with this notorious smuggler in Thailand. He was probably paying the guy to smuggle him into Andakar, but they don't know that."

"So let's tell them. I mean, what are we doing? This is crazy—we're being questioned by the *CIA*! If they know the truth, maybe they'll help him."

"We can't, Kasey." Danny suddenly realized he might have made a mistake getting Kasey involved. She had a point—this was out of hand, and now he'd made her a part of it.

"Why not?"

"Because what they do—this whole Emergency Rescue Committee thing—it *is* illegal. They use fake passports to sneak into countries. Probably bribe officials and hack into government records. Sneak across borders. Who knows what else? They could get arrested for any of those things."

"That's stupid—they're *helping* people," Kasey insisted.

"I know. And they could pay a terrible price for it if we're not careful." Danny understood her frustration. "Look, don't worry about checking out that building tonight. I'll probably just blow it off anyway."

"No, you won't," Kasey said. "You're just saying that because you think I'm freaking out. And I guess I am a little."

"It's a completely justified freak-out."

"Hey, Kasey!" They both turned to see Drew Stieglitz, Kasey's brother. "Come on, let's go!"

Kasey grabbed her backpack. "If I can get out, maybe I'll see you tonight."

"You don't need to," Danny said, and he meant it.

"Text me if anything changes." She took off, running to join her brother. Steeg glared at Danny like he wanted to rip his head off. Danny smirked and waved, just pissing off the muscular jock even more.

And that gave Danny the only smile he'd had all day.

CHAPTER
35

**MOUNT BANA,
ANDAKAR**

ake up. They're coming."

Ryan turned over as Lan shook him. He was groggy and his body ached from sleeping a few hours on the stone floor. But the alarm in Lan's expression snapped him into focus.

"Soldiers?"

Lan held up the radio they had taken from the jeep. "I had to go outside to get a signal. But I heard them talking. The two guards we tied up didn't report in, so they're sending a squad."

Ryan realized that Lan was whispering. She also had her backpack on. "What are you doing?"

"Making a run for it before they get here."

"That's crazy. We'll stay here—they didn't find you before."

"That's only because they thought we'd escaped. That we were heading to the border. I know the ASI. If they think there's a chance we're here somewhere, they'll burn all the temples to the ground." She looked over at John, who was still sleeping. "And your father can't travel yet. He needs at least another day or two."

Ryan knew she was right, but he still didn't understand her plan. "So what're you gonna do?"

"Lead them away," Lan said. "I'll make sure they see me. If they follow me, then they'll leave you and John alone. They won't even know you're here."

"They'll kill you."

"Maybe. I just don't want them to catch me. That would be much worse." Lan stood and Ryan got up, going after her.

"Don't do this—we can all wait it out together."

"I made the choice to become Myat Kaw, not you or your father. I'll deal with it." She turned back. "Tell your dad *thanks*."

Ryan didn't know what to do as she disappeared into the tunnel that led to the exit. This was suicide. Or worse—he'd seen the kind of torture the ASI used. What would they do to someone who had spilled all their most-guarded secrets? Ryan didn't even want to imagine.

This wasn't his problem. So why did he feel responsible? He'd just met this girl! But it didn't seem right. She'd been so brave, standing up to these tyrants and risking everything. And now they were probably gonna catch her and make her suffer and—

Ryan reacted without thinking. He grabbed his own bag, stuffing a flashlight and a couple of the meal bars inside. He heard the grinding of the stone moving at the entrance as he closed the bag and slung it over his shoulder.

"What's going on?" Ryan turned to find his dad sitting up. "Where's Lan?"

"The ASI's coming. We're gonna lead them away from here."

"No, you're not!" John tried to stand, but Ryan went to him. He put a hand on his dad's shoulder, keeping him from rising.

"I am, Dad. Lan's already gone and I can't let her try to do it on her own. She's got a better chance if I'm there to help."

"It's too dangerous—you're not ready."

"I found you, didn't I? I got here on my own, and, somehow, I'm gonna get Lan out of Andakar. Besides, what choice do we have? If the ASI catches Lan, what do you think Aung Win will do with Mom? You think he's really gonna just let her go?"

John wanted to argue, but Ryan could tell that he agreed. Once Aung Win had what he wanted, he'd make sure there was no one left alive who could reveal what had happened. They had to keep Lan safe, not just for her own sake, but for Jacqueline's.

"Get my bag," John barked.

John sat against the wall as Ryan grabbed the pack and handed it to him. John dug inside, pulling out a passport, some Baggies, and a roll of fabric tape. "This is Lan's passport. It's fake, but it's top-quality. It'll get her across the border into Thailand."

"Okay," Ryan said, about to put it in his bag.

"No." His dad stopped him. "Always keep everything important wrapped up tight and taped to your body. Passports, cell phone, emergency money."

Ryan nodded, glancing toward the exit. "I have to go."

John held his arm tight. "You need to make your way down the mountain to the town of Hodaw. You should get cell reception once you cross to the other side of Mount Bana. Memorize this number." John spouted out a ten-digit number.

"Why?"

"Just do it." John was all business, giving Ryan the sense of what he must be like on a mission. He said the number once more, then made Ryan repeat it.

"Tell the man who answers to initiate the extraction out of Hodaw. His name is Simon McClelland. He'll tell you what to do next."

"Is he the smuggler?" Ryan asked, remembering the CIA's questions.

John was obviously surprised Ryan knew, but didn't waste time on it. "You can trust Simon. I helped him out of a bad situation once."

Ryan stood. He had to go now or risk losing Lan. "There's enough food and water here for a week. Will you be okay?"

"Don't worry about me. I'll follow as soon as I can put pressure on my leg. When Aung Win calls, try to stall him. See if you can buy us a couple of more days so I can deal with him."

"I'll try." Ryan headed for the tunnel.

"Ryan." Worry and fear were etched across his dad's face. "Be careful. You know how much I love you, right?"

Ryan remembered his father's same words all those years ago when he was a boy. He tried his best to offer the reassurance his dad had once given him: "We'll be together again before you know it."

But neither one of them seemed convinced that was the truth.

CHAPTER
36

**MOUNT BANA,
ANDAKAR**

They had been traveling since just before dawn. As the temperature rose, the sun finally burned off the morning fog. This side of the mountain was rockier, the descent slippery and treacherous. Lan had boots, but Ryan's high-tops sucked for this kind of climbing, and they still had another four hours of trekking ahead.

They didn't talk much, hiking together in silence. Lan had pretended to be upset when Ryan joined her, but he was pretty sure she was secretly relieved. As they left the temple grounds, they made sure the tied-up guards saw which direction they headed. They needed the squad to follow them so Ryan's dad would be safe.

Lan had the soldiers' radio turned low. "I'm sorry about what's happening," she said. "It's my fault your mother and father are in danger."

"No, it's not. They chose this kind of life. I think danger comes with the territory."

"Sounds like you don't approve."

"I just want a normal life. Getting chased by soldiers with machine guns is definitely *not* normal." As they continued along the rocky path, Ryan realized he knew almost nothing about Lan. There was undoubtedly a lot more to her than her blog posts. "Where are your parents?" he asked.

"They died. A car crash." Lan kept walking, not looking at him.

"That's terrible. I'm sorry." Ryan didn't know what else to say. Maybe he should've just kept his mouth shut.

After a few steps, Lan spoke. "I think the idea of a 'normal' life is a lie. It was for me, anyway. It's like living inside a bubble. All these horrible things are going on around us, but we just pretend they're not there."

"We can't solve everyone's problems," Ryan said.

"We can't just pretend everything's fine, either."

Ryan had seen a lot in his travels. He knew firsthand how hard some people had it. He had to admire that Lan had actually done something to help. And it had cost her—she was on the run from the only home she'd ever known. He was starting to understand the sacrifice she had made when she became Myat Kaw.

"I think what you did was really brave," he said.

"Brave or stupid." Lan smiled as Ryan offered her a hand, helping her down from a ledge. "I'm still not sure."

"Sometimes brave and stupid aren't that far apart."

Over the next half hour, they talked. She told him about living with Aung Win and how she learned to sneak around the Kali Thawar. He told her about New York City and the kids who went to his school. Lan was fascinated by all the places he'd lived around the world.

"That's what I want to do," she told him. "Travel everywhere. See new things all the time. It sounds great."

"There were a lot of cool things about it, I guess," Ryan admitted. "Definitely better than living with your uncle."

"Anything's better than that. He was so angry when he found out I was Myat Kaw."

Ryan stopped short. "He knows it's you?"

"That's why he's desperate to get me back. He doesn't want his bosses to find out who I am. If they learn Myat Kaw is his niece, they'll know exactly where all that top secret information came from. He'll be ruined. Probably even executed."

They could use that to their advantage, Ryan thought. "Maybe if you agreed not to post anything else, he'd agree to let my mom go? As long as he leaves you alone, you promise not to tell anyone who Myat Kaw really is."

Lan didn't respond, but it was clear she didn't think much of that idea.

"It might work," Ryan added.

"I wish it were that easy. It would be safer for me if the world never found out who I really am. But my uncle won't ever stop. Not if he thinks I pose a threat to him. Eventually, he'll find me."

Ryan knew in his heart she was right. He'd seen Aung Win in action. He was ruthless and not the kind to leave loose ends.

Lan's hand flew to her mouth as she thought of something. "Oh my god . . . the phone."

"What phone?"

"Your dad's." Lan turned to him, looking

horrified. "I've been trying to figure out how my uncle discovered your father was involved. We were always careful—all our messages were encrypted. But the night he was shot, I was so scared. I wasn't thinking straight, just trying to get away. We barely made it to the temple and it was too dark to see. I felt the phone inside his pocket. So I grabbed it and turned it on— just for the light, to be able to find that secret door. When John saw what I'd done, he made me shut it off immediately."

Ryan understood what had happened. "Cell phones can be traced and the number identified. Even when you're not making a call."

"Which means it really *was* my fault. Them finding you, your mom getting taken . . ."

"Don't say that," Ryan said. "You were just trying to survive, doing what—"

"Ryan!" Lan leaped forward, shoving Ryan so hard that both of them tumbled to the ground as—*boom!*—a shot echoed across the mountainside. As they scrambled to their feet, she pointed down the hill. "There!"

Far below, Ryan saw soldiers spreading out across the landscape. They weren't getting past them. Ryan looked uphill instead. "This way!"

Ryan veered toward a thick clump of trees as

more shots rang out. Using the foliage as cover, they ran, jumping rocks and fighting through underbrush. Lan stumbled and hit the ground hard. Ryan ran back, grabbing her hand and forcing her to shake off the pain and keep going.

They made it to the top of a ridge. In the distance, Ryan spotted more military vehicles racing toward their location. As he tried to figure out which way to run, Lan held the radio to her ear, listening closely. "They called for helicopters," she reported.

They couldn't go back down the mountain. But up above, the jagged cliffs appeared impossible to scale. That left no choice but to keep moving around the side of the mountain, the opposite direction from where they wanted to go. Every step was taking them deeper into Andakar and farther from the border with Thailand.

"They're getting closer," Lan warned.

"Let's go." Ryan forged a trail, choosing at every fork to go deeper into the underbrush and, hopefully, make it harder for the soldiers to follow. They might be able to hide if they could put enough distance and obstacles between themselves and the enemy.

After fifteen minutes of relentless running, Lan was out of breath and struggling to keep up. A dull roar became noticeable as they made it through a rough patch of underbrush. "Is that a helicopter?" Lan asked, looking up.

Ryan searched the sky but couldn't see anything. The roar seemed to be coming from all around. Ryan was starting to get a bad feeling about it when he burst through a thick growth of trees and into a clearing. He came to an immediate halt, not believing what he was seeing.

"They're catching up," Lan said as she crashed through the underbrush. She rushed into the clearing and nearly knocked into Ryan.

Lan froze, seeing what Ryan was staring at: Ten feet ahead, the ground abruptly ended in a sheer drop into a deep chasm. The source of the roar became clear. Fifty feet below, a raging river with white-tipped rapids swept its way through the jungle.

They were trapped. There was nowhere left to run.

CHAPTER 37

**MOUNT BANA,
ANDAKAR**

W e don't have time for this—we have to run!" Lan glanced nervously back at the trees.

Ryan ignored her. He put the fake passport his dad had given him into a plastic Baggie and sealed it up. "Hold this against your stomach."

Lan was confused, but lifted her shirt and did as Ryan requested. Quickly, he wrapped the fabric tape around her middle, circling her body twice to secure the Baggie. "Do we have to do this now?" she asked impatiently.

"We can't risk losing the passports." Ryan pulled his cell phone from the pocket of his jeans and transported it into another Baggie with his own passport, resealing it quickly. "This phone's supposed to be waterproof, but I'm not risking it."

Lan suddenly understood: "Waterproof?" She looked at the rapids below them. "I'm not a very good swimmer."

"Bet you're better at it than dodging bullets." Ryan taped the Baggie with the passport and phone around his own torso, and then took Lan's hand. He had to practically drag her to the edge of the cliff. Down below, the river snaked along the canyon, cutting through the bamboo and boulders with ferocious power. "When you hit the water, cross your arms over your chest and try to stay on your back. Keep your feet out ahead of you so your boots hit the bottom first. Okay?"

"No, not okay!"

Ryan tried to sound like this was no biggie, but he didn't quite pull it off. "One—two—" Ryan yelled, grabbing her hand once more.

"I can't—" Lan jerked her hand away as a bullet struck the tree just behind them, scattering leaves everywhere.

"THREE!" Ryan yelled and they leaped from the cliff. For a moment, it felt as if they hung suspended in air. Then, both screaming, they plummeted to the water below.

Ryan hit the river at an angle, slicing through the current. He spun around as the water tossed him end over end. Unable to tell which way was up, he struggled to keep his mouth closed. If water got in his lungs, he'd be done. He had to get to the surface.

His shoulder slammed into a boulder, knocking the air out of him. But then he saw bright light above—the sun! The current slowed slightly and Ryan kicked, propelling himself toward the light. He was running out of breath, but he forced himself to keep kicking.

Ryan finally burst to the surface, gasping for air. Paddling hard, he turned himself around so he was facing forward and tried to float on his back. It was nearly impossible—and now he was heading right for a series of rapids.

He tried to slow himself, paddling backward furiously as he looked around for something, anything to slow him down.

"Lan!" he yelled, though it came out more a strangled cry than the shout he was attempting. Ryan felt the first stirring of panic that she might have drowned—

But then Lan popped to the surface ten feet ahead of him! Her arms thrashed in desperation as her head bobbed up and down under the water. She wasn't going to make it, Ryan realized. She'd swallowed a lot of water and would drown unless he did something. "On your back," he yelled, but she either couldn't hear him over the rapids or wasn't paying attention to anything but her own survival.

The next set of rapids was just ahead. Lan needed help. With a surge, Ryan swam toward her, the river's momentum helping him close the distance.

Ryan was going so fast, he practically slammed into her. He grabbed Lan and the look of utter panic in her eyes was all the motivation he needed. Exhaustion creeping in, he spun her around so she faced the sky. "I've got you. Just relax—trust me!"

Ryan pulled her close on top of him and wrapped his arms around her waist. She was small enough that his legs extended beyond her own and, as they hit the next set of rapids, he was able to use his feet to help them navigate the boulders.

They rode the white water, twisting through the curves like they were riding an Olympic toboggan. Ryan's hip slammed into a rock and his head bashed against a branch, but he held her tight. No matter what, he wouldn't let go.

At last, they shot out of the final rapid and into a quieter section of the river. For several seconds, they floated, but Ryan could already feel his feet starting to sink. Not wanting to let Lan go, he held her with one arm while using the other to keep them above the surface.

"You okay?" he asked in a hoarse whisper.

Lan gasped, having difficulty catching her breath. "Fantastic."

Ryan couldn't help but smile. Up ahead, he could see the wide river made a sharp turn. On the side closest to them, an island of rocks and broken bamboo stalks offered the best opportunity to land. He paddled in that direction, but as they approached, the current accelerated.

"Ryan," Lan said, "do you hear that?"

A sound like low, rolling thunder was coming from around the bend. Ryan used his one free arm to stroke even harder, steering them toward the island. Stretching out, Ryan managed to grab hold of a thick bamboo pole, hoping to use it to pull them to safety. But the bamboo wasn't rooted in anything and it wrenched free in his hand.

As they whipped around the bend, the river flowed faster and the lip of a waterfall came into view. Knowing he wouldn't be able to keep hold of Lan against that kind of force, Ryan dragged the bamboo pole under their arms.

"Hold on!" he yelled, as they raced toward the falls.

The bamboo offered just enough resistance to allow them to keep their legs raised high, avoiding the rocks below the surface.

Screaming in unison, they flew over the edge!

CHAPTER

38

**NEW YORK,
USA**

anny glimpsed the shadow of someone sneaking up behind him just as a
hand grabbed his shoulder. Certain he
was about to be killed, he screamed, spinning
around so fast he lost his balance and fell backward, landing on his butt.

But it was only Kasey, who shook her head.
"Jumpy much?"

Danny picked himself up, checking to make
sure he hadn't damaged his remote control in
the fall. He was happy to see her, even if he
wasn't going to let her know that. "Get in here
before someone sees you!"

Danny stepped aside so Kasey could join him
in the alcove where he was hiding. Across from

them was the final address on the list of properties owned by Andakar's government that
Danny had found. It was an old building on this
cobblestone street in SoHo, a trendy section
of New York that had once been nothing but
factories and sweatshops. Though some of the
stores along the block had been updated and
turned into stylish shops, the area maintained
its oppressive, industrial feel.

Danny and Kasey were hidden in the shadows of a stairway that led down to the basement entrance of a bakery. The shop was closed
for the night, so Danny thought it was probably
safe.

"I didn't think you were gonna come," Danny
said.

"My brother was watching me pretty close. I
finally told him I was going to do homework and
go to bed, and just shut my door. Didn't you get
my text?"

"I left my phone at home," Danny explained.
"My mom's out late tonight, but she checks the
GPS on my phone so she always knows where
I am."

"I thought you were this tech genius. Can't
you just disable it?"

"Of *course* I can—give me a little credit. But

sometimes it comes in handy. Like tonight, because she thinks I'm still at the apartment doing my homework."

Kasey noticed the remote control Danny carried. It had a short antenna, two separate joysticks, and a screen right in the middle. "What's that?"

"It's how we're gonna see inside without you doing anything crazy again." From the ground, Danny picked up a remote-control flying drone that had mini helicopter rotors at the end of each appendage. "The XTL Specter with a few Danny Santiago upgrades!"

Underneath the rotors was an electronics rig that housed a tiny camera mounted on a swivel platform. Danny moved the joysticks on his controller and the camera pivoted back and forth. The camera's video feed appeared right on the controller's display screen.

"Your very own spy cam." Kasey looked across the street at the building. "The apartments all look empty. Is anybody even living there?"

"We'll find out. Everything's closed up in the front, and there's no way to get around the sides."

"So what do we do?"

"We go over the top." Danny punched a button on the Specter and the rotor blades started to spin faster and faster, until the drone suddenly lifted straight up. Kasey stepped out of the way as Danny told her, "I made it superquiet—like a stealth drone. Plus, I improved the electronics so it has a five-hundred-yard range and can fly faster than thirty miles an hour."

Eerily silent, the Specter rose above the empty street, zipping sharply from side to side as Danny tested his reflexes with the controls. Kasey looked over his shoulder at the display screen, amazed at the crisp images the camera transmitted.

Danny guided the Specter up the front of the five-story building. All the windows had drapes or blinds pulled across them, and there were no lights on anywhere.

"Weird in New York not to have anybody home," Kasey said.

"I know." Danny manipulated the controls and the drone flew up and over the roof. In back of the building was a private courtyard. He carefully steered the Specter down, allowing it to hover so they could inspect the apartments.

Kasey peered at the screen. The windows back there weren't covered up, but they were still dark. "Go down to the next floor," she said. "I think I see a light." Danny directed the Specter down into the courtyard.

"See?" Kasey pointed. Sure enough, there were lights on inside, but the curtains were drawn, keeping them from seeing much. "Maybe someone's in there, but they don't want anyone to know."

Danny tried to get a better angle, moving the drone in different directions. Suddenly, the curtain jerked aside and a man's face peered out! Danny impulsively pressed both joysticks forward so the Specter rocketed up into the sky.

"It was a guy, but I couldn't see him very well."

"That's okay, I saw him enough for both of us." Danny was urgently guiding the Specter back toward them. "I know who it was."

"You recognized him?"

"It's the same guy who kidnapped Ryan's mom. The big one—the bodyguard."

"We have to call the police."

"We can't. They said no cops." The Specter soared down as Danny brought it in for a landing on the stairway next to their hiding place.

But Kasey was adamant. "Danny, think about it. Ryan's on the other side of the world and his mom may be *right there*. If they're able to save her now, it means this'll all be over."

"But what if they can't? What if she's not there, or something goes wrong and these guys get pissed off?"

"They're the police. They're good at this. A lot better than we are."

Danny knew that Kasey was making sense. He didn't know what to do. He needed to talk to Ryan. "You have your phone, right?" Kasey nodded. "Call Ryan. Maybe we'll get lucky and he'll answer."

Kasey took out her phone and hit a button—Danny noted that she already had Ryan on her Favorites screen—and waited. Please answer, Danny thought, don't make us decide this on our own!

But Kasey shook her head. "Voice mail."

Disappointed, Danny looked at the dark apartment building. "Okay, he finally said. "Let's call the cops."

CHAPTER 39

**LAZU RIVER,
ANDAKAR**

Ryan soared through the air, arms wind-milling uselessly, then plunged into the water. He hit feet first, going deep. The current tugged him forward, and he was somer-saulting underwater—again.

When he finally made it to the surface, Ryan coughed and gasped for air. He scanned the water around him but saw no sign of Lan. The current was slowing, but continued to pull him relentlessly forward. Just ahead, the river they had been traveling along merged with a much larger body of water, wider and slower moving. Ryan finally spotted Lan, clinging to the bamboo pole like a lifeline. She had drifted even farther out into the larger river than Ryan. He swam to her, knowing he needed to calm her before she got more water in her lungs.

"You're okay—take deep breaths," he said, easing her onto her back. The shore was far away in both directions. This river was wider than a football field, and they were dog-paddling right in the middle.

"Look . . ." Lan wheezed, gazing over his shoulder. Ryan shifted around, relieved to see a large fishing trawler heading in their direction, its occupants calling out to them. The vessel was old and dilapidated, but had been painted bright blue and green. It had a festive appearance even though it looked ready to fall apart.

Lan was worried. "What do we do?"

"I don't think we have a choice. Let's just hope they're friendly."

When the trawler eventually pulled alongside them, the fishermen lowered nets from the side of the boat. Ryan helped Lan grab hold of one and, climbing it like a ladder, she made her way to the boat's deck where the fishermen pulled her aboard. Ryan followed, aware that out here in the middle of nowhere they'd have no easy way to escape if this went bad. At the top, rough hands grabbed him and hauled him over the rail.

Ryan and Lan lay on their backs, drenched and panting. Curious faces surrounded them on all sides, many of them decorated with white paint on their nose and cheeks. There were rough-skinned men and women here, and Ryan even saw several children. An extended family, all living together on this fishing boat. They seemed to view the rescue as something pretty remarkable.

Lan tried to speak to them, but she was having trouble communicating. After a moment, she explained: "They're Nachine—River Gypsies. They have their own language."

"How many languages does Andakar have?"

"Fifty or sixty. Maybe more. Their language and traditions are the only freedom some people have. They don't let go easily."

A gruff, weathered-looking man squatted in front of them, openly appraising these two strangers. He motioned for them to take off their shoes and socks to let them dry, then turned back to his family and crew, snapping orders. With backward glances and whispered exchanges, they did as told, preparing the nets and manning the boat.

"Do they all live onboard?" Ryan asked, checking out the boat. In addition to the fishing gear, the trawler had clotheslines with laundry hanging to dry, an outdoor cooking area, and a sitting area with small chairs. They'd even hung twinkly lights and colorful flags all around.

"They do for several months each year," Lan told him. "The rest of the time, they live in temporary villages along the riverbanks, usually with a bunch of other families. They work together to make it through the rainy months. It's not an easy life."

A woman approached with two wooden bowls filled with yellow rice and chunks of fresh, white fish. She smiled, urging them to eat. Ryan scooped a bite into his mouth and nodded his enthusiasm. The dish was delicious, garlic and spices giving it a tangy flavor.

"Are they always this nice to strangers?" he asked after swallowing.

"For Buddhists, being a good host is a form of reverence. We take it very seriously." For a few peaceful moments, they ate in silence, the heat from the morning sun quickly drying their soaked clothes.

Now that they had food, the captain, as Ryan now thought of him, wanted answers. He directed his questions to Lan, each of them struggling to make the other understand, and she managed to communicate that they were in trouble. The man's expression darkened. He could guess who was after them, and he kept looking at his family as if he was already worrying for their safety.

One of the fishermen called out, pointing across the horizon. The captain moved swiftly to the back of the vessel. Ryan and Lan set their bowls down, following.

In the distance, sweeping along the hills above the waterfall, a military helicopter headed in their direction. Ryan and Lan traded a worried glance. To Ryan, the captain's face was unreadable as he watched the helicopter making its way toward them, weaving erratically in its search.

Abruptly, the captain turned to his family and shouted more commands. They jumped into action, some casting nets while others threw out lines with yellow buoys attached. The woman who had brought the fish and rice gestured for them to follow her quickly.

She led them to the middle of the boat's deck where two young boys slid open a wooden portal, revealing a dark cavity. She indicated they should get inside, her gaze darting to the skyline as the *whomp-whomp-whomp* sound of the helicopter came closer. Ryan couldn't see inside, but they didn't have much choice. Going first, he dropped into the shadows, landing unevenly on several burlap bags.

A moment later, Lan landed beside him and then the door above slammed shut, leaving them in near-total darkness. It was a compartment used to store supplies—cramped, claustrophobic, and wickedly hot. Lan took Ryan's hand and held on tight. They stayed completely still as the powerful buzz of the helicopter got nearer, until it was right overhead.

For several nerve-racking seconds, the helicopter didn't move. The entire boat shook as it circled. Then, miraculously, the shaking subsided and the sound faded. The chopper was moving away.

Ryan let out a sigh of relief, not even realizing he'd been holding his breath.

CHAPTER
40

**LAZU RIVER,
ANDAKAR**

Ryan didn't know how he was going to get them out of Andakar now. The Thai border would be swarming with ASI soldiers, making it impossible to connect with the smuggler who was supposed to get them across.

One of the fishermen was rowing Ryan and Lan to shore in a small skiff that had been tied up at the back of the trawler. The helicopter had continued its search downriver, so they had taken the opportunity to make it to land. But once they got there, Ryan had no idea which way to head.

They needed a plan.

He removed the plastic Baggie with his passport and cell phone from around his stomach.

The Baggie was still sealed, everything inside just as dry as when he'd taped it on. Turning on the phone, Ryan hoped he could get a signal out here in the open. Thirty seconds later, with the skiff just reaching shore, Danny's number began to ring.

Ryan waited, but there was no answer. After four rings, it clicked over to voice mail. "Hey, it's me," Ryan said. "If you get this, I could use your help. Check your email, okay?" Thumbs flying over the keyboard, Ryan composed a message to Danny updating him on the situation. He needed a way out of Andakar, but he didn't even know exactly where he was. His phone had less than half the battery left, but Ryan told Danny he'd leave it on for a while. With any luck, Danny could use the cell tracker app and the phone's GPS to locate them and help find some way across the border.

Ryan hit send just as the boat touched the riverbank. Before they disembarked, the River Gypsy who had been rowing them handed them each a plastic bottle of water and a folded piece of cloth. Ryan unwrapped his package, finding several strips of dried meat and pieces of flatbread covered with sesame seeds. They thanked him for the food and jumped off, happy to be back on solid ground.

Lan looked up a small hill. "The captain said there are train tracks up top. They lead back toward the border."

"That has to be at least ten miles away."

"And they'll be looking for us everywhere."

Ryan wished he could think of some alternative. But the truth was, he didn't have any other ideas. Maybe his parents would have known what to do, but he had absolutely no clue.

Hearing the sound of the helicopter, Ryan turned and saw it heading back in their direction. The chopper had made its quick, initial sweep down the river but was now backtracking, moving slowly and searching more carefully. "We need to find cover," he said, guiding them toward the trees and brush that lined the shore.

The crack of gunfire exploded across the river. Ryan and Lan dove behind a tree. But the shots weren't aimed at them.

"No!" Lan called in alarm. The helicopter circled the fisherman in the skiff like a shark stalking its prey. The man was panicked, paddling furiously back toward the trawler.

Machine gunfire tore into the small boat and the fisherman was struck multiple times. Lan instinctively turned away from the slaughter, but

Ryan stared in horror.

The ASI had killed the man in cold blood.

And they weren't done yet. The chopper hovered, now focusing on the trawler and the rest of the River Gypsies. The tinny sound of a bullhorn carried across the water as the soldiers communicated with the fishing vessel.

Lan saw what was happening. "They're forcing them to land."

Downriver, Ryan spotted a clear area where it appeared the boat was being directed. As he watched, a small convoy of military jeeps raced along a winding road that led down to the landing point. The vehicles screeched to a stop and soldiers jumped out, weapons drawn as they waited for the trawler.

"The ASI," Ryan said.

"They'll torture them until someone breaks and admits they helped us. Then they'll kill them all."

Ryan looked up the hill. He knew the best chance for getting Lan and himself out of Andakar safely was to run the opposite direction and stay low. If they could get on a train, they'd be miles away in minutes.

Ryan thought of all the people he'd met over the last couple of days who had helped him: the monk with his string bracelet, the men at the café who didn't give him up, the prisoners at the ASI command center, the girl in the Hello Kitty shirt and her father. He would have never made it this far without each one. If he ran away now, it would feel like he was abandoning all of them.

Lan was right. Ryan couldn't live in a bubble. He couldn't just turn his back and pretend like this brutality wasn't happening. If he didn't help these people, who would?

"Get to the train tracks," Ryan told Lan. "Take whatever train comes along—just get out of here."

"We have to do something," she said.

"I'm gonna try, but you should go while you can. Otherwise, we'll probably both die here."

Lan held her ground. "I'm not going anywhere."

Her mind was obviously made up. Ryan looked back at the trawler, which was being forced to shore by the gunmen aboard the helicopter. ASI soldiers waited for them, rifles pointed threateningly.

"You're sure?" Ryan asked.

"Positive."

"All right. I've actually got an idea. But I'll need your help."

CHAPTER
41

**NEW YORK,
USA**

Kasey didn't understand why the police sent only one squad car. When she made the anonymous call from the pay phone around the corner, she told the guy that she had heard a woman's scream coming from inside the building. She thought they'd send a SWAT team or something.

But it was just two uniformed officers who came to investigate. They knocked and rang a couple of buzzers. One of them stood on the sidewalk, peering up at the dark windows.

"What'll they do if no one answers?" Danny wondered.

"Maybe they'll call in reinforcements and search the building," Kasey said.

The front door unexpectedly opened and a light came on in the small foyer of the building. An Asian man in a cardigan sweater and reading glasses smiled at the officers. His back was slightly stooped and his movements were relaxed and deliberate. Kasey couldn't hear the conversation, but it all seemed very friendly.

"That's him," Danny said. "That's Aung Win."

Kasey was surprised. "That guy's a spy?" Aung Win invited the officers inside, then closed the front door.

"That's not what he looked like before. Believe me, he's totally evil."

"He just let the cops come in. Like he didn't have anything to worry about."

"Which means they're probably not gonna find anything. He's too smart. Maybe this was a mistake."

Kasey felt a sudden twinge of panic. Should they have waited to hear from Ryan? What if they had basically signed his mom's death warrant by calling the police? The next ten minutes felt like forever as they waited in silence. Occasionally, a light would come on in one of the empty apartments for a minute, then abruptly go back out.

Eventually, the front door opened again and

the officers and Aung Win emerged. Kasey's heart sank when she saw them all laughing. It hadn't worked.

The officers returned to their vehicle and drove away as Aung Win waved from the door. The moment the squad car disappeared, so did his smile. Aung Win stood up straight and pulled the glasses off.

"Get back!" Danny whispered, pulling Kasey deeper into the shadows.

They didn't move a muscle as Aung Win angrily glared up and down the block. After a few tense seconds, he stepped back inside and shut the door. The foyer light went out and the building was dark once more.

"What do we do now?" Kasey asked.

"We go home and pray we didn't screw everything up." Danny quickly began to disassemble the camera from his drone. "On a low setting, the camera records up to ten hours. We can hide it here aimed at the front door."

"You're gonna spy on the spy. Nice."

"I'll swing by before school in the morning and replace the memory card. At least we'll know if they leave."

They found a spot behind some pipes where the camera would be practically invisible and

Danny hit record.

They made sure nobody was watching from the building across the street. When they felt sure it was safe, they darted out of the alcove and turned to head down the sidewalk.

But their path was blocked by a tall, imposing figure.

"You're dead."

Danny gulped. It wasn't Aung Win, but it might be even worse: Kasey's brother Steeg glared at them, punching his fist into his free hand.

CHAPTER
42

**LAZU RIVER,
ANDAKAR**

An ASI officer, medals across his chest and gold epaulets adorning his shoulders, watched the trawler with a cold stare. As the boat approached shore, Ryan could make out the frightened faces of the River Gypsies, drifting ever closer to their doom.

This was his chance. All the soldiers were looking away from the jeeps and toward the water. Ryan nodded to Lan and they darted out of the trees, scurrying down the hill as quietly as possible. They crept in behind the last jeep.

"Is this enough?" she asked, showing him the handful of sticks and dried bamboo she had gathered.

"Perfect," Ryan said. "You ready? It's gonna happen fast."

"You really think this will work?" Lan looked dubiously at the plastic Baggie in Ryan's hand.

"I sure hope so." Ryan wasn't overly confident. They were going to need a big distraction to get the ASI's attention away from the fishing boat and this was the best idea he had.

Ryan had emptied the plastic Baggie holding his passport and phone, then filled it with the drinking water the fishermen had given them. He raised the Baggie of water up to the sun. As he hoped, the water inside the pouch created a makeshift lens, like a homemade magnifying glass. Holding it up to the sun's rays, Ryan created a laser-like beam of concentrated heat. It was an old survival trick he'd learned from his dad during a camping trip in Indonesia after their matches got wet in a storm.

Ryan focused the beam on the kindling. Seconds later, it burst into flames. "Okay," he whispered, "time for the bamboo. Be careful, it burns fast."

Lan put one end of the long, dry bamboo stick into the fire Ryan had created and it lit. Ryan peered around the jeep. The soldiers were still focused on the fishing boat.

He crept around the side of the jeep and un-screwed the gas cap. Lan slipped in beside him and placed the bamboo stick into the gas tank, leaving the burning end up top. The bamboo made a great natural fuse, the fire racing down its length.

But they had to get out of there *fast*! Ryan was running for the trees until Lan grabbed his hand and steered him behind a boulder. "Safer," she said.

With a *whoosh*, the gasoline in the tank ig-nited and the jeep burst into flames! Soldiers spun around in alarm, startled and confused by the sudden eruption.

Lan looked worried, though. "One jeep on fire won't stop them for long."

"The thing is, when you put fire in the gas tank, cars don't really explode like they do in the movies." Ryan grinned, making sure they were both fully behind the rock. "But the *hand grenades* in the back sure do. Cover your ears."

Lan did, as—*ka-boom!*—the first vehicle ex-ploded in a ball of fire! Soldiers scattered in all directions, jumping for cover. The officer was struck by the concussive blast, flying several feet in the air before he splashed down into the river. It was utter chaos, the fishing boat suddenly forgotten.

"Go!" Ryan yelled, pointing up the hillside. He and Lan took off running, getting as far away as possible while they could. As Lan continued, Ryan paused to look back.

After the initial pandemonium, the helicopter was wheeling around to come after them. But down below, a second jeep suddenly caught fire, triggered by the explosion of the first. As the chopper soared in their direction, the second jeep blew sky-high!

A chunk of flying metal hit the tail rotor and the helicopter began to veer wildly. It spun in circles, spiraling around and around until the tail hit a tree with a thunderous boom. The chopper plummeted to the ground like a brick, crashing right where Ryan and Lan had been hiding.

On the river, Ryan saw the fishing vessel swerve away from the shoreline and head back out to open water. Ryan hoped they'd get far, far away before any reinforcements could arrive.

Charging once more up the hill, Ryan caught up with Lan just as she made it to the top. Stopping to catch their breaths, they saw smoke billowing everywhere. It looked like a war zone.

Lan shook her head. "You sure you've never done this before?"

"Beginner's luck," Ryan said, with a smile. The sound of a train whistle stole their attention from the destruction by the river. They had made it to the tracks the captain told them about, and a train was chugging right toward them. Ryan was excited, thinking they'd finally caught a break.

But Lan immediately dashed his hopes. "It's heading the wrong direction—*away* from the border. Toward China."

Ryan thought through their options. The explosions would only distract the ASI long enough for them to radio for help. And he knew the Thai borders were basically impossible to cross. So maybe it was time do something unexpected. Maybe it was time to leave his father's plan behind and trust in himself.

With the train coming closer, they had to act quickly. "We should take it. It's our best chance to shake the ASI."

Lan didn't hesitate. "I'm with you."

Together, they sprinted toward the passing train.

CHAPTER
43

**THANLIN,
ANDAKAR**

*T*asha hoped she wasn't too late.

It had taken most of the night to shake the ASI soldiers chasing her. Twice, she'd been cornered and feared it was the end. But Tasha Levi never gave up. She knew how to fight with a viciousness that stunned the soldiers. Underestimating her was a serious mistake. She'd left a few dead bodies behind her, but had no regrets.

Whatever it took to accomplish her mission.

When she was finally safe, Tasha had doubled back around to Thanlin. She found the villager she had seen with Ryan and forced him to tell her about the temple with the secret chamber. Moving fast, she had traversed the mountain in a couple of hours, hoping to find Ryan and John Quinn still in hiding.

The temple grounds appeared to be empty. Tasha identified the golden dome the villager had mentioned and headed that way. But the rumble of a motor stopped her in her tracks.

A jeep was approaching from the opposite end. Tasha pressed up against a temple wall and tracked its progress. It pulled to a stop and two soldiers got out. The men wore gray uniforms, which meant they weren't ASI. Probably just a regular guard patrol. They appeared relaxed as they set off in opposite directions.

Tasha needed that jeep. If John and Ryan Quinn weren't already gone, it would make the next leg of the journey much simpler. She couldn't afford for the guards to raise the alarm and bring more soldiers. Which meant they'd have to be eliminated.

Silent as a cat, Tasha followed the driver as he wound his way through the temple structures. After a few minutes, he stopped and unstrapped his rifle, leaning it against a wall. He took a couple of steps around the corner, unzipping his pants. This was going to be too easy.

Thinking he was alone, the soldier peed, whistling softly. Tasha crept forward, closing the distance between them. She picked up his rifle, holding it like a club. He was zipping his pants back up as she advanced, swinging the weapon like a baseball bat. *Whack!* The butt of the rifle hit the driver on the back of the head and he crumpled to the ground. When he tried to get up, Tasha struck him again.

She dropped the rifle and took the soldier's handgun instead, tucking it into her pants against the small of her back. Searching his pockets, she found the jeep keys, then hurried to locate the second soldier.

Hearing his heavy steps, Tasha slipped into the shadows of a temple entrance. After the soldier passed, she snuck behind him and wrapped her forearm around his neck in a choke hold. The startled guard struggled, but her grip only tightened. He dropped to his knees, fingers clawing at her arm. A few seconds later, his eyes rolled up into his head and he went limp.

That's what happens when you're careless and undisciplined, she thought.

Tasha drove the jeep to the entrance of the gold-domed temple and jumped back out. Inside, she found the wall sculpture the villager had described and pushed. Slowly, it opened, pivoting to reveal the tunnel's entrance. Absolute silence greeted Tasha.

She was too late—they'd already gone.

But as she stepped into the chamber, her senses went on high alert. She whirled around, drawing the handgun from her pants with one smooth motion.

"Don't shoot. It's just me." John Quinn leaned against the wall.

"Quinn!" she said, not disguising the relief she felt at seeing him alive. Then she glanced around and realized, "You're alone?"

"Ryan found me. I was surprised when he said you'd helped him get here. How did you know where I was?"

"I didn't. I went to find you and sort of walked into a mess. Where's Ryan?"

"With any luck, he and the girl I was helping are in Thailand by now. I need to call Simon McClelland and make sure they made contact."

"We'll call as soon as we can get a signal." Tasha noticed the bandages. "You're injured."

"I'm getting stronger," John insisted. "With your help, I can travel."

"Good," Tasha said, coming around behind him. "Because we have somewhere to be."

Tasha pulled what appeared to be a pen out of her pocket. She'd been carrying it since they landed in Andakar. But it wasn't a pen at all. It was a well-disguised hypodermic needle filled with enough tranquilizer to subdue a sumo wrestler. It would be plenty for John Quinn.

She plunged the needle into John's neck. He turned to her in shock and confusion as the drug flooded his body.

"What?" he stammered, already unsteady. "Why . . . ?"

"You'll find out soon enough," Tasha said without a trace of compassion. John crumpled to the ground, unconscious. Tasha smiled.

Mission accomplished.

CHAPTER
44

**CHINDI PROVINCE,
ANDAKAR**

The train rattled along, rocking back and forth so gently that it had lulled Lan to sleep. For the first time since they'd met, Ryan thought she seemed at peace. He looked back out the window. Along the way, the scenery had shifted from verdant mountain jungle to flat plains and was now changing once more. If things were different, Ryan imagined the rolling hills and forests they were passing through would be fun to explore.

The train was huge, probably close to a hundred cars long, and filled mostly with locals who appeared to be from rural areas. Jumping onboard hadn't been hard. The train was slow enough that Ryan and Lan were able to run alongside and grab the handrails on the back car. Luckily, nobody was checking tickets, so they were able to find empty seats and blend into the crowd.

Ryan's phone vibrated in his pocket. He slipped it out, thankful to see he finally had a signal again. It was Danny. It was almost noon here in Andakar, which meant it was close to midnight back in New York. Not wanting to wake Lan, Ryan moved down the aisle before answering.

"Hey."

"Dude, you're going the wrong way!" Danny said, skipping hellos. "I've got your GPS up on my tracking program—you need to turn around, like *now*."

Just hearing his friend's voice made Ryan feel a little better. "We ran into a few problems."

"The kind where you're dodging bullets?"

"Plus some white-water rapids, military choppers, and exploding hand grenades. And that's just since this morning."

"You're joking."

"So not joking."

"Wow," Danny said. "And here I was feeling all impressed with myself that I fought with Steeg tonight."

"You fought Steeg?" Ryan knew that couldn't have gone well. "Are you okay?"

"Well, by *fought*, what I really mean is, 'ran as fast as possible in the opposite direction.' So, yeah, I'm fine."

"You need to stay away from that guy." Ryan glanced over at Lan, still sleeping. "Did you get my email?"

"Yeah—so Myat Kaw is a girl, huh?" Danny said, and Ryan knew what was coming next: "Is she hot?"

"You're unbelievable."

"She is, isn't she? Text me a pic!"

"How about I just let you see her for your-self? All you have to do is find us a way out of here."

Ryan could hear Danny clicking away on his keyboard as he spoke. "Are you on a train?" he asked.

"Yeah, how'd you know that?"

"I've got your GPS location on satellite now. I can see the tracks."

"Lan says we're headed for China." Ryan glanced over and noticed one of the passen-gers, an older man with a brutish face, watching him. Ryan nodded a friendly hello, then turned away, hoping the man would lose interest.

"She's right. You're actually within a few miles of the Chinese border now."

"How close is the nearest airport?"

Danny typed again. "In Jinhong, about fifty miles from the border. They have an international airport that gets lots of tourists. You wouldn't stand out."

"Then that's where we need to go. If I send you the names on our passports, you think you could figure out a way to get us a couple of tickets?"

"I'll make it happen. And I'll send you a satellite map of the border area. It looks like a lot of forest and hills around there."

"I'm not sure how long my battery will last. I'll have to turn off the phone until we're close, make sure I have enough juice left to get whatever info you send about flights."

"Listen," Danny said. "Things have been pretty crazy here, too. I may know where your mom is being held."

Ryan totally forgot to keep his voice down. "You saw her?"

"No, but I saw Aung Win and that big dude with him." Danny told him about the apartment building. They didn't know for sure if Jacqueline was inside, but it seemed likely. The fact that

Kasey was now involved came as a shock. But just then another call started beeping through.

He glanced at the screen and his stomach churned: "Blocked."

"I gotta go—I think it's him calling," Ryan told Danny.

"Ryan, wait!" Danny's tone was so urgent that Ryan hesitated. "We called the cops. We were just trying to help—but it didn't work."

"Oh no . . ." Was Aung Win calling to tell him that he'd already done what he promised? Was his mother dead?

"I'm sorry, we really thought—"

"I have to go." Ryan hit the accept button on his phone, fearing what was to come. "Hello?"

"My instructions were very clear." Aung Win's voice was unmistakable. "You were not to speak to anyone."

"I only talked to my dad, just like you told me." Ryan hoped it was convincing since it was the truth.

"You called the police!"

"I didn't. I promise."

Aung Win remained suspicious. "It would be foolish of you not to do as I say."

"I know that. My dad told me to just do exactly what you tell me to. Is my mom okay?"

"What does it matter? You are out of time."

"We have one more day! You said five days—
that's tomorrow." Ryan knew one day wouldn't
be enough time for Dad to get back, but he'd
worry about that later. Right now, he had to
make Aung Win believe everything was fine.
"My father said to tell you he has Myat Kaw. He
has your niece."

Aung Win said nothing. Ryan let it sink in
that he knew Myat Kaw's identity, then continued, "He said he'll make the trade. Your niece
for my mom. As long as my mother isn't hurt.
I'm supposed to talk to her, to make sure she's
okay."

"He wants to know if you're okay," Aung Win
said, but he wasn't speaking to Ryan.

And then he heard his mom's voice: "Don't
trust him, Ryan! Tell Dad not to—" But her final
words were muffled, like a gag had been placed
over her mouth. Ryan was surprised at how
calm he remained, not rattled like the last call.

"If anything happens to her, the deal is off,"
Ryan said.

"And if anyone learns Myat Kaw's true identity before she is in my possession, then she is
useless to me. And so is your mother." Aung
Win's tone became brisk and efficient. "Tell

John Quinn I will contact him at this number to-morrow. He will have one opportunity to make the trade according to my instructions. Alone. Any deviation and I will simply disappear. Along with your mother."

"Ryan!" Ryan turned to find Lan just behind him. She was worried, glancing back the way she'd come. At the end of the train car, the older passenger who had stared at Ryan was pointing him out to a uniformed police officer.

"Do you understand?" Aung Win snapped in Ryan's ear. Ryan felt like a traitor, arranging to trade Lan to a man who wanted to kill her while she looked at him as an ally.

"I got it," he said to Aung Win. The connection was immediately terminated. Lan gave him a curious look. "That was Danny," he lied. "He's gonna help us get out of here."

The officer was now talking into a radio—they had to move.

"This way," Ryan said, moving to the back of the car. He opened the exit door and stepped out between the train cars. Beneath his feet, the ground rushed past as wind whipped his face. He grabbed hold of the handle on the opposite side and stepped across the open space to the next car.

They charged down the aisle, passing from car to car. But the police officer was gaining on them. Pushing Lan ahead of him, Ryan grabbed a couple of suitcases and baskets of vegetables that lined the sides, knocking them into the officer's path to slow his pursuit.

Passengers jumped up and yelled after Ryan angrily, causing even more difficulty for the officer. Ryan made it to the back of the car, just as Lan opened the next door. But she froze in the doorway: They were at the end of the line, nothing beyond but empty air.

They didn't even hesitate. Ryan and Lan jumped!

CHAPTER
45

**CHINDI PROVINCE,
ANDAKAR**

Ryan knew to hit the ground in a roll to lessen the impact. But when he got up, he saw that Lan had landed harder. He helped her up, and she winced.

"Your ankle?" he asked.

"It's all right." She put weight on it, but it obviously hurt.

Screeeeech! The squeal of the train's metal brakes was ear-piercing as it slowed to a stop. Ryan pointed toward the forest up the hill.

"There. We can hide." He offered Lan a hand, but she refused. Moving as fast as they were able, they hurried toward the cover of the trees. Behind them, passengers stuck their heads out the windows and watched the unexpected excitement.

The forest was dense, and the train was soon out of sight. They stopped so Lan could rest her ankle a few minutes and Ryan could check the map Danny sent. The Chinese border was only a few miles away, but it was hilly terrain. Unfortunately, Ryan's phone now showed a single bar left on the battery. Not only would they lose their map, they'd also lose all contact with Danny if it ran out of power. Ryan took another minute to try and memorize the map, then reluctantly turned the phone off.

For the next hour, they trekked through the forest, moving steadily uphill. Hungry and exhausted, it took all their strength, both physically and mentally, to just keep moving forward. When a helicopter buzzed by overhead, they knew the ASI had been alerted and was now searching the area.

Making it to the top of a ridge, Ryan scanned the valley below. It was a rustic area, full of trees and jagged boulders. Cows, oxen, and horses grazed in grassy clearings. At the bottom of the basin was a small community of wood-thatched homes and simple barns. Rocky hills encroached on both sides, and there was just one road in and out—a road that looked like their only possibility of escape. It led to the border crossing at the far end of town, where heavily armed soldiers stopped anyone trying to leave Andakar.

"We can't get across here," Lan said, disheartened. "There are too many of them."

Ryan felt his own doubt grow as a chopper flew past. Down below, more soldiers arrived, jumping out of their jeeps. They searched the houses and barns, treating the citizens roughly. Ryan and Lan were severely outmatched. It would be suicide to attempt a border crossing here, but there was nowhere else to go.

Ryan thought of Varian Fry and the original Emergency Rescue Committee, who helped save so many people from the Nazis, knowing they'd be killed if they were caught. They must have been scared, too. There must have been times when escape seemed impossible. His own grandfather probably felt like this—and his parents, too.

He glanced over at Lan, whose eyes were closed, her head slightly bowed as she muttered under her breath. After a moment, she looked up and saw Ryan watching her.

"Were you praying?" he asked.

"Buddhists don't pray. I was giving thanks for a blessing."

Ryan was confused. "Is there a blessing in this that I'm missing?"

"You're the blessing," she said. "You and your father. Whatever happens next, the two of you allowed me to hope again—if only for a little while."

Ryan fixed her with steely gaze. "That sounds a lot like you're giving up."

Her only answer was to look up at the helicopter, which was sweeping toward them. As it spun around, the chopper's side door slid open and a soldier appeared, shouting through a bullhorn. Another soldier appeared beside him and aimed a rifle their direction.

"They want us to come out," Lan said.

No way, Ryan thought. He wasn't giving up—and he wasn't letting Lan give up, either. He'd spotted something down the hill that had sparked an idea, a way they might still be able to get out of this. Ryan grabbed Lan's hand, pulling her after him.

"Run!" he yelled. "Stay close to the trees!" A shot rang out, splintering a branch behind them, as Ryan pulled her into a thicket. They heard another couple of shots, but they weren't as close.

He kept changing directions, always keeping the trees between them and the helicopter.

"Where are we going?" Lan asked breathlessly, fighting the pain in her injured ankle. "There's no way we can get through the border crossing."

"We're not going to," Ryan answered. "We're going around it!" Ryan veered sharply to their right, taking them in a completely different direction than they'd been heading. Since the chopper couldn't see them through the trees, he hoped this would confuse their hunt.

It worked. The helicopter moved away, not realizing its targets were now on a different path. But Ryan could hear the rumble of truck engines racing up the narrow roads. The ASI soldiers were on the way.

Ryan stopped abruptly as they neared the edge of the trees. He had skirted around the hill with this destination in mind. Fifty yards away was one of the ranches he'd spotted. That's where he hoped to find their possible ticket to freedom.

"There." Ryan pointed, enjoying the light that came to Lan's eyes when she realized what he was thinking:

"Horses!" Lan looked genuinely excited. "I'm

an excellent rider," she said. "You, too?"

"No," Ryan admitted, "I'm terrible. But if you can swim the rapids and run on a hurt ankle, I can stay on a horse."

Three horses were tethered on the far side of the clearing. Crouching low, Ryan and Lan used the huge humpbacked cows as cover, weaving among them as they approached the horses.

As they arrived, Ryan realized the horses had reins, but no saddles. Riders here only used simple blankets thrown over the horse's back. Lan seemed used to that, leaping onto the back of a beautiful chestnut-colored mare in one agile motion. Ryan wasn't as graceful, hoisting himself onto a gray stallion and nearly sliding off the other side. He finally got settled and pulled on the reins, prodding the horse with his heels to get it running. The horse bolted forward, nearly throwing Ryan off as it chased after Lan.

"Across the field and up the hill," Ryan called. "We make it to the other side and we'll be in China!"

Lan was a confident rider, and she charged across the open clearing. Ryan barely stayed seated as his gray stallion flew after her. But after a few seconds of breakneck galloping, he fell into the horse's rhythm and the ride felt more natural. He glanced back, seeing the helicopter execute a wide arc in pursuit of them.

"They're coming!" he yelled. "Get to the trees!"

Lan knew what she was doing, using the reins to guide her horse in that direction. Thankfully, Ryan's stallion seemed happy to follow, allowing him to focus on hanging on. They had almost made it across the field when the chopper swooped in, soldiers firing from the open doorway. Bullets hit the ground on all sides, a few of them barely missing before the horses reached the tree line and disappeared into the forest. The chopper flew overhead so low that Ryan felt his whole body shake.

Gripping the horse with his legs and the reins with his fists, Ryan struggled to keep upright. These were mountain horses, used to the rocky hillside they were now climbing. They darted between the trees, nimbly keeping their footing over the rough terrain. Limbs and twigs struck Ryan's body and face as Lan led them ever higher, taking them around the border crossing down below.

Finally, they crested the top, pausing for a moment to look back. From up here, they could see the frustrated ASI soldiers in their jeeps, unable to follow because no roads led this high. The chopper continued crisscrossing the sky, trying to find them.

"Do you see where we are?" Ryan asked.

Lan looked at the border crossing down in the valley and then realized: "China! We're over the border—we made it!"

Ryan grinned, then glanced warily at the helicopter. "We'd better keep moving. They probably won't risk flying into Chinese airspace, but I wouldn't want to bet on it."

Reining the horses around, they started down the other side, using the forest for cover. As they rode on for the next hour, the reality finally settled in: They had actually done it—they were out of Andakar.

But Ryan's relief was short-lived as he remembered the impossible choice that would soon face him. He had promised to trade Lan for his mother. Aung Win had given him only until tomorrow, which meant that his dad wouldn't make it back in time to help. Which was a disaster because Ryan had no idea how to handle this.

When he left New York, he believed he would do whatever it took to save his mom. His family meant everything to him. There was no sacrifice he wouldn't make.

But then he'd met Lan. Small and delicate on the outside, but with a rebel's heart. She was just a teenager, but she'd already been through so much and faced it with strength and courage.

Aung Win demanded a trade. It had to be one or the other.

Would he save Lan or his mother?

How was he supposed to choose?

PART FOUR

DO OR DIE

CHAPTER
46

**NEW YORK,
USA**

Home.

For Ryan, it was weird to think of any one place that way. But as the taxi sped from the airport toward Manhattan and he caught his first glimpse of the skyline, that's exactly how he felt. For the last couple of years, Ryan had been craving a home and now he had one.

But what good was a home without the family to fill it?

Lan rode next to him, her face pressed against the glass, taking in the strange, new surroundings with a mixture of awe and panic. It was Saturday morning in New York, a crisp autumn day without a cloud in the sky. Traffic was light as they zipped along the expressway. On the long flight back, they had both eaten and slept, though Ryan's slumber had been filled with fitful dreams.

Thanks to Danny's hard work, catching the plane out of China had been the smoothest part of this entire experience. He had booked tickets under the fake identities on the passports Ryan and Lan carried. At the airport, they had blended into the crowds of tourists without any issues. Danny had also wired money to the Western Union station at the airport, enough for them to buy food and new clothes at the gift shops. A sandwich and a fresh change of underwear and socks had been desperately needed!

Ryan checked his phone once more, making sure he hadn't received a message from his dad. No text, no email, no voice mail. No contact at all. Ryan hoped he was all right, but mostly, he wished he'd get in touch to tell Ryan what to do. Aung Win could call at any moment to arrange the trade of Myat Kaw for Jacqueline. When he did, Ryan would have to act quickly.

Lan turned from the taxi's window. "On the train, that was my uncle you were talking to, wasn't it?"

The question caught Ryan off guard, but he

didn't even consider lying to her. They'd been through too much together. "Yeah."

"And he'll trade your mother for me?"

Ryan nodded. "That's what he says, anyway. My mom yelled out not to trust him."

"She's right." Lan had a determined look on her face. "But you have to make the trade anyway. We have to do whatever we can to save your mom."

Ryan could tell she meant it. Despite the risk, Lan was ready to go with her uncle, to do anything necessary to help—to give up her own life to save someone else.

And in that moment, Ryan knew there was no way he could ever let Aung Win get his hands on Lan.

Ryan flashed back on all that had happened: He'd used a fake ID to sneak into a hostile country, broken into the command center of a spy agency, and journeyed across rivers and mountains while being chased by jerks with machine guns. Five days ago, he would've never believed any of that was possible. But he'd done it. And somehow, he'd figure this out, too.

There had to be a way to save them both.

Daylight vanished as they plunged into the Midtown Tunnel, which led under the East River and into Manhattan. White tiles flashed past in the dimly lit underpass. Ryan wished he had a deck of cards. Practicing his sleight-of-hand tricks always helped him think.

Ryan opened up the email program on his phone, which was now fully recharged. Danny had sent him photos of the building where they believed his mom was being held. Danny's camera had been recording the entrance ever since the failed police search. Neither Aung Win nor the bodyguard had come out, but the driver of their car had stopped by twice. He brought several bags of groceries on each visit, which made Ryan believe they were still holed up inside. Probably lying low until the trade.

Suddenly, Ryan stopped.

The trade . . . the driver . . . sleight-of-hand . . .

His thoughts came in a jumble as a plan began to form. He couldn't do it on his own. He'd need the help of his friends to pull it off, but Ryan finally felt a glimmer of hope.

As the taxi pulled out of the tunnel and into traffic, Ryan started putting the pieces together.

CHAPTER
47

**NEW YORK,
USA**

Back home, Ryan ran straight for his parents' room and unearthed the canister of pepper spray from his mom's gym bag. She kept it with her workout clothes and running shoes—just in case.

Stuffing the canister in his pocket, he hurried down the hallway of his family's brownstone to his bedroom. He went straight to the pegboard that held all his baseball caps. Without hesitation, he grabbed his Roy Halladay–signed Philadelphia Phillies hat and pulled it on. Halladay had thrown a no-hitter his very first time pitching during the playoffs—the first post-season no-hitter in over fifty years. It was the kind of once-in-a-lifetime success that Ryan needed today. He hoped the cap brought him the same luck.

As he came back downstairs, the doorbell rang. He glanced through the peephole, then opened the door, happy to see Danny on the front steps.

"Thanks for coming," Ryan said. Just seeing his friend standing there gave him a boost of confidence, which he sorely needed.

"Yeah, it was either join my parents for a day of antiques shopping, or come here and help you kick some butt. You're lucky antiques suck."

"Antiques may sound better before today's over."

Danny's cool bravado disappeared as he grabbed Ryan in a spontaneous hug. "Dude, it's good to see you. I thought for sure you were a goner."

Ryan grinned. "Thanks for keeping that to yourself."

"Ryan!" The guys pulled apart, turning to see Kasey arrive. "I'm so glad you're okay."

"Sorry you got pulled into all this," Ryan said.

"I'm not. And whatever you need, we're here for you." She turned as Steeg came up behind her, scowling.

Danny instinctively stepped behind Ryan,

using him as a human shield. "Back off, man, or Ryan'll go all ninja on you!"

"Ignore him," Ryan said, stepping forward and stretching out his hand to Steeg. "We never officially met. I'm Ryan—thanks for helping."

"I haven't agreed to anything yet." But Steeg reluctantly shook Ryan's hand.

Danny looked between them, confused. "What's going on?"

"That's what I want to know." Steeg glanced at his sister, then back to Ryan. "All this stuff she told me—it's some kinda prank, right?"

"I wish. I know it sounds crazy, but it's real."

"We brought my parents' car like you asked," Kasey said.

"We're not going anywhere with these guys." Steeg was adamant, used to being in charge. "No way I'm risking my license on some stupid scheme that's probably a bunch of bull anyway."

"Before anyone decides to do anything or not, I want you to meet someone." He ushered them inside the brownstone, quickly scanning the street for anyone suspicious before he closed the door.

Ryan led everyone down the hall to the kitchen where Lan was typing on Ryan's laptop. He said Lan's name to get her attention, and she looked up with a fierce expression. All it took for her to change from a frightened teenager to the crusading blogger Myat Kaw was a laptop and internet access.

"I started several rumors that Myat Kaw had been taken prisoner by an American," she said. "That should make my uncle more confident the trade is happening."

"Good. Everyone, this is Lan." Ryan introduced Danny and Kasey, adding, "These are the two who managed to get us out of the country."

"Thanks," Lan said. "Ryan's lucky to have such smart friends."

Danny grinned. "And handsome—don't forget how handsome his friends are. And very available to show you around this amazing city."

"Seriously?" Steeg just shook his head.

"Well, I don't mean, like, *right now*."

"Danny showed me the blogs you've been writing," Kasey said. "It's amazing. You're really helping people."

"I just write the truth."

"Well, the truth can be powerful in the right hands." Kasey didn't hide her admiration.

Ryan noticed that Steeg was uncharacteristically quiet, his eyes never leaving Lan. "This is Kasey's brother, Steeg."

"Nice to meet you." Steeg held out his hand, which Lan took delicately, not used to the gesture. "And it's, uh, Drew. My name—it's Drew."

"Hello, Drew." Lan actually blushed as Steeg broke into a goofy smile, the two holding hands longer than necessary. "It's nice to meet you, too."

"You gotta be kidding." Danny rolled his eyes. Maybe convincing Steeg to help wouldn't be that hard, after all.

Ryan brought everyone up to speed on all that had happened, answering their many questions. Ryan was impatient, knowing they might not have much time. But if everyone wasn't on the same page, they didn't stand a chance of succeeding.

Finally, Ryan was ready to tell them what he had in mind.

"When I was a kid," he started, "my dad encouraged me to learn magic. Sleight of hand, card tricks, making things look like they can float. You know what the most critical part of any magic trick is?"

"Finding someone to watch who's not bored to tears?" Danny suggested.

"Distraction," Ryan said. "You have to get your audience focused in one direction"—Ryan snapped with the fingers of his left hand and they all glanced that way—"while the *real* trick is happening someplace completely different."

Ryan's strategy required an element of surprise, so they'd only have one shot to get it right. A million things could go wrong. But he forced himself not to think about those now. This plan had to work.

His mother's life depended on it.

CHAPTER 48

**NEW YORK,
USA**

Ryan's cell phone rang as the screen lit up with the word he'd been anxiously awaiting: "Blocked."

The call had finally come. Still no contact from Dad or Tasha. Ryan was beginning to give up hope that she'd escaped or that his father would make it out of Andakar. But he couldn't allow those worries to control him. He had to keep moving forward. Ryan picked up the phone and held it out to Steeg.

"You ready?"

Steeg took it, nervous. "This whole acting thing, I don't know . . ."

Kasey gave his arm a reassuring squeeze. "You can do it, Drew. Just be tough and determined—pretend it's the final seconds of a playoff game."

Steeg nodded, psyching himself up. The three of them were on the second floor of a massive used bookstore, tucked in a private corner next to a picture window. The bookstore was across the street from the building where they'd seen Aung Win and the bodyguard. Danny had checked the camera one last time and believed they were all still inside.

As the phone rang again, Steeg answered, putting the call on speaker so Ryan and Kasey could hear. He took a deep breath and said, "This is John Quinn."

Ryan prayed this would work. Being seventeen and a big guy, Steeg's voice had already changed, giving him the lower register of a grown man. They needed Aung Win to believe he was dealing directly with Ryan's father.

"You have Myat Kaw?" Aung Win's gravelly voice was unmistakable.

"I want to speak to my wife." Steeg did well, his tone confident and assured. "I won't hand over your niece unless I know she's okay."

For an interminable few seconds there was no response, and Ryan felt a twinge of panic. He heard a scuffling sound as the phone was moved, and then his mom's voice, tense but controlled: "John, is that you?"

Ryan pointed to the name *Jackie* written on a notepad for Steeg. Ryan's father always called her Jacqueline, never a nickname. He hoped this would send a signal to his mom to play along.

"It's me, *Jackie*," Steeg said. "Are you okay?"

Jacqueline only hesitated a moment, then said, "I'm fine, Johnny." Ryan gave a silent cheer—his mom had understood, sending back her own signal by calling his dad Johnny. Hopefully, that meant she'd be on the alert, ready for them when they moved into action.

Aung Win was back. "You will deliver Lan to me. You have her?"

"I do," Steeg answered. Kasey gave him a thumbs-up. She made a mean face, encouraging her brother to stay tough and in character. "My wife better not be hurt."

"As long as you don't contact the authorities, she will be unharmed. Come alone." His tone was cold and detached. Ryan wished he could reach through the phone and punch him.

"Where?" Steeg asked.

"There is a private airfield on Long Island. The East Shore Aerodrome. Bring her there."

"You have to promise me you won't kill Lan.

She's just a girl." That was a nice touch, Ryan thought. Steeg was really selling it.

"You have two hours," Aung Win said, and the call was disconnected.

Steeg gave the phone to Ryan, then looked at his hand. "I'm shaking. I never shake."

"You were perfect," Ryan assured him. "He totally bought it."

Kasey was already standing. "We need to get in position. I'll find Danny and Lan." She took off to collect the other two, who had been killing time while they waited for the call, lost in the vast collection of used books.

Ryan got up, but Steeg stopped him. "Listen, I get that it's a lot to deal with, what your parents are going through and all. But are you sure this is the right play? Maybe we should just leave it to the cops."

"Aung Win will be on the lookout for police. I can't risk him getting spooked. But he won't be expecting any problems from a bunch of kids."

"That's because a bunch of kids shouldn't be doing this."

Ryan understood Steeg's reluctance. He still felt it himself. "You want me to tell Kasey to go home?"

"Nobody tells Kasey to do anything she

doesn't want to do. But since my job is to be with Danny and Lan, it's up to you to watch out for her, got it? Forget about this Aung Win dirtbag—anything happens to Kasey and you've got *me* to worry about." After a beat to let that sink in, he walked away.

Steeg was right. Ryan was putting his friends in danger. Sure, he thought he had figured out a way to keep everyone safe, but what if things didn't go as planned? What if everything fell apart and someone got hurt?

"You coming?" Kasey was once again at Ryan's side. Beyond her, he saw Danny, Steeg, and Lan waiting at the top of the stairs.

"I can't ask you guys to do this."

"We're all here because we chose to be," Kasey said.

"But it's not your problem."

"Of course it is. You're our friend, and you need help. That's what friends do."

"It's too dangerous."

"How dangerous was getting Lan out of Andakar? And what about your parents? Who knows how much they've risked helping people over the years."

"That's different," Ryan said. "They knew

what they were getting into."

"So do we," Kasey insisted. "Isn't that the point of the Emergency Rescue Committee? That sometimes it's worth taking risks to help people when they really need it?"

"Your brother thinks we should just leave it to the cops."

"That's what I thought, too," Kasey said. "I was the one who pushed Danny to call them that night, and it was almost a disaster. These guys are smart and careful. I think your plan is the best chance we've got to get your mom away from them safely."

"You do?" Ryan was surprised by how much her vote of confidence meant to him.

"Absolutely."

Ryan felt a renewed sense of commitment. "All right—let's do this. But just in case, have 911 ready to dial, okay?"

"Will do. But this is gonna work."

"I hope you're right."

"I better be," Kasey said, "because we have a date for the Autumn Carnival Dance tonight."

"That's tonight?" Ryan had completely forgotten.

Kasey arched an eyebrow playfully: "Don't

think for a second that all this gets you out of dancing with me."

Together, they joined the others and headed downstairs.

There was no turning back now.

CHAPTER
49

**NEW YORK,
USA**

Timing would be everything. Their crucial advantage was that Aung Win would not anticipate any problems here at his safe house. If something were to go wrong, he'd expect it to happen at the airfield during the trade.

At least, that's what Ryan hoped.

Ryan and Kasey were at the corner, a short distance from the building's front door. Ryan had checked the video Danny recorded and confirmed that there was no back entrance. They would have to bring his mother out the front.

"When it goes down, everything's gonna happen fast," Ryan told Kasey. "Stay here and wait for my mom. I'll try to buy you as much time as I can to get her to the car."

"Got it," Kasey said, opening her bag. "I grabbed everything I could think of that might help cut her free. Scissors if her hands are duct-taped, wire cutters if they have her zip-tied. And if she's in handcuffs"—she produced a bobby pin bent into an L-shape—"one ready-to-go lockpick."

Kasey was full of surprises. "You know how to pick a lock?"

"I have three brothers who love to play tricks on me. I learned a while ago how to break into their rooms and get my revenge."

"Remind me not to mess with you," Ryan said. "Okay, you're the lookout. I'm gonna get set."

Ryan pulled his Phillies cap out of his back pocket and put it on, tugging the brim down low. He grabbed the sleeping bag and cardboard box he'd brought from home. The box was a big one from their recent move. Ryan had pierced several holes in it for spying. In a nook a few doors down from Aung Win's building, he set it up to look like a homeless person's shelter. He left the end of his sleeping bag visible and threw some fast-food wrappers down to make it convincing.

Danny had downloaded an app on all their phones that allowed them to be used as walkie-talkies. Ryan put one headphone in his ear and, with the press of a button, had instant communication with the group.

"Everybody in place?"

"It's cold up here." Shrill and loud, Danny's voice bellowed through the headphone, causing Ryan to quickly lower the volume. "Can you see me?"

Ryan peeked out of his cardboard hideout, looking toward the roof. Leaning against the edge, five stories up, he saw Danny waving. The brick building was narrow, only four windows across, with a fire escape that had a landing at each level. After the top platform, a metal ladder led to the roof.

"I see you," Ryan confirmed. "How's Lan?"

"Great. We're getting to spend some quality time together." Danny's voice lowered to a whisper. "I think she's really into me."

Steeg's voice broke through. "You know we can all hear you, right?"

"Jealous, big guy?" Danny mocked, enjoying himself.

"Hey, everybody," Kasey interrupted. "Heads

up. Somebody's coming out."

Ryan ducked back inside his cardboard box. Through a hole, he watched as the door opened. A moment later, Aung Win appeared. He had on the cardigan and glasses Danny had described. Stooped over, he carried a broom in his hand. He began sweeping, but Ryan could tell he was actually scanning the area for signs of trouble.

His gaze swept toward Ryan's makeshift homeless shelter. Ryan pulled away from the eyehole, staying completely still. He held the canister of pepper spray, ready to fire.

But nothing happened.

"He's going back in." Kasey's voice was quiet. Several minutes passed. It seemed like forever to Ryan.

And finally: "Diplomatic plates coming this way."

Through an eyehole, he watched the familiar black Town Car pull to a stop in front of the building. The driver stepped out and scanned the street. He waited until a couple of pedestrians had walked past, then moved around to the rear door.

Ryan pressed the button on his cell-walkie, his voice barely a whisper. "It's showtime."

CHAPTER
50

**NEW YORK,
USA**

L an had a secret.

She wasn't sure why she hadn't told Ryan. There'd been plenty of time as they traveled. Maybe it was because it still hurt too much.

But now, she was going to use that secret to hopefully do some good.

Up on the roof, Danny turned to her. "You ready?"

She nodded, sticking one headphone into her ear, then slipped the phone he'd lent her into a pocket. She climbed onto the ladder and started down. It was old and rickety, shaking a little as she descended to the top level of the fire escape.

She heard Danny's voice in her ear. "Lan's on the move."

Though everyone had a part to play, Lan's role was critical. She was to provide the distraction Ryan needed. If she accomplished her goal, it would give Ryan enough time to grab his mother and get her away from Aung Win and his men.

Now, it was Ryan's voice in her ear. "Don't go any lower than the third story," he said. "I don't want you getting too close to him."

"She knows," Danny assured him. Lan liked Danny. He was funny and independent in a way that the kids of Andakar couldn't be. Not when any careless joke could bring the authorities to your door to haul you away.

Arriving at the third-floor landing, Lan walked to the rail and looked down. She hadn't seen her uncle since the night he caught her. She'd been terrified during their confrontation, but now the fear was gone. She was ready to face him.

"They're coming out," Kasey reported.

The cardigan and eyeglasses had been removed as Aung Win came back out. Her uncle motioned to someone inside. Ryan's mother appeared, squinting against the bright sunlight, her hands clasped together in front of her. Lan assumed the jacket draped over her wrists hid some kind of restraints. She recognized Kang, her uncle's oversized bodyguard who was never far from his side. Ryan's mom stumbled, wobbly on her feet, and Kang grabbed her arm to keep her from falling.

"Something's wrong with her." Ryan's voice was strained.

"She looks like she's been drugged," Kasey said, her tone reassuring. "They probably just gave her something to keep her calm. Stay focused, Ryan."

The driver opened the rear door. It was finally time for Lan to confront the man who had ruined her life.

"Uncle!"

Aung Win looked up at the third-story fire escape in astonishment. Lan stared down, both hands on the rail. Up here, she was far enough away to be safely out of reach, but close enough to see the uncertainty on his face.

"I know what you did. I know you were responsible for the car crash that killed my parents."

The guilty expression on Aung Win's face confirmed her suspicions. Only days before her uncle had caught her, Lan had accessed Aung Win's private emails and discovered several old messages arranging an "accidental" crash. She realized with horror that it was dated a week before her parents had died.

In an instant, she had understood. Her uncle had never had a family of his own. He had always been jealous of his brother's intelligent wife and energetic daughter. And so he had decided to make them his own. Only it didn't go as he had planned. Lan's mother wasn't supposed to be in the car that day. She wasn't supposed to die.

"That's absurd," Aung Win said. "Is that what this has all been about? It was an *accident*."

Lan saw that he had regained his composure. Her uncle was moving closer to the building.

"I found the emails. Proof that you murdered your own brother," Lan said to him.

"You're mistaken. Come down—let's talk about this. We're still family."

"No, I lost my family. And I'm going to make sure you lose everything you care about, too. I'm going to tell the world that *you're* Myat Kaw. And you know how easy it will be for them to believe me—because every secret I stole came from you!"

Lan headed back up the fire escape stairway. She had set the hook the best she could.

Now, if only her uncle took the bait.

CHAPTER
51

**NEW YORK,
USA**

Aung Win's face twisted in rage. He noticed the ladder Ryan had unhooked earlier from the bottom of the fire escape. Bottom ladders were usually kept too high to reach from the street, but Ryan had lowered this one. And sure enough, Aung Win went for it, leaping up and pulling himself onto the rungs.

Lan slowed down at the stairs that led up to the next level. She needed to stay far enough ahead to not be caught, but close enough to keep her uncle in pursuit.

The distraction had worked. This was Ryan's chance.

When he'd first seen his mother, he'd been

momentarily overwhelmed. She was unsteady and disoriented, with dark circles under her eyes. And Lan's revelation that Aung Win was responsible for the deaths of her parents stunned him. But he couldn't afford to be sidetracked. He had to act fast.

Springing forward, he yelled, "Mom, duck!" Jacqueline reacted instantly, bending down. Ryan now had a clear shot at the bodyguard.

Ryan sprayed a stream of pepper spray right into the huge man's eyes! He screamed, hands covering his face, coughing and wheezing.

"Run!" Ryan yelled, grabbing his mom and pointing her down the street.

"Ryan, look out!" Jacqueline was looking over Ryan's shoulder. He spun around, raising the pepper spray. But the driver of the Town Car was too close. Before he could press the nozzle, the man batted his hand away, knocking the canister out of Ryan's grip. He punched Ryan in the stomach with enough force to make him double over, gasping.

The driver was about to strike again, when Jacqueline looped her hands around his neck and jerked him back. Her wrists were bound with plastic zip ties, which she now used as a weapon. His mom wasn't quite as drugged as she'd been pretending.

Ryan kicked the driver as hard as he could right in his crotch! The man's eyes opened wide, his cheeks puffed out, and he dropped to his knees. Mom knocked him out for good with a nasty kick to the side of the head. The bodyguard was stumbling around, swinging blindly at whatever he heard. Ryan dodged a near hit, then grabbed his mom's hand, pulling her after him.

"Around the corner," he urged, trying to catch his breath.

Kasey ran to meet them. "Hold your hands up." Jacqueline did, and Kasey quickly snipped the ties with the wire cutters. "Come on, we have to meet the others at the car!"

Jacqueline turned to Ryan. "Is Dad here?"

"No."

"You did this on your own?"

"I got help from my friends." Ryan saw the driver was already shaking off the blow and back on his knees. "We have to go."

As they turned the corner, Ryan glanced back at the roof of the building, hoping the rest of the plan was working as well as this part did.

CHAPTER
52

**NEW YORK,
USA**

anny leaned over the edge of the roof, watching anxiously as Lan dashed up the fire escape. Aung Win was close behind, quickly reducing the distance between them.

Danny could sense things turning bad. Aung Win was much faster than they'd guessed. Danny held a length of heavy pipe he'd found. He was ready to use it on Lan's crazy uncle if he had to.

"Hurry—he's catching up!" Danny shouted as she cleared the last set of stairs. Aung Win yelled at his niece and she glanced down. Lan's next step hit the rung of the ladder wrong. Her foot slid off the slick metal surface and she nearly fell. Aung Win leaped forward, grabbing for her ankle. But she dodged just in time, scrambling to the top where Danny hauled her over the edge.

"Get to Steeg," he said, turning back to the ladder with his heavy pipe. Time to play Whac-A-Mole on this dude's head!

But when Danny leaned over, he got a surprise: Aung Win had drawn his gun and was pointing it straight at him. Danny hurled the pipe as hard as he could. It slammed into Aung Win and knocked the gun from his hand. The weapon clattered along the fire escape, bouncing two levels down before coming to a rest. Aung Win roared with anger and surged upward.

Danny sprinted across the rooftop toward the office building next door, where it would be an easy drop from one building to the next. The plan was to make it to the office building's stairwell. Once they were inside, they could lock the metal door behind them and they'd be safe.

When Danny made it to the edge, Steeg was below, helping Lan drop from one roof down to the next. "Come on," Steeg urged, reaching up a hand to help Danny.

But before Danny could jump, Aung Win

shoved him. He toppled over, off-balance, and fell into Steeg. The boys tumbled to the ground. Danny rolled to his back and looked up as Aung Win loomed above them. The older man's eyes were poisonous as—*snit*—a switchblade snapped open in his hand.

"Move!" Lan yelled from the stairway door, which was propped open. Danny sprung to his feet and ran. As he closed the distance, he saw Lan looking in horror behind him. "Drew!" she screamed.

Danny stopped short, whirling around in time to see Aung Win leap down at Steeg. Steeg was big, but he was agile. He rolled out of the way as Aung Win landed. Crab crawling backward, he tried to get away, but a large air-conditioning unit blocked his way. Steeg was trapped as Aung Win advanced with the knife.

Danny charged at Aung Win with a ferocity he didn't know he possessed. He tackled the older man around the waist, trying to pull him down. But Aung Win was too strong. He stumbled, then quickly regained his balance and swung his knife.

Danny felt the blade slice his shoulder. He let go of Aung Win and staggered, stunned that he had actually been hit. His hand touched the wound and came away covered in blood.

Aung Win turned to Lan. "Do I need to kill them both?" he asked. Steeg tried to stand, but Aung Win's hand shot out, the point of the knife aimed right at the boy's chest. "Their blood will be on your hands . . . Myat Kaw."

Lan stepped forward, her face pale. "Let them go. You win, Uncle. I'll go with you."

"No," Steeg said.

Aung Win ignored him, striding toward her. "You will pay for your betrayal." He grabbed her roughly, pulling her through the stairwell door. The metal door slammed shut, locking Danny and Steeg out.

"We have to stop him," Steeg said, pulling out his cell phone.

"Yeah, we should . . . warn . . ." Danny's eyes fluttered before he fainted, collapsing to the roof.

CHAPTER
53

**NEW YORK,
USA**

D anny's hurt." The panic in Steeg's voice was evident, even through the cell phone. "And Lan's gone—her uncle took her."

Ryan and Kasey locked eyes as she pressed the talk button: "Are you okay?"

"Yeah. I've got Danny. We're coming down the fire escape. There's a lot of blood."

Ryan looked at the Stieglitzes' Lexus, then turned to his mom. "Can you drive?"

Jacqueline shook her head, woozy. "I can barely focus."

"Kasey, call 911—tell them we need an ambulance," Ryan said, already running. He was thankful they'd rescued his mom, but knew that whatever happened to Danny or Lan was his fault.

Ryan rounded the corner just in time to see Aung Win forcing Lan into the back of the Town Car. "Hey, stop! Somebody help!" The street was mostly empty, but a couple walking a dog turned to stare as Ryan ran toward the car.

Aung Win got in and the car started moving even before the door was closed. The Town Car turned right at the intersection and disappeared around the corner. Ryan watched, helpless once again, as Aung Win sped off with someone he cared about.

"Put me down!" Danny's voice pulled Ryan's attention back to the fire escape. Steeg had the smaller boy thrown over his shoulder, using a fireman's carry to get him down the ladder.

"Shut up and keep still," Steeg said, grunting with each step. Ryan ran over and helped lower Danny the rest of the way to the pavement. Steeg had taken off his jacket and used one sleeve to tightly wrap Danny's wound. Both the jacket and Danny were caked with blood.

Ryan's stomach clenched, fearing the worst for his friend. "Aw, man, what did he do to you?"

But Danny shrugged it off. "It's not that deep. I'm just kind of a wimp about blood. I've fainted at the doctor's office a few times."

"You probably saved my life up there," Steeg said. "You're no wimp."

"Remember that the next time you want to stuff me in a locker." Danny turned to Ryan. "Lan's uncle is nuts. You have to go after her."

"We need to get you to a doctor first." Ryan glanced down the street, where Kasey and Jacqueline were approaching. "I should've never let Lan help. I knew it was too dangerous."

Danny grabbed Ryan's arm. "Lan could've saved herself—she had the chance. But she didn't. She went with her uncle to save *us*."

Jacqueline knelt on the other side of Danny. "Stay still, Danny—let me take a look." Even in her disoriented state, her movements were assured and efficient.

Danny's eyes never left Ryan's. He thrust his own cell phone into Ryan's hand. "The phone I gave Lan—it's got my tracking app on it."

Ryan looked at Danny's phone and realized what his friend meant. He jumped up, turning to Steeg. "Will you drive?"

Steeg was already moving. "Hell yeah."

Ryan pulled off the Roy Halladay–signed baseball cap and put it on Danny's head. "For luck," he said, then raced off after Steeg.

"Drew!" Kasey yelled after them.

Hearing the alarm in Kasey's voice, Jacqueline looked up. "Ryan, no!"

Around the corner, Ryan jumped into the passenger seat of the Lexus as Steeg fired up the engine. With screeching tires, the sedan took the corner without slowing. They raced off in pursuit of the Town Car.

CHAPTER

54

**NEW YORK,
USA**

Steeg floored it, cutting in and out of traffic. Approaching a stoplight just as it turned red, Steeg hit the gas and the Lexus shot through the intersection. Angry drivers honked, forced to brake abruptly.

"Please, god, do not let us pass any cops," Steeg said, veering around a slow truck in front of them and jetting forward.

"Try not to crash," Ryan said, glancing down at Danny's tracker app and setting it to find Lan's phone.

"Brilliant. Wish I'd thought of that." Steeg accelerated around two more vehicles, swerving in and out of lanes to find a clear path.

A blinking red heart appeared on the map.

Ryan grinned. Of course that's the symbol Danny would give Lan. Looking up, he pointed ahead.

"Left up here. They're not that far ahead."

At the corner, Steeg took the left. The boulevard contained a shifting sea of delivery trucks, yellow taxis, and cars. Ryan forced himself not to examine each individual vehicle, focusing instead only on the color black.

Finally, he caught sight of the Town Car turning at the next block. "There—Spring Street!"

Steeg was on the wrong side of Broadway and had to cut across two lanes of traffic to make the turn. Spring Street wasn't as busy, and Ryan could see that the Town Car was slowing to a stop at the next red light.

Ryan's phone buzzed and he saw Kasey's name pop up on his screen. Probably his mom calling to tell him to stop. He didn't have time to argue with her now, so he declined the call.

"What do we do if we catch them?" Steeg asked. "They've got guns."

Ryan hadn't actually thought that far ahead, simply moving on adrenaline. "We'll do what you said before. Follow them to wherever they're going and then call the cops."

Steeg glanced over. "I'm not sure how much

good that's gonna do."

"Why not?"

"Lan's still a teenager and her uncle's her legal guardian. Plus, he's got diplomatic immunity. There's nothing the cops can do except maybe give him a speeding ticket. If he wants to take her back to Andakar, the police can't stop him." As he narrowed the distance between the two cars, Steeg clutched the steering wheel tightly. "I should've stopped him. I let him take her."

"No, it's my fault. You guys were never even supposed to be that close to Aung Win. I thought you'd be gone long before he got to the roof."

They drove in silence, Ryan racking his brain for a way to save Lan. Steeg looked over at him. "I was a jerk to you and Danny at school," he said. "Sorry. You guys are okay."

"You were just looking out for your little sister. Protecting her."

"Yeah, that's probably what Lan's douchebag uncle says to himself, too. That he's just protecting his people, looking out for them. But he's really nothing but a bully." Steeg glanced over at Ryan. "I'm not like him."

Ryan was surprised by the conviction in his tone. "I never thought you were."

As they made their way across the Bowery, Steeg stayed close to the Town Car, keeping behind a brown UPS truck so they wouldn't be visible. The UPS truck abruptly shifted lanes, leaving the Lexus exposed. Ryan was shocked to see Aung Win turned around in his seat, looking out the back window right at them!

"He saw us," Ryan blurted, as the Town Car swerved hard to the right, taking off down a side street. Steeg pounded the brake, spinning the wheel so the sedan skidded into a turn. They fishtailed, but he managed to straighten out and keep going.

Now that they knew they were being followed, the driver of the Town Car was much more aggressive, weaving in and out of traffic. Steeg trailed behind, matching his moves, though he wasn't nearly as fast. The Town Car driver had obviously done this before.

"He's turning again," Ryan said. "Left—left!"

Steeg attempted the turn, but didn't quite make it, popping over the curb and hitting a green trash can next to the streetlight. The trash can smashed off the bumper as the Lexus bounced down the other side of the curb, heading right for a parked car. Steeg jerked the wheel, barely avoiding a collision.

"Man, I'm so gonna be grounded for this."

Ryan saw something fly out of the Town Car's back window. Almost instantly, the blinking red heart on the tracking app disappeared.

"He threw her phone out. Don't lose them!"

The Town Car executed a series of sharp turns. Steeg did his best to keep up, but he was no match for the professional driver, who clearly didn't care if he hit any pedestrians. After several minutes, the Lexus pulled into an intersection, Ryan looking one way, Steeg the other.

"Where'd they go?" Steeg asked.

"I didn't see." Ryan glanced down as his phone began buzzing once more. Kasey's ID again—probably his mom. He ignored it, searching the streets for the Town Car.

But it was gone.

Steeg pulled the Lexus to the curb. "What do we do now?"

Looking out the front window, Ryan noticed the metal towers of the Williamsburg Bridge in the distance. With all the erratic turns, he hadn't realized where they were. But as he looked at the sweeping expanse of the bridge that connected Manhattan to Long Island, something struck him: "When Aung Win called to set up the trade for my mom, he wanted to meet at the East Shore Aerodrome."

Gazing at the bridge, Steeg made the connection. "So they could have been coming this direction to get on the Williamsburg Bridge. But that place isn't a real airport, is it?"

"No. It's more of a club for people with old planes," Ryan said, feeling like he was on the right track. "But it's got a runway and lots of old hangars and buildings."

Steeg got it, already shifting the car back into gear. "A good place to hide a private jet."

"If he gets Lan on a plane, we'll never get her back."

Steeg said what they both feared: "If he hasn't killed her already."

CHAPTER
55

**NEW YORK,
USA**

Kasey hung up her phone, frustrated. She'd tried to call Ryan and Drew both, but neither had answered. The sidewalk was now busy with onlookers who were curious about all the excitement, and the sounds of sirens could be heard approaching. Things were about to get even more complicated.

Jacqueline had attended to Danny's cut with the proficiency of a field medic. She'd stripped off Drew's bloody jacket, and then appropriated a scarf and bottle of water from one of the bystanders to clean and bandage the wound. Despite her ordeal and the drugs in her system, Ryan's mom stayed focused. This was a woman used to handling a crisis, Kasey thought.

As the paramedics arrived, Jacqueline turned to Kasey. "Your bag," she said. "Do you have a hair band or any makeup?"

Kasey was surprised by the request. "I think I have both." Opening the bag, she pushed aside the scissors and tools, grabbing a scrunchie from the bottom and some blush and lip gloss from the zippered compartment.

Jacqueline pulled her disheveled hair into a ponytail and slid the scrunchie into place. As she applied the lip gloss and a quick dab of blush to her cheeks, she whispered urgently to Kasey. "Danny was robbed. The attacker was a white male in his twenties, wearing a green hoodie. He took off down the street. Got it?"

Kasey nodded, feeling like she was in a spy movie.

"Keep trying to reach Ryan." Jacqueline handed back the makeup as she stepped toward the arriving paramedics. "Thank goodness you're here! This poor boy says he was mugged, but I think he's okay."

Jacqueline's transformation was amazing, the weary victim replaced in a few moments with an energetic Good Samaritan. Kasey marveled at how quickly she had adapted to the situation.

Kasey stepped away from the crowd as Danny took to the story like a fish to water and hammed it up for the crowd: "I could've taken him, but he was huge—like, seven feet tall— maybe *bigger*!"

Instead of phoning Ryan again, she texted, *It's Kasey—call me!* Moments later, her phone vibrated, and she answered instantly. "Are you guys okay?"

"We lost Lan," Ryan said. "Sorry I didn't pick up. I thought it was my mom."

Kasey glanced over at Jacqueline, who was now busy with the paramedics as they checked out Danny. "She's got her hands full right now. Where are you?"

"Long Island. Headed toward the East Shore Aerodrome."

Kasey heard the frustration in Ryan's tone. "That's where Aung Win wanted to make the trade, right?"

"Yeah. I'm hoping maybe he has a plane hidden there."

"It makes sense he'd want to trade somewhere he could get her out of the country right away." Kasey thought of something else. "Remember that warehouse Danny and I investigated? They had all that top secret, high-tech equipment hidden away that they weren't supposed to have. Maybe a private plane is how they get it all out of the country."

"If Aung Win was caught smuggling top secret tech out of the United States, his diplomatic immunity could be stripped."

"I've got an idea," Kasey said, digging in her bag. She retrieved the business card Agent Calloway had given her, flipping it over to see the CIA agent's handwritten cell phone number on the back. Glancing over, she saw that Danny was being wheeled away on a gurney. "I gotta go—I'll call you back."

Without waiting for an answer, she hung up, pushing her way through to Danny. "Where are you going?"

"The hospital—but I'm fine. I just need a few stitches. Hopefully, I'll have an awesome scar."

Kasey leaned in close, walking along with the gurney. "I need the video of the warehouse."

Sensing her urgency, Danny pulled out a thin wallet and handed it over. "All the memory cards are in there. What's going on?"

"It's time we got a little help," Kasey told him. The paramedics hauled Danny up into the truck and slammed the doors closed.

Kasey dialed Agent Calloway's number.

CHAPTER
56

**NEW YORK,
USA**

A huge sign read East Shore Aerodrome—Aviation Historical Society. Below that was another sign: No Trespassing!

"Looks deserted," Steeg said.

Ryan got out of the Lexus to take a look. The afternoon was turning into evening, twilight coming on quickly. Tall trees lined the fence in both directions. On the other side of the gate, the road veered off to the right, making it impossible to see the actual airfield.

The gate was wrapped with chains and locked up tight. Ryan checked to see if he could climb the fence, but the top was lined with barbed wire. Steeg got out and followed as Ryan left the road and walked the property line.

He hoped to find a spot where he could see the runway or possibly find a tree to climb.

"Maybe he took her somewhere else," Steeg suggested.

Then, a high-pitched whine echoed through the trees. They froze in place, listening.

"That sounds like a plane," Ryan said.

Steeg pivoted and ran for the Lexus. "They're gonna take off!"

Ryan dashed after him, getting in the passenger seat just as Steeg shifted into reverse. He backed the car up several feet, then slammed into drive. "Hold on!"

Ryan grabbed the handhold above him, bracing himself as the car surged forward. They hit the entrance with a violent impact, snapping the lock and flinging the gates wide open!

Inside, the road changed from asphalt to dirt. They still couldn't see the runway because of the surrounding trees, but the sound of the plane's engine was getting closer.

"Stop here," Ryan said. "We don't want them to see us."

Steeg pulled to the side of the road and they both got out. Using the trees as cover, they crept forward until they had a view of the airfield.

A collection of hangars and small buildings

ran alongside a grass runway, which stretched off into the distance. Halfway down, one of the hangars was open and a sleek, private jet emerged into the twilight.

"They're here." Ryan pointed to the Town Car, parked just outside the hangar. The bodyguard and driver stood watching the jet as it taxied forward.

"If they get her in that plane," Steeg said, "she's gone forever."

Ryan noticed an old bi-wing plane, like something the Red Baron would have flown, tethered close to one of the sheet metal structures. The vintage plane was probably part of the historical society mentioned on the sign. Looking past it, he realized that the buildings along the runway formed a line. From the airfield, it would be impossible to see the road.

"We can drive around behind the hangars," he said. "They won't be able to see your car from the runway. If we come up between the buildings, we might be able to surprise them."

"And then what? What exactly is our play here?"

"Kinda making it up as I go along," Ryan admitted.

Steeg shook his head. "How did I end up taking directions from an *eighth grader*?"

They hurried back to the car and Steeg drove behind the row of buildings, where they couldn't be seen. As they approached the hangar with the jet, the whine of the engine drowned out all other sound. Steeg got as close to the back of the hangar as possible before Ryan stopped him and jumped out. "Wait here."

Ryan ran to the front of the hangar and peered around the corner. The jet was very close, a small but stylish private plane. The stairs were down, and two cargo doors in the back were now open. The bodyguard and the driver helped the pilot and two other men load crates. Ryan recognized the logo of LTV Technologies from the video Kasey and Danny had taken at the warehouse. Aung Win was smuggling the stolen, top secret technology out of the country on the same flight he was taking with Lan.

The back door of the Town Car opened and Aung Win got out, giving orders to his men. He gestured impatiently as Lan slid across the seat. Aung Win motioned for her to get on the plane, and she began to shuffle forward slowly. Ryan darted back to the open passenger window of the Lexus.

"They're putting her on the jet," he said. "Can

you keep them busy?"

"What're you gonna do?"

"I'm gonna get her out of there."

Steeg peeled out, lying on the horn as he zoomed by. The Lexus exploded from between the hangars and headed right for the jet! Steeg was driving like he was insane.

Ryan sprinted, knowing he'd only have seconds before Aung Win spotted him. Up ahead, Aung Win and Lan dodged out of the way as the sedan swerved back and forth. The huge bodyguard was already drawing a gun as Steeg steered right toward him.

The Lexus plowed into the open door of the Town Car, wrenching it off its hinges. The bodyguard tried to jump from its path, but he was too slow. The Lexus clipped his legs—he rolled over the hood before crashing to the ground.

"Lan!" Ryan closed the distance as she looked up, shocked to see him there. "This way!"

Lan reacted a moment too late, giving her uncle time to grab her. He pulled her close, but was caught off guard when she slammed the back of her skull right into his jaw! Aung Win shrieked in agony, letting go. Lan shoved him away and took off running.

Ryan indicated the dark hangars. "In there!"

As they ran, he glanced back. Steeg was spinning the Lexus around to come back for them. But the Town Car driver fired a shot, shattering the Lexus's side window. Ryan froze—did the bullet hit Steeg? But the Lexus did a quick U-turn, letting him know Steeg was still driving. Another shot rang out, forcing him to speed off away from the hangars.

Ryan made it to the hangar as Lan disappeared inside. Aung Win and the driver were coming after them, guns drawn and closing in fast.

CHAPTER
57

**NEW YORK,
USA**

Inside, the hangar was cavernous and dark. It must be some kind of maintenance area, Ryan thought. It was crammed with racks full of airplane parts and tools. He and Lan ducked behind a tall, mobile staircase used by mechanics to reach the airplane engines.

"You shouldn't have come after me," Lan whispered. "He'll kill you, too."

"Only if he catches us," Ryan said.

Ryan took her hand and they ran behind a row of steel shelves, crouching low to keep out of sight. The door to the hangar burst open. Aung Win and the driver entered, their raised weapons silhouetted against the evening sky. They split up, the driver moving away while

Aung Win came in their direction.

Spread across the length of the hangar were three vintage planes; two were bi-wings like the one outside, and the other was a Piper Cub with a big propeller on its front. Ryan motioned toward the Piper Cub, and Lan moved that way. Passing a rolling metal tool chest, Ryan had an idea. He grabbed the first thing he found—a screwdriver sitting right on top—and hurled it across the hangar.

The screwdriver hit the far side of the building with a loud bang. Aung Win fired instantly, the sound echoing in the confined space. He headed off in search of Ryan and Lan, as they continued in the opposite direction.

"I think I see an exit." Lan pointed to the far corner of the hangar, which was mostly lost in shadows. The faint outline of a door was barely visible.

"All right," Ryan whispered. "Halfway there."

The clatter of a screw skittering across the concrete caused Ryan to swivel around. The driver was right behind them! Ryan pulled Lan out of the way as another shot rang out. Before the driver could fire again, Ryan was on him, using his forearms like a battering ram to knock the wiry man down.

"Get to the door," Ryan said. He turned to follow Lan, but the driver grabbed his leg, tripping him. He fell, the driver on top of him before he knew what was happening. The guy was fast, straddling Ryan and wrapping both hands around his throat. Ryan gasped, but he couldn't get any air, the driver choking him viciously, trying to crush his windpipe.

Wham! Lan swung a wrench into the side of the driver's head and he toppled over, out cold before he even hit the floor. With a fierce look in her eyes, she reached out to give Ryan a hand up. "Let's get out of here."

"So brave." They both whirled around to discover Aung Win, his pistol aimed at Lan's head. "But so stupid. Did you think two children could outwit a colonel of the ASI?"

Ryan stepped in front of Lan, instinctively shielding her. Aung Win scrutinized him, curious. "Why do you care? Why risk so much for someone you barely know?"

Ryan met his gaze head-on. "Call it a family tradition."

"In the end, Myat Kaw is nothing but one sad little voice against the power of Andakar's generals."

"Well, she certainly scared you," Ryan said.

"When she's gone, no one will remember she ever existed."

"Then someone new will step up to take my place," Lan said, defiantly. "There'll always be someone to stand up to tyrants like you."

Annoyed, Aung Win stepped forward, raising his gun . . . but then, hearing something, he hesitated. It was the roar of a helicopter outside, getting closer by the moment.

"This is the FBI," a voice from a bullhorn bellowed. "Lay down your weapons and lie on the ground!" Confused, Aung Win looked to Ryan.

"Sounds like they're talking to your men," Ryan said. "But I think *you're* the one they really want."

Aung Win sneered. "Your FBI and police can't touch me. I have diplomatic immunity."

"You also have a plane full of stolen top secret military technology sitting on the runway." Ryan saw Aung Win's bravado falter. "That's espionage. Immunity won't protect you."

Aung Win couldn't disguise his panic as the reality of his situation set in.

"Lower your weapons immediately!" the bullhorn thundered once more. Aung Win involuntarily glanced toward the door and Ryan sprang forward, knowing this might be his only chance.

He grabbed Aung Win's wrist, jerking his arm straight up as Aung Win fired. The blast so close to his ear was disorienting, but Ryan managed to rip the gun from Aung Win's grasp, knocking it away. Ryan tried driving an elbow into Aung Win's stomach, but the older man was too fast. He ducked the blow and punched Ryan hard in the small of the back.

Ryan stumbled as Lan charged, the wrench held high. Her uncle easily sidestepped the attack, using Lan's own momentum to send her sprawling onto the concrete. Turning to Ryan, Aung Win produced the switchblade. The knife flicked open in his hand.

"You should have just given me the traitor." Aung Win lunged, the blade barely missing Ryan as he twisted out of reach. He took off running, hoping to lure Lan's uncle away so she could escape. But within a few feet, he realized he couldn't outpace Aung Win.

Changing direction, Ryan sprinted toward the bi-plane. As Aung Win reached him, Ryan dropped into a slide, gliding on the smooth concrete floor underneath the plane's body. It bought him a few seconds, as Aung Win had to go around.

As he ran, Ryan's shoulder grazed a tall metal

rack filled with airplane parts, and it swayed, pieces falling to the floor. On the top shelf, a small propeller rattled precariously, giving Ryan an idea. He backed up to the corner of the rack, waiting.

Aung Win came around, stopping as he spotted Ryan. Ryan grabbed the edge of the rack and pulled with everything he had. The propeller tumbled off the top shelf and hit Aung Win's head. The rest of the rack followed as Ryan brought the entire thing crashing down, pinning Aung Win underneath!

As Aung Win moaned, Ryan came around and stared down at him. "That's for my mom."

"Ryan, come on!" Lan yelled.

Ryan glanced once more at Aung Win, who was stunned and immobile, then joined Lan across the hangar. They made it to the far door, exiting just as the FBI stormed in. They surrounded Aung Win, taking him into federal custody.

CHAPTER
58

**LOCATION
UNKNOWN**

Tasha didn't like the man in the bow tie. But he was a necessary evil. She had learned that you don't always have to like the people you work for.

And he did pay well.

The room they were using was dark and dingy, but the smell of sea salt in the air made it almost bearable. Hopefully, they wouldn't be here long. Just long enough to get the information they needed.

John Quinn struggled against the leather cuffs that secured him to the chair. It was probably a good thing he was gagged, Tasha thought. Based on the hate-filled glare he was giving her, she didn't want to hear anything he had to say.

"This will be easier if you don't resist," said the man in the bow tie. He was short and bald with pale skin. People who met him often guessed he was a professor, timid and brainy. But Tasha had learned not to underestimate him. The man in the bow tie was the most dangerous person she had ever met.

He held up a syringe with a thin needle. "Sodium thiopental. Commonly called truth serum. But this is my own formula—I think you'll find it's quite effective."

Quinn thrashed harder against the cuffs. But it did him no good. He wasn't getting away.

"You're going to give us names," the man in the bow tie told him. "That doesn't sound too difficult, does it? Names, addresses, contact information. And the best part is, when we're done—you won't remember a thing. Two days from now, you'll be back home with your family. Safe and sound with no memory whatsoever of what went on here."

John Quinn went still. He had finally realized what was happening. The Emergency Rescue Committee was about to be destroyed. And he was the one who would bring it down.

Quinn looked to Tasha, begging her with his eyes not to let this happen. But it was too late to turn back now.

The man in the bow tie turned to her. "I think it's time you made the call. We don't want his family to worry. Tell them he'll be home soon."

Tasha took out her phone and dialed. She turned away. The betrayal in John's eyes made her uncomfortable. Thankfully, her call was quickly answered.

"Tasha?" said Jacqueline Quinn, miles away in America.

"Jacqueline—thank goodness! Are you all right?"

"I am now. Are you with John?"

"Yes," Tasha said. "We made it across the border. He's with the doctors, but they're fixing him up. He's going to be fine."

Behind her, John Quinn roared beneath his gag. But it only lasted a few seconds. After that, there was silence.

CHAPTER 59

**NEW YORK,
USA**

Ryan finally got to hug his mom.

They held on for a long time, knowing how close they had come to losing each other. Finally, Jacqueline pulled away, smiling.

"Dad's okay. He's out of Andakar."

Ryan couldn't believe it. "He called?"

"Tasha Levi did. She found him and helped him cross the border."

"She made it!"

"Tasha can be challenging, but she's tough. They're in Thailand now. Dad was in surgery for his wound, but Tasha says he'll be out soon and he's doing well. They'll fly home tomorrow or the day after."

Ryan turned to Lan, just getting out of the

banged-up Lexus at the curb of the brownstone. "My dad got away," he told her. "You did it—you saved him."

He'd never seen Lan smile so brightly. She hugged him with relief as Steeg joined them on the sidewalk.

"Mom, this is Lan," Ryan said, as they parted.

"I know exactly who she is." Jacqueline took Lan's hands in her own. "You're a courageous young woman. We're going to do everything we can to help you."

"Your family's already done too much."

Ryan looked up at Kasey on the brownstone's front steps. "How's Danny?"

"Loving the attention. He'll probably be on every evening newscast before he's done. I think it's now up to four muggers that he single-handedly fought off."

Ryan laughed. Steeg just shook his head.

"Happy to see you're feeling better, Ryan." They all turned to discover Agent Calloway. Ryan and his mom instinctively moved closer together. "Have to say, you both look like you've been through quite an ordeal."

Her gaze was piercing, but Jacqueline didn't miss a beat. "Is there something we can help you with, agent?"

"I just came to say thanks." She turned to Kasey. "I thought I might find you here. We were so appreciative to get that video you sent."

"I'm happy to help," Kasey said without any hesitation. "It was pure luck I happened to go into that particular warehouse."

"With your camera running," Calloway added. "Very lucky."

"Sometimes things just work out." Ryan had to keep himself from grinning. Kasey was playing it so cool.

"Our associates at the FBI caught Aung Win and his men red-handed. And the Andakar military leadership is denying all knowledge of his activities. So he'll be going away for a long time." She suddenly focused on Lan. "And who are you?"

"Emma Manado," Lan said, using the name on her fake passport. "I'm visiting."

"She's a foreign exchange student," Jacqueline offered.

"From Indonesia," Ryan said. "She'll be staying with us awhile."

They were a united front. Agent Calloway nodded, looking at each in turn, letting them know she didn't believe them for a second. "Well, welcome to America, Emma Manado. I hope you like it here." She looked at Jacqueline. "I'll be anxious to talk to your husband when he returns. We still have a lot of questions."

She turned and walked off.

"Man, I don't know how much of this I can take," Steeg said. "I thought playing for the junior varsity championship was intense. But it's nothing compared to this."

Ryan grabbed his shoulder. "You kidding? You were awesome out there tonight."

"It *was* pretty exciting." He turned to the Lexus. "Though I don't think my dad's gonna be nearly as stoked."

"Don't worry about the car," Jacqueline said. "We'll get it fixed, along with a good cover story for your father."

Ryan turned to Kasey. "We better hurry or we're not gonna make it."

She was confused. "Make it where?"

"The Autumn Carnival Dance—it starts at eight, right?"

"Ryan, I was just kidding earlier," Kasey said. "We don't have to go—not after everything that's happened."

"I want to go. Lan's free, my parents are safe, and we just pulled off the craziest idea I've ever had in my life. Tonight, I just want to be a normal kid and go to my very first school dance." He turned to his mom. "If that's okay?"

"I think it sounds like a great idea."

Kasey looked down at her shirt and jeans. "Well, I can't go looking like this." She headed for the car, grabbing Steeg. "You've got to get me home to change!"

Steeg looked to Lan, nervous. "I don't— I mean, this is probably weird, but . . . if you wanted to—"

Ryan smiled as the big jock fumbled, then saved him. "I think what he's saying is, how'd you like to go to the dance with him?"

"Yeah." Steeg nodded. "What he said."

Lan was excited. "I've never danced with a boy."

"We don't have to dance if you don't want to."

"Oh, I want to!" They both had those goofy grins again.

Kasey opened the door for Lan. "Then get in—I've got the perfect dress for you to borrow." Lan climbed in as Steeg hurried to the driver's side. Kasey got in and slammed the door, then looked at Ryan. "See you soon."

As the Lexus raced off, Jacqueline put her arm around Ryan.

"I'm so proud of you. I hope you know that."

Ryan still felt some resentment about his parents' lifelong deception, but there'd be time to work through that later. "I'm just glad everybody's okay."

"We'll have a long talk when Dad gets home. There are things you need to know. But tonight, just have fun. Be a teenager—you deserve it."

Ryan had a feeling there was something else bothering his mother, something other than the Emergency Rescue Committee and its work. But for tonight, he was gonna take her advice and not worry about it.

Tonight, he was gonna have fun.

EPILOGUE

**NEW YORK,
USA**

The Autumn Carnival Dance was a riot of yellow and orange, with streamers draped everywhere and pumpkin-shaped paper lanterns suspended from the school cafeteria's ceiling. The floor was covered with countless red-and-gold maple leaf cutouts, giving Ryan the impression he was walking on a forest floor.

The party had been in full swing for a while now as he entered, a bass beat thumping and kids dancing to a hip-hop song Ryan didn't recognize. He searched the crowd and spotted Kasey, already heading toward him.

"You look incredible!" she said, taking in his new clothes. Ryan wore a sleek black blazer with gray skinny jeans and cherry-red high-tops.

"I didn't have much time to shop," he admitted. "Mom helped me pick everything out. Except for the high-tops—those were all me."

"Well, you've got excellent taste."

"That's what I kept telling her." Kasey laughed as Ryan admired her dress, a shimmering, silver, 1920s flapper style, with fringe that sparkled as it moved. "Wow. You're like a disco ball."

Kasey twirled, the fringe flaring and creating little flashes of light. "This was my costume for a musical production of *The Great Gatsby* last year. I know it's kind of gaudy, but I love it."

"It's perfect," Ryan said, totally meaning it.

"They're cute together." Kasey nodded across the room, where Lan clung to Steeg's arm, both of them dressed up now and looking great. Steeg was over a foot taller than Lan and held her close, protective as she marveled at the dancing kids, the loud music, and all the decorations.

Ryan understood how strange and bewildering this all must be for her—it still felt that way to him a lot of the time. But the truth was, kids around the world weren't actually all that different. They just wanted the freedom to be themselves, whoever that might be.

"Have you seen Danny?" Ryan asked.

"This way." She took his hand, leading him through the crowd. "Your mom made him a hero."

They found Danny sitting on a cafeteria table that had been pushed to the wall, surrounded by guys and girls, all listening with rapt attention. His arm was bandaged and hung in a sling around his neck.

"The guy was trying to rob this little old lady and I was like, 'Dude, back off, or I will take you down!'" Ryan smiled as Danny acted out his story. "So I'm all ready to do some karate on him, and then he pulls out this machete!"

"A machete?" Ryan said.

"Ry-ry!" Danny winked at a pretty girl who was smiling at him, then joined Ryan and Kasey. "Today was *so* worth five stitches."

Ryan laughed—Danny's enthusiasm was infectious. "Apparently."

"So what happens next? Are we, like, official members of the ERC now? Do we get to go rescue people and stuff?"

"I don't know." Ryan looked to Kasey, too. "All I know is, working together we managed to do something that none of us could have accomplished alone. So, thanks."

"Enough shop talk, boys. We came here to dance!" With a playful grin, Kasey beckoned them both to the dance floor. Danny followed, already grooving, even with his arm in a sling.

Ryan was nervous. Would he look like an idiot trying to dance with all these kids who knew what they were doing? He took a deep breath, telling himself to just get it over with, when Principal Milankovic stepped in front of him.

"Mr. Quinn. It's good to see you're feeling well again."

"Oh, uh—yeah. Thanks." Principal Milankovic wore a stern expression, and Ryan could tell he was skeptical. "I'll be sure to bring a note from my parents on Monday."

The principal nodded, his attitude softening. "I'm glad you're okay. I was worried."

"Thanks." There was something odd in his manner, Ryan thought, like it was personal to him. But Ryan had known Milankovic for only the past couple of months. Shaking off the weird feeling, he started toward the dance floor, when the principal suddenly grabbed his elbow, stopping him.

"You have to talk to your parents," he whispered urgently. He looked up, scanning the room as if to make sure no one was watching them. "There's so much you don't know."

"About what?"

"It's not my place to say. But you deserve the truth." Now, he looked Ryan right in the eye. "The truth about who you really are. Ask your parents."

Abruptly, Principal Milankovic let go and walked away. He strode off through the crowd, leaving Ryan confused.

What did he mean, the truth about who you really are?

Ryan started to go after him, but Kasey was suddenly at his side, taking his hand.

"Come on," she encouraged. "It's not that scary!"

Ryan glanced toward Milankovic's retreating figure but finally allowed her to lead him toward the dance floor. A sea of dancing teenagers quickly engulfed him.

"It's okay to let go," Kasey shouted over the music. "It's all over now."

Ryan knew in his heart it wasn't over at all. In fact, this felt more like a beginning. But she was right. For tonight, everyone was home and life was good again.

So Ryan made himself forget about what might be ahead and focus on where he was right now. He knew he wasn't a very good dancer, but that didn't seem to matter much. Surrounded by his friends, Ryan finally let loose, the music and laughter washing over him, and, for a little while at least, life was perfect.

TO BE CONTINUED . . .

CHRONICLES
OF THE
RED KING
Leopards' Gold

JENNY NIMMO

SCHOLASTIC PRESS / NEW YORK

For Richard Simpson

Nimmo, Jenny.
Leopards' gold / Jenny Nimmo. — 1st ed.
p. cm. — (Chronicles of the red king ; 3)
Summary: It is years since King Timoken, his sister, Zobayda, and his friends settled in the enchanted
Red Castle, but now they are all threatened by the evil beyond the castle's protective spells — and it
will be up to two of Timoken's nine children, Petrello and Tolomeo, to find out which of their
siblings is the traitor in their midst, and defeat their enemies.
ISBN 978-0-545-25185-3 (jacketed hardcover) 1. Magic — Juvenile fiction. 2. Kings and rulers —
Juvenile fiction. 3. Brothers and sisters — Juvenile fiction. 4. Castles — Fiction. [1. Magic — Fiction.
2. Kings, queens, rulers, etc. — Fiction. 3. Brothers and sisters — Fiction. 4. Castles — Fiction.]
I. Title. II. Series: Nimmo, Jenny. Chronicles of the Red King ; bk. 3.
PZ7.N5897Leo 2013
813.54 — dc23
2012043508

10 9 8 7 6 5 4 3 2 1   13 14 15 16 17

Printed in the U.S.A. 23

First edition, November 2013

Book design by Elizabeth B. Parisi

CONTENTS

CHAPTER 1   The Vanishing   1

CHAPTER 2   The Investigator's Message   15

CHAPTER 3   The Hall of Corrections   29

CHAPTER 4   Caught in the Forest   41

CHAPTER 5   Wolves and Eagles   55

CHAPTER 6   The Missing Crystal   69

CHAPTER 7   Guanhamara's Demon   85

CHAPTER 8   A Sword Fight   101

CHAPTER 9   The Enchanted Helmet   117

CHAPTER 10   Breaking the Spell   131

CHAPTER 11   Lilith's Punishment   143

CHAPTER 12   A Serpent in the Solarium   161

CHAPTER 13   Touching the Future   173

CHAPTER 14   A Cloak of Feathers   187

CHAPTER 15   Quelling the Storm   199

CHAPTER 16   Wizards' Smoke   211

CHAPTER 17   The Royal Tower   225

CHAPTER 18   Zobayda's Ring   239

CHAPTER 19   The House on Stilts   255

CHAPTER 20   Leopards' Gold   269

CHAPTER 21   Dragonfire   285

CHAPTER 22   The Damzel and the King   299

CHAPTER 23   Petrello's Storm   313

CHAPTER 24   A Celebration   327

ABOUT THE AUTHOR   337

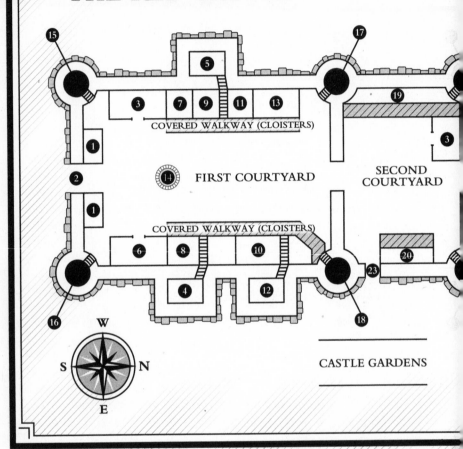

GROUND MAP OF
THE RED CASTLE

COVERED WALKWAY (CLOISTERS)

FIRST COURTYARD

SECOND COURTYARD

COVERED WALKWAY (CLOISTERS)

CASTLE GARDENS

W
S   N
E

1	Guardroom	**9**	Children's Dining Hall
2	South Gate	**10**	Great Hall
3	Stables	**11**	Chancellor's Office
4	Library	**12**	Children's Bedchambers
5	Chancellor's Apartments	**13**	Meeting Hall
6	Kitchens	**14**	Pump and Well
7	Schoolroom	**15**	Gray Men's Chambers
8	Hall of Corrections	**16**	Bell Tower

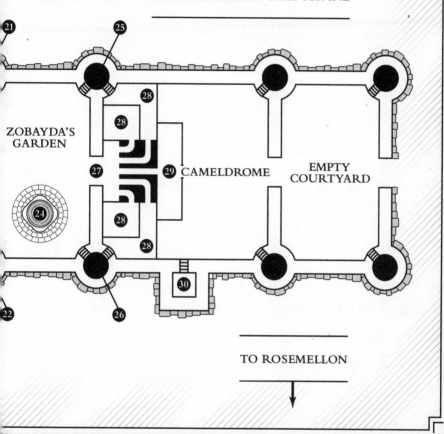

RIVER AT BASE OF DEEP RAVINE

ZOBAYDA'S GARDEN

CAMELDROME

EMPTY COURTYARD

TO ROSEMELLON

17	Armory / Helmet Room	25	Royal Tower / Solarium
18	Aerie / Sanatorium	26	Zobayda's Tower
19	Blacksmiths' Forges	27	Entrance to Passages
20	Carpenters' Workrooms	28	Secret Room
21	Knights' Apartments	29	Golden Room (Chamber of
22	Families of Workmen		Pictures)
23	East Gate	30	Plants, Herbs, Seeds
24	Fountain		

CHARACTERS

In the Red Castle

TIMOKEN

An African King. When he was born, his mother wrapped him in the web of the last moon spider. It was a gift from a forest-jinni who said that it would give Timoken immortality and exceptional powers. When he was eleven, Timoken's parents were killed by another tribe, aided by demons from the forest. Timoken escaped from his kingdom with his sister, Zobayda, and together they traveled the world, eventually coming to Britain. Timoken is now nearly three hundred years old. The moon spider's web has become his cloak.

ZOBAYDA

Timoken's sister. She wears a ring made from the web of the last moon spider. This gives her some protection but does not make her immortal. She is clairvoyant and has aged faster than her brother.

BERENICE

Born in the Spanish kingdom of Castile, her father was the greatest swordsman in the land. She was kidnapped when she was twelve, but rescued by Timoken. They were later married.

ERI

A wizard. He and Timoken escaped from Castle Melyntha when it was taken over by the conquerors. Eri is one of the ancient Welsh/Britons.

LLYR

Eri's grandson, and also a wizard. Llyr's parents were murdered by the conquerors.

THORKIL

Son of the Saxon earl Sigurd, who was murdered by the conquerors. He is now King Timoken's chancellor.

EDERN, MABON, PEREDUR, AND FRIAR GEREINT

Welsh/Britons who were kidnapped when they were children and were about to be sold as slaves when Timoken rescued them. They are now his most faithful knights, except for Gereint, who was brought up in a monastery.

RIGG

Bellman of the Red Castle.

WYNGATE

Investigator of the Red Castle. He escaped from the town of Innswood when it was burned down by the conquerors.

CHIMERY

Married to Thorkil's sister, Elfrieda. The chancellor's right-hand man.

The King's Children

BORLATH

Age nineteen by the time of this chronicle. He can burn objects with his fingers.

AMADIS

Age eighteen. He can communicate with animals.

LILITH

Age sixteen. She can bewitch others with clothing.

CAFAL

Age fourteen. A were-beast.

OLGA

Age thirteen. She can move objects with her mind.

GUANHAMARA

Age eleven. At the beginning of this chronicle, the king's younger children have not discovered their talents.

PETRELLO

Age ten.

TOLOMEO

Age nine.

VYBORN
Age six.

In the Forest

TUMI
Friend of Timoken and son of a fisherman.

SILA
Tumi's wife.

KARLI
Tumi's friend.

ESGA
Karli's wife.

All four were children when the conquerors burned down their homes in the town of Innswood. They escaped and lived in the forest.

OSBERN D'ARK
Steward to Prince Griffith of Melyntha Castle. When the
prince was killed in battle, Osbern, a conqueror, began to take
control of the castle. All Welsh/Britons had to leave or be
killed.

THE DAMZEL OF DECAY
An evil spirit who lives in the forest. An enemy of sunlight, she
embodies all the death and decay that occurs in the damp and
the dark. She hungers for the Red King's cloak.

THE CONQUERORS
People of Norman/French descent referred to as conquerors
because their ancestors invaded England in 1066. Since then
conquerors have occupied the English throne.

Animals

GABAR
A camel. He came from Africa and has traveled the world with
Timoken. He is also nearly three hundred years old, having
drunk some of the Alixir the forest-jinni gave to Timoken's
mother.

ENID

A dragon. She feels that she belongs to Eri, the wizard. She loves Gabar.

GREYFLEET

A wolf. Leader of his pack and friend to Amadis.

SUN CAT, FLAME CHIN, AND STAR

Leopards. Timoken wrapped them in the moon spider's web when they were cubs. Now they are immortal and magical.

ISGOFAN

Amadis's black horse.

ELIZEN

The queen's white horse.

CHAPTER 1
The Vanishing

The spell began at their feet. Eri, sitting on a tree stump, hummed; his voice broke often and he paused in his chant. He was now very old and couldn't hold the notes for long. Today it was his grandson, Llyr, who murmured and sang as he walked beside the wall of leaves.

Every autumn, children from the castle would gather freshly fallen leaves and build up the wall until it reached their knees. It would remain throughout the winter, but in the summer months the leaves would sink a little and the wall had to be built up again, and then, when the wizards chanted, everything inside the wall would become invisible.

The spell-wall extended deep into the forest. It encircled the castle whose sixteen towers rose above the trees. As Llyr sang, the spell crept through the grass until it reached the great yews that stood on either side of the high castle gate. The yews and the gate were slowly swallowed. The spell drifted over the castle gardens; it covered the bank of roses and the marble statues. Hedges of rosemary, hawthorn, and sage were gently shrouded in a white mist.

The pond melted into gossamer, the stone steps dissolved, the great castle doors disappeared along with the high red walls and, finally, the sixteen towers.

The castle and its inhabitants were now invisible to the outside world. Humans and animals were also floating. This was the only drawback to invisibility and a bell was always rung to warn the people that soon they would be swept off their feet, or out of their beds.

Llyr returned to Eri. "It is done. You can rest now, Grandfather."

"Did you hear the bell?" asked Eri.

"I was listening to our chant. I heard no warning. But I told the bellman the spell would soon begin."

"It never came. Timoken will be annoyed. His sister is frail and shouldn't be tossed out of bed without warning."

"It could be worse," said Llyr. "At least the beds don't move now, and the chairs all stay in place."

A hint of a smile touched Eri's lips. "No. You've done well, Llyr."

"A little more work," said his grandson, "and I'll be able to keep them all grounded when the disappearing starts."

Eri looked toward the vanished castle. "I wonder how they're doing in there. Without the warning bell there'll be a few bruised heads."

"And what has become of the bellman?" said Llyr with a frown.

Petrello woke up to find himself in the air. His brothers were floating just beneath him. Tolly, his brown curls bobbing, twisted and turned, his arms flailing, his hands reaching for something to grab. Vyborn lay on his back, spread-eagled inches above his bed. He glared up at Petrello accusingly.

"It's not my fault," said Petrello.

"The bell didn't ring." Tolly kicked in the air. "I'd have held the bedpost if I'd had a warning."

"Perhaps we didn't hear it. Or perhaps the wizards had no time to call the bellman."

Petrello's feet skimmed the floor and his head jerked back, hitting a bedpost. "Ouch! That doesn't usually happen. What's going on?"

Vyborn's small body had drifted higher. He had rolled over and was now staring down at Petrello. Petrello hoped his brother wasn't going to be sick. Vyborn was often sick. He was only six years old and sometimes ate more than he should, though he was still a scrawny boy. He had a face like a bad-tempered owl.

Petrello swam over to the window and, reaching for the sill, clung on. In the pale dawn light he could make out the lines of rose trees in the castle gardens and the low hedges of medicinal herbs. Two stately yews marked the end of the garden and the track that led east to the small town of Rosemellon. To the south, the great forest of Hencoed spread as far as the eye could see; to the north, the mountains rose like ghostly towers, their snowcapped peaks lost in the night clouds.

Two men appeared between the yews. Both wore blue cloaks edged in gold. The men carried long staffs that glimmered softly as they moved through the garden.

"The wizards are returning," Petrello observed. "They have a lot of ground to cover now that the castle has grown so vast."

"And it's still growing." Tolly gulped air as the wizards' spells tossed him to the ceiling.

It was true. Even the king had begun to wonder if his castle would continue to expand. It had been built by his African spirit ancestors twenty-seven years earlier. For some reason, they considered the building incomplete and would arrive now and again, in the dead of night, called, perhaps, by an old song the king had thoughtlessly hummed on his way to bed, a rhythm that had remained in his head ever since he had fled his secret African kingdom.

Try as he might, the king could never discover the precise sounds that called his spirit ancestors. The great Red Castle now sprawled for almost a mile, along a cliff that rose sheer from the river Dolenni.

Petrello couldn't see the river, but he never tired of the view from his window, and he marveled that, while he could see so much, the castle and all its inhabitants were invisible to anyone outside.

The wizards were responsible. Their spells kept the castle safe. If the king of England were ever to know that in the northern forests there was a castle larger than his own, he would consider its owner, especially a foreign king, a threat to his throne. An army of conquerors would be dispatched and the castle burned to the ground. If they survived the fire, who knew what would happen to an African king and his family once they were prisoners of the conquerors' king?

"I wish the spell wouldn't do this," said Tolly as Vyborn floated above him and dribbled onto his bare foot.

"Llyr will refine it," said Petrello. "It's already better than it was. Remember we used to see through all the walls, as if we were in a giant bubble. And the furniture floated. Now it's just us."

"I don't remember," grumbled Vyborn.

"You were only two," said Tolly. "But I remember because I was five and Trello was six."

An angry roar echoed down the passage outside the boys' bedchamber. "Senseless! Ludicrous! Pointless!"

"Borlath!" Tolly made a face.

Borlath, the king's eldest son, was always angry. If he'd had his way, the wizards would have been banished long ago and the castle left to be defended by the king and his knights. Borlath's fingers could burn like fiery pokers. It was an endowment inherited from his father, though the king never used his fingers in anger. In Borlath's bad moods it was best to avoid him.

"Sometimes, I wish he'd burn himself on his own fingers," Petrello murmured.

The wizards were drawing closer. Llyr supported his grandfather on his arm. Old Eri limped badly, his back was bent, and the hem of his cloak heavy with dew, but he still wore a mischievous smile.

Llyr was tall, his face paler than his grandfather's. Llyr wasn't smiling. Spells were a serious matter. If they were not right, their